Gene Tapia, United States Marine Corps Raider. A Veteran of Guadalcanal, Guam and Iwo Jima Battles.

From The Author

Two weeks before this book was scheduled to go to the printers, I received a call from Gene Tapia.

"Be sure we can corroborate everything that is printed in the book," he said. "If there's anything in it we can't back up or verify, take it out."

That's Gene Tapia.

Gene's memory of his wartime experiences are extraordinary. In all cases, he remembers the battles and what happened, but sometimes he couldn't recall the dates or sequences certain battles occurred in.

I have used the Third Marine Division Journal published in 1948 by the Infantry Press to substantiate and date his experiences on New Caledonia, Guadalcanal, Guam, Iwo Jima, and scouting missions, plus other reference works by different authors.

Jeff Dickrell, a historian on the Japanese attacks on Dutch Harbor, Alaska, June 3-4, 1942 was able to verify Gene's experiences during that period.

NASCAR has many records on file of Gene's races, and his Florida State Championship.

The information on Georgia Tann and her theft ring was taken from Memphis, Tennessee newspaper records, magazine articles, and personal conversations with Jalena Bowling, one of the three women who operated, "The Tennessee Right To Know Organization."

This is the story about an individual who started out in life just like you and me. He says, 'I am not a hero, the heroes are still over there.' Yet, he lived a hero's journey.

This is not my story, it is, **Gene Tapia's Story.**

Gerald Hodges/The Racing Reporter
Friday, September 6, 2002

Published by Hodges News Services
Gerald Hodges Agency
913 Lakeside Drive
Mobile, Alabama 36693
251-660-1555

Copyright © Gerald Hodges, 2002
All rights reserved

This book is true, but certain names have been changed and some conversations paraphased in order to avoid intrusion on the privacy of certain individuals or their familiies

This book is sold subject to the condition that it shall not, by way of trade or otherwise, be lent, re-sold, hired out, or otherwise circulated without the publisher's prior consent in any form of binding or cover other than that which it is published and without a similar conditon including this condition being imposed on the subsequent purchaser.

*The Gene Tapia Story is a joint effort between
Gene Tapia and Gerald Hodges*

*"Never Be Ugly To A Child,
Because They Won't Ever Forget It."*

Eugene Henry Tapia, 1952

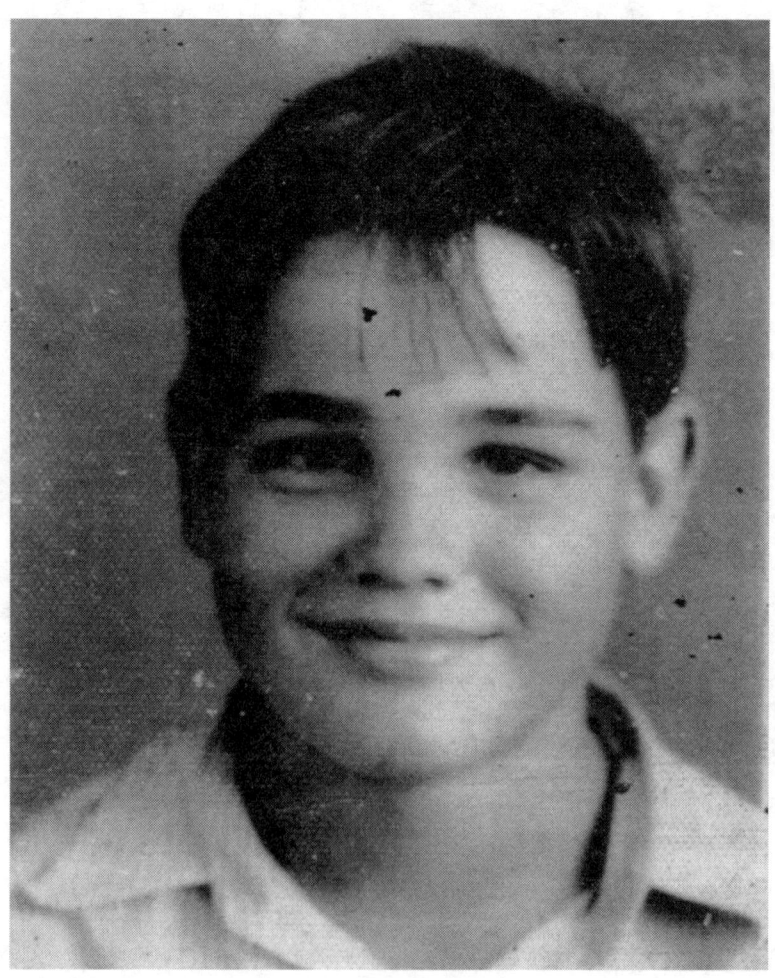

INTRODUCTION

ABOUT GENE TAPIA

Gene Tapia is best remembered as the smiling and congenial driver of supermodified No. 327. Very few of his fans and even close friends know the other side of his life.

Obsessed with adventure, he has lived on the edge nearly all of his life. After being involved in a car wreck at the age of sixteen that almost took his life, he shot a man in self-defense on the way to the hospital. Told by the District Attorney 'he better get out of town,' Gene wound up in Dutch Harbor, Alaska. After being wounded during the Japanese attack on Dutch Harbor, June 3-4, 1942, he crossed an ocean to fight back. But his biggest field of combat was against personal demons of guilt raging inside him over the loss of a baby son, stolen at birth from his wife while he was in Alaska. Later, he battled bureaucrats, and NASCAR drivers to win over 600 races, and be known as "King of The Supermodifieds."

This is a true and fascinating look at the extraordinary personal life from which Gene Tapia lived out a hero's journey, first on the battlefields of Guadalcanal, Guam and Iwo Jima, and then to help promote NASCAR stock car racing.

"I was not a hero," said Tapia. "My life has been an interesting journey, but most of the real heroes never made it through. They're still over there."

Gene's world was not made up of avant-garde or highly educated people. After completing Marine Corps boot camp at San Diego, California, he was sent to Marine scout sniper school, and from there, to Marine Raider School. By the time he shipped out of San Diego for his first World War II duty station, he was capable of handling any type warfare situation.

The travels, experiences, and fighting on Guadalcanal, Guam and Iwo Jima had turned him into a first-class killing machine by the time the war ended. Unable to work when he returned home because of coral reef cuts, jungle rot, malaria and dengue fever, he was like a lost ball in high, high weeds.

A chance encounter with automobile racing forged a connection within him that gave his competitive spirit an outlet. In his first NASCAR race in 1948, he went up against NASCAR's biggest stars, Buck Baker, Gober Sosebee and Lee Petty. He helped the struggling NASCAR organization develop, then turned his back on it because he had a need to race more than once a week, often competing up to five times a week at different tracks. After saying good-bye to NASCAR, he turned his talents to modified racing at short tracks.

His style of racing was copied by many short-track drivers, including Red Farmer, Donnie and Bobby Allison, and superstar, Marty Robbins. When Tapia and the legendary No. 327 supermodified hit the track, the other drivers had hell to pay if they beat him.

He survived both a military and racing career, but Tapia admits that without a bunch of the Captain's angels, his life would have been cut short.

Gene Tapia's life could never have been complete without the help, support and faith of his wife, Francine. It was her absolute belief that God would some day answer her prayers, and allow her to hold the son that she had never seen-- a baby that was stolen at birth from a Memphis, Tennesse hospital by the infamous baby merchant-- Miss Georgia Tann.

Contents

I	UNFORTUNATE CIRCUMSTANCES		1
	Don't Bring a Knife to a Gunfight	4	
	North To Alaska	12	
II	THE GREAT ADVENTURE		17
	The Feel of Hot Lead	22	
	The Akutan Zero	24	
	Alaskan Photographs	26	
III	THE ALASKAN ADVENTURE ENDS		29
	Mary Francis Hays	30	
	A Long Line of Horse Thieves	32	
	Possum in The Henhouse	35	
	Life Outside Mobile	39	
	The Omen is True	42	
	Out On His Own	44	
	Family Photographs	47	
IV	THE BIG THEFT		57
	Miss Georgia Tann	59	
	The Baby Is Gone	60	
	Politician, Edward H. Crump	61	
	Juvenile Judge Camille Kelley	63	
	A Fine Jewish Boy	65	
	Midnight Flight To Memphis	67	
	The Return Home	68	
	Greeting From Uncle Sam	71	

V	**586TH PLATOON, U.S. MARINES**		73
	Scout Sniper School	75	
	Marine Raider Training	77	
	Destination: South Pacific	79	
VI	**GUADALCANAL**		82
	A Strange Enemy	85	
	Shortland Island Mission	87	
	The Boy Grows Up	92	
	Shifting Battle Fronts	96	
	A Request From The Homefront	97	
	Photograph on Guadalcanal	99	
VII	**INVASION OF GUAM**		100
	Danger in The Sea	101	
	Rescue of The 27th Army Division	105	
	Battle of Sugar Loaf Hill	107	
	The Fate of Jesus Chamacho	109	
	Only Mechanized Battle on Guam	114	
	There's My Man	116	
	Tokyo Rose	117	
	Jungle Diseases	118	
	A Surprise Visitor	120	
	Two Face To Face Encounters	123	
	Terror in The Sea	124	
	Photographs of Guam	125	
VIII	**IWO JIMA, THE SULPHUR ISLAND**		128
	Welcome To Hell	131	
	General Graves B. Erskine	136	
	Suicide Mission	140	
	No More Prisoners	143	
	The Big Two-O	148	
	The War's End	149	
	A Fork in The Road	152	
	Don't Make A Raider Mad	154	
	Photographs of Iwo Jima	156	
IX	**HOME TO AN INNER HELL**		159

	Chief Wiley Shatopa	164
	Moonshine Runner	167
	Stock Car Racing	171
	NASCAR Bigshots	175
	Don't Mess With My Man	177
X	AN ANGEL WITH LIGHT	180
	A Lap Girl	185
	Serious Racing	186
	Kangaroo Court	187
	New York, New York	191
	King of The Cow Pasture	194
	Early Racing Photographs	198
XI	A DEATH AND REBIRTH	216
	A Lost Ball in High Weeds	220
	On The NASCAR Circuit	222
	The King of Rock and Roll	229
XII	ANOTHER TWIST OF FATE	231
	Saga of The School Bus	233
	Joe Caspolich	237
	Superstar, Marty Robbins	241
	The NASCAR Strike	243
	NASCAR's Top-10 Drivers	244
	Gulf Coast Racers	245
	King of The Supermodifieds	247
	Photographs	251
XIII	THE CHECKERED FLAG	260
	Thunder and Lightning	261
	Photographs	267
XIV	ONE MORE MOUNTAIN	271
	The Call	275
	Family Photographs	285
	Conclusion	291

CHAPTER 1

UNFORTUNATE CIRCUMSTANCES

"He's dead, I just know he's dead. Ohh, he's been killed," Bea Pierce screamed.

A light fog swirled around the inside of the twisted hulk of what was once a 1932 Ford sedan. Engulfing the limp body of Gene Tapia was a thick mixture of steam and smoke. As motorists and nearby residents came running up to the accident scene, they were unable to see inside. A gray cloud of vapors streamed upward, merging into the blackness of the cold January night.

Bea Pierce continued to stand on her front porch, shrieking and wailing hysterically. Tears rolled down her face.

A few days after New Year's Day of 1942, sixteen year-old Gene Tapia was heading home about eight-thirty on a Friday evening. He had been working on his car at a garage near Schillinger and Moffatt Roads, just west of the Mobile, Alabama, city limits and about five miles from his home.

I had gone out to Cy Hardy's garage and filling station to tinker on the engine of my car. I knew my wife, Francine would be mad at me if I was too late for dinner, so I headed home pretty early. I pulled out on Moffatt Road and was listening to the engine. I felt proud of myself because I loved to hear the engine purr like it was sounding that night. I was traveling along about forty-five, and had gone less than a mile on Highway 98 when I saw a set of headlights in my rear view mirror. They were coming up on me fast. I moved over to the right shoulder because I could see he was taking up half of my lane. My first thought was that he was drunk and I needed to give him plenty of room. As soon as his rear bumper got even with my front one, he cut over, almost forcing me to hit the ditch.

The vehicle that had nearly sideswiped was an olive drab army ambulance. I reacted by shifting into second gear and mashing the accelerator all the way to the floor. Pretty soon, that light Ford coupe was on the bumper of him. It didn't take me long to catch him even though I almost wound my speedometer cable off the dial. When I did catch up and started to pull alongside, he cut me off.

The impact of the army ambulance as the driver swerved left on the narrow two-lane road sent me and the little Ford into a ditch. I managed to control the car and keep it from turning over, but as we crossed the shallow ditch, the car went airborne and when it landed, it hit a concrete driveway culvert—head on. It was an abrupt stop for both the car and myself. The left wheel and axle were knocked all the way back to the driver's seat. The dashboard and steering column were pushed back into my chest. Since cars of that era were not equipped with seatbelts, or safety glass, I was thrown upward and forward. My head was rammed into the top of the car. The windshield and left door glass shattered. I was bleeding profusely from broken glass that had cut my face, forehead, and upper body.

If I hadn't had on my fiberglass shipyard hat it would have been a lot worse. When it pushed the axle back into the car, it caught my knee and I couldn't move it for a while. I was pretty bunged up. There was a lot of steam and smoke all around me, which I confused with real clouds. For a few minutes, I wasn't sure if I was alive or in heaven. I didn't know if I still had all my arms and legs. All I was able to do was sit there and wait for the feelings to return to my body and see if everything was still in place.

All I could hear was this woman screaming. I didn't know who I was, where I was, and it suddenly struck me that maybe this was an angel because the sound was so unreal. Bea Pierce, who had been sitting at her window, saw the entire thing. She was just standing there screaming, shouting and crying at the top of her voice. I didn't think she would ever shut up.

Eventually, I was able to control the physical pain and began working my knee back and forth. A wrecker had arrived and after the car was pulled from the ditch and hooked up, I crawled in the front seat with the driver.

Francine later said my face looked like it had lost a fight with a hamburger meat grinder.

By the time I made it to the dining room table, my left knee was hurting and had begun to stiffen up. To make matters worse, a cut on my forehead was still bleeding. I very patiently explained to Francine what had happened as she tried to doctor me.

"You're going to the hospital," Francine said. "You've got cuts that have to be sewn up, and there are probably some broken bones. Mommy is still at work, but we can go in Preacher Colson's car. Can you still drive? If you aren't able to drive, I'm going to call someone to take you. You're going to the hospital right now."

I grabbed the keys to Homer Colson's car and a .38-caliber pistol off a shelf on the back porch, and stumbled down the steps. Francine caught up and ran alongside trying to steady me. It was hard getting into the driver's seat and even harder pushing the clutch because of the pain in my leg, but I got it in gear and headed for one of momma's restaurants, the White Spot Café less than two miles away on Springhill Avenue. I parked on the side street while Francine went inside. This is a hell of a thing to have happen as I glanced in the mirror and saw the bloody lump on my head.

"Your momma says she can't go with us because some of her help didn't show up and she's having to do the cooking," Francine said as she jumped back in the car. "She said to get to the emergency room as quick as you can. Come on, Gene, let's go."

DON'T BRING A KNIFE TO A GUNFIGHT

In order to get back on Springhill Avenue, I had to circle the block. The car began to move, and at the end of the block i turned left. What I didn't see as we made that left turn was a gang of about twenty young men, most of whom were black. They were blocking the street about halfway down the block, across from Crichton Elementary School.

I won't say I was dazed, but I wasn't really aware of things as I should have been, or I wouldn't have allowed myself to get in that mess. I knew who this bunch of thugs were. They were a lot older than me, but they didn't like me, and I knew there was going to be trouble. The street was narrow and they had it blocked off. I guess I could have started to back up when I saw the knives, but it wasn't in me to run, so I just stopped.

Francine, Hand me the gun out of the glove compartment.

"No, Gene, you'll hurt somebody."

"Give it to me, Francine."

"No, Gene, let's see what they want first."

"Hell, I know what they want. They want me."

Gene pulled open the glove compartment and felt around until he laid his hand on the .38-caliber Smith & Wesson revolver. It was in a holster, but he jerked it out.

Things got pretty fuzzy there for awhile. There were some shots fired, but as soon as the shooting started, they scattered like quail. That is, all except one. As I began backing up, I saw him lying on the ground. I kept backing up until I got to the street that ran alongside the White Spot, and then I stopped.

"Let's go, Gene," Francine said. "Please, let's get out of here. They're going to come after you if you don't leave. And the police are going to be here soon."

Gene drove slowly back to his mother's restaurant. "Get out," he said.

"What do you mean, get out," asked Francine?

Just that, get out. I can't leave that man lying there. And I'm not going to let you get involved in it. Now get out and go inside with Mommy and stay there.

After making her get out of the car, I waited until I saw her go inside the restaurant before leaving and heading back to the scene of the shooting.

It was entirely different when I rounded the corner. There were no crowds, yelling or cursing, all was quiet—too quiet. I could see the figure of a man half leaning and half sitting against the front steps of a house. He was alone and it looked like he was in a daze, but blood was shooting out of his leg. I was worried. I told him, 'Buddy, for God's sake, don't move that leg any more than you have to.' I loaded him in the car and took him to Providence Hospital's emergency room. While they were sewing him up, they checked me out and said I didn't have any broken bones. After about two hours, they got him sewed up. He couldn't walk, and even though I don't know whose bullet it was that hit him, I still felt partially responsible.

As soon as the hospital released us, I took the black man home, and then went back by the White Spot Café where Francine and momma were waiting. My head still hurt, my knee was killing me and I still had on the same bloody shirt. When we got back home, I saw my prized Ford was a pile of junk. It had been a hell of a night.

The next day was Saturday, and there was a lot of questioning and confusion and explaining that went on between Francine, momma and myself.

Monday morning, Mommy and I went to see the Mobile County District Attorney. His office was in the Van Antwerp Building at Dauphin and Royal Streets. After telling our story to a detective, a lady took us into a small office at the end of a corridor and told us to wait.

Even though it was January, the windows were open, allowing both the wind and noises from the street to filter into the room. The green drapes on one side of the room flapped. Both the feel of the wind and sounds were comforting. One of the things, I thought, as I watched my mother, is that people are too pretentious. Maybe it was the plain gray walls that gave me the feeling, I don't know.

After another waiting period of between fifteen and twenty minutes, this middle-aged man dressed in a blue business suit came in and introduced himself as Mr. Inge. He was the District Attorney, the "big man," in Mobile politics.

Things were a lot different than they are today. As far as the District Attorney's secretary could tell the police hadn't been called in to make a report. Inge told us, if a report were filed, he would have to investigate. And he made it plain that if he began an investigation I would have to answer a lot of questions. He said if I wasn't in town and couldn't be found, then of course he wouldn't have to call me in to answer all his questions.

Inge leaned across the big mahogany desk. His horn-rimmed eyeglasses had slid down a little on his nose, as he looked menacingly into my eyes and said, 'Son, the best thing for you to do is get out of town right away.'

Momma and I both understood what the man meant. She got up, thanked him, and shook his hand. Then I shook his hand and we both headed for the door. But as I began walking out of the courthouse that morning, I was suddenly keenly aware of my predicament. It was not so complicated to understand.

I had a job, I could work as much overtime as I wanted and I had a good-looking wife. I wasn't disappointed in either. The thought of leaving my wife, just for a brief time, wasn't in my mind. Leaving her and Mobile was the last thing in my mind, but I also knew it was the most likely way to stay out of jail.

After we got back home, Momma suggested I go to Houston, Texas, and stay with my uncle Sam Johnson until she could arrange to settle the problems in Mobile. Not only would I be able to live with them and their family, but they could probably get me on in one of the Houston shipyards.

Now, for the first time in his young life, unable to think through his problems, he lunged blindly out of the house, with the intention of going—where? When his temper settled and he was in his mother's car headed uptown, the question nagged him. Where? He was like a little boy running away from home—to teach them a lesson—but quite at a loss as to which direction to take.

Gene tapped his fingers on the steering wheel as he headed toward downtown Crichton on Springhill Avenue. His destination was Paul Botter's Shell Service Station on the corner of Springhill and Randolph Streets. He felt a need to talk with Homer, a part-time preacher/mechanic, who usually stayed in part-time trouble but he was still the one person Gene could count on when he needed advice about women or cars, or both. He turned the wheel right at the intersection of Randolph and pulled straight into the back of the station where Homer worked.

Homer Colson was a real good mechanic. He was one of those people who came into my life that I learned a lot from. He had showed me how to really soup up my 1932 Ford I had at the time. He was about ten years older than me, but I really liked old Homer. We just hit it off.

The shop at the rear of the station wasn't much. On the outside it was a white block building that needed scrubbing. Burglar bars had been installed over the two small side windows, but the big front door was open most of the time. The only times it was closed were at night and when it rained. Inside there was room for only one car. Two could have been fitted into it, but for the spare parts, used parts, junk, and tools piled around the sides of the concrete floor.

Homer had the hood raised on a big Packard and was revving the engine. I sat down on the couch next to the door between two cats and a pile of clothes. I immediately got cat hairs on my pants and down the back of my shirt.

Homer came over in a few minutes and sat down.

Don't you ever get tired of working on other people's cars? Or the urge to see what life is like outside Mobile?"

"Man, of course I do. What are you getting at? I've been to New Orleans. Their banana docks are three times as big as Mobile's. And there's a lot more loose women over there. Why, you thinking about leaving?"

"I don't really have anything up my sleeve, or care about the women now that I have Francine, but sometimes I just want to go places and see and do other things. I get a headache from sitting around and doing the same old stuff. And besides, I have to get away for awhile. I don't feel like a bastard, or betrayer, either, but it's just something I've got to do until things blow over. Besides, it might be a long wait."

"Well, don't raise your hackles at me. If you've got a plan let's hear it."

"I don't really have anything, but I got some uncles in Houston," Gene continued.

"Houston? Man what are we gonna do in Houston? I've never been to Houston, but I've heard it's a lot like Mobile, only, bigger,"

"That's just the point," Gene said. "You see, I need to leave Mobile and I've been thinking about going over there, and if I can't find something, then uncle Sam can get both of us on with him."

"What about Francine and your family?"

She doesn't know anything about the problem I'm up against, and besides she's got her daddy, a sister and mommy. She won't have any problems. What do you say? Let's go.

That defect of character, believing that good things come to those who wait, was to afflict Gene Tapia for most of the first half of his life. He did things in good faith, but the pull he felt inside wouldn't allow him to look beyond the circumstances. A mysterious alchemy took place and he was drawn into situations, never actually seeing where he was going, or the meaning of what was happening to him.

"It was just something I felt and had to respond to," he said later in life. "But the answer always came. Whatever I needed to complete a task always came just at the right moment. It was not something I could sit back and think out."

Gene Tapia needed help and whether it was fate, circumstances or both, Homer Colson was the man that was to help lead him on his first journey outside Mobile, Alabama. After several more hours of talking, the two decided they would leave for Houston, Texas as soon as Homer could finish the repairs on two cars he was currently working on. This way, they might not have much money, but they would at least be able to buy gas for Homer's 1934 Chevrolet.

Gene backed his mother's car out of the Botter's driveway and headed home. As he turned west on Springhill, back towards his country home, he suddenly experienced a strange sense of peace and awareness. He often said that just before some meaningful event in his life, he would go through a spell of intense anxiety. Afterwards, when he had "heeded the call," and the answer had arrived, a serene calm would be felt. "When I felt my peace return, then I knew I was headed in the right direction and on the right path."

It was after nine when he arrived home that night. There was no one up. He knew his mother had to get up at three-thirty to work the early morning shift at her restaurant. Francine would be in bed

The house felt depressing, and Gene paced around downstairs turning on several lights as he searched for a brown suitcase that had belonged to his father. The morning paper still lay on the big coffee table in the living room, and there were no fresh flowers in the vases. When every thing was going well, there were always fresh flowers.

He climbed the stairs to his bedroom, flicking on the hall light. He heard the iron frame bed squeak as Francine began stirring "Where have you been all evening? You've been away a long time. Your mom and I were worried about you. When are you coming to bed?"

Even though they had been married for over a month, Francine still fascinated Gene. She was a rather quiet girl, but she had so many assets, and some of them stuck out so delightfully. There had been no trouble with sex, and this night was no exception. After showering, Gene slid under the covers and began to explore her fascinating body. Everything went naturally and with a high degree of excitement. After a rapturous climax, the young couple drifted off to sleep. The events of the past few days seemed far, far, away as the couple fell into a blissful sleep locked in a lover's embrace.

Gene did not make it home for dinner the next night. He lost his nerve at the last moment. His mother knew where he was going, and he was sure she would tell Francine. Thereafter, he tried to put Mobile, his troubles, and family out of his mind.

"When Gene's mother told me what Gene had decided to do, I was shocked," said Francine. I had always looked at him with wonder and amazement. He was the handsomest thing I'd ever laid eyes on."

She loved him, of that she was sure. But even at her early age, she became afraid. If inside himself Gene was really a mass of troubled personalities, what would the future hold. What was a man really like if he couldn't tell his own wife good-bye?

"You know we had a together thing," says Francine. "A boy and girl kind of relationship. He always made love to me like he meant it. I felt safe when he was around. It wouldn't be so bad if I had known he was leaving. I liked the way things had started off-if-if only I could get my husband out of whatever he was trying to do.

"I hated him for going off and leaving me like that, but I still loved him."

By the time Francine had learned the truth about her husband's plans, Homer's 1934 Chevrolet sedan was nearing the outskirts of New Orleans, Louisiana. It didn't matter that they had very little money. Gene recalls that he had less than fifty dollars, including a twenty-dollar bill he kept hidden in his billfold for emergencies only.

The two young men drove all the next day, and once they reached the outskirts of Houston, it took another two hours to find his Uncle Sam's house. Darkness and a biting wind blowing in off the Gulf of Mexico met them as they stepped out of the car. Gene shivered in his short sleeve shirt and glanced around. The size of the house was small. Inside, the three and one-half room bungalow cottage was even smaller than it had appeared from the outside.

"You can put your things here in the living room; have a cleanup and I'll get you something to eat," said aunt Lois after everyone had said their hellos. "Make yourselves at home."

The plan was for Gene to sleep on a pallet on the floor while Homer slept on the couch. The house was plain, but comfortable, just suitable for a couple. A large colored print of Uncle Sam's family, which included Ada Johnson, Gene's mother hung on one wall. On the opposite side of the room was a small Victorian table with a radio on it. Two more chairs and an oval braided rug on the floor was all the furnishings in the living room.

"Are you ready," came the call from the kitchen.

The dining room was cramped, but Lois Johnson had prepared generous portions of food: several bowls of vegetables, fresh bread, a bowl of butter, and milk. Gene and Homer sat opposite each other, while Sam slid into the chair next to his nephew. Lois remained in the kitchen making a pot of coffee for everyone.

Sam Johnson only knew that Gene and Homer had come to Houston looking for a job. He knew nothing of Gene's other problems. Over coffee, he began to tell them the procedures for getting on at the Houston Shipyard. As a foreman, he said he would be able to help them land a job in the best department once they passed their physical and other pre-employment screening. All gulf coast shipyards were screaming for workers, so landing a job was almost assured.

It was nearly midnight when all the small talk had ceased and everyone was ready to go to bed. Gene had a slight headache, and headed for the bathroom first.

"You can't stay in there all night," Homer said. "Give someone else a chance at that shower, will you?"

Gene's eyes remained open for a long time. He wasn't much for sleeping in strange places. Suddenly, Francine appeared in his mind. The image of her the day he left in a simple sweater and tweed skirt made his loins tingle. The sweater showed off her curves and hinted at what was really underneath. God, how he longed to squeeze one of her breasts now.

"Coffee's ready if you would like some," said Lois coming into the room in a long robe. "Did you sleep at all? I'm so sorry that you have to get up early, but your Uncle Sam has to be on the job pretty early."

"Slept like a log," Gene lied.

The next two days both young men spent filling out forms and taking physical examinations at the Houston Shipyard. Gene had applied for a pipefitters job, and Homer was trying to get on as a mechanic in the shop.

On the fourth day, which was Friday, Gene had successfully completed all the paperwork and was told to report to the personnel department on Monday with a hard hat and steel toe shoes.

The young Houston war widows, if they happened to be attractive, had two choices. She either did or she didn't. If she did, there were plenty of bars and honky-tonks where she could find a willing partner.

"After spending five days in Lois and Sam's small house, we were both becoming overheated," said Gene "To make matters worse, Uncle Sam had taken on the responsibility of seeing that I didn't touch any alcohol or get into any hanky-panky."

Saturday morning while Gene was discussing how to get along in his job with Uncle Sam, Homer got up and walked to the front door.

"Walking is good exercise for my thinking," said Homer. "Be back in a little while."

Once in Houston, Homer learned there was a company in Seattle, Washington, called Siems Drake Puget Sound Bridge and Bridge Company that was hiring men for jobs in Dutch Harbor, Alaska.

That seemed like an awful exciting place to me. I'd always been good at geography, so I knew where the Aleutian Islands were. Homer had gotten hired to go to work at this Navy base and airfield under construction, but by the time I got to the Houston hiring hall, their quota was filled.

Gene had missed out on Pearl Harbor; now it seemed as if he would miss out on a second great adventure. Like most Americans, he felt the Japanese attack on December 7, 1941 was an act of treachery.

I was wanting to get into something to get back at those fellows. I was boiling mad. I hadn't been in the world long enough to learn to forgive and forget, so Pearl Harbor just seethed inside me.

My daddy had told me in 1934, after we sold some scrap iron, that it would be shot back at us by the Japanese. I didn't believe him at the time, but in some ways my daddy was smarter than I gave him credit for.

I wanted to get back at them. I had tried to join the Army, but they wouldn't take me because of my age. So going to Alaska and helping build a Navy base was the next best thing.

There weren't any more Alaskan jobs available in Houston, but the personnel officer told him there were plenty of jobs still available at the main office in Seattle.

NORTH TO ALASKA

Homer was not given any kind of advance or travel expenses. Once he arrived in Seattle, he would be fed and clothed and furnished passage to Dutch Harbor. Gene had only the promise of the personnel man— if he could make it to Seattle.

Gene went back to his Uncle Sam's house where he and Homer were staying. He packed his suitcase, and as soon as he had the opportunity, put the small suitcase under his arm and headed down the steps to where Homer was waiting. Opening the door on the passenger's side of the four door Chevrolet, he told Homer, "Step on it."

Homer put the accelerator down and the car sped away from the curb. And so Gene Tapia's first journey into the unknown began in the middle of January 1942.

Getting across the State of Texas seemed like eternity for the pair. The journey itself might have been monotonous, but for Homer and Gene there was plenty of excitement.

During the war years, there were a lot of people hanging out on street corners, in barbershops, in train stations and in the Greyhound bus stations.

The Travelers Aide Society usually set up a desk in bus or train stations and had someone on hand to help low income or indigent people travel across country. Instead of riding a bus and paying full fare, a traveler could go to a Travelers Aide desk and pay about half that.

People in cars would stop by and see if there was anyone going in their direction they could help.

These people would pay the Travelers Aide maybe a dollar and fifty cents. They in turn would pay us about half that and we'd take the person to the town where they wanted to go, if it was on our route. When we dropped that person off, we'd hit the next station. We went from station-to station and from city-to-city. That's how we got gas money.

By the time they reached Needles, California, the two were out of money, gas and food.

We had picked up this old man at a Travelers Aide in San Antonio and took him to California. We finally made it to Los Angeles, but we just couldn't figure out how we could go any farther. This man realized our situation and what a bind we were in. He asked Homer if he might want to sell his car.

The boys thought about it for a few minutes and realized that once they got to Seattle they wouldn't need a car. By selling the car, they could buy bus tickets up the west coast to Seattle.

Homer allowed the old man to take the car and their clothes with the promise of coming right back with a buyer. That was the last time they saw the car or the clothes.

As they headed north, hitchhiking, one family gave them coats because in early February the weather is cold in the higher altitudes in northern California, especially as they approached the Trinity Mountains. They arrived at Redding, California, and noticed that nearby, on Lake Shasta, a dam was under construction

The U. S. Government had sold the timber to the timber companies, who were cutting it down before the lake was formed. They gave us a chance to work, and we showed them what two Southern boys could do. It was hard work and we really had to put out. I marveled at the log trucks coming up out of that valley. They weaved back and forth on that narrow road that made several circles between the bottom and top. Several trucks lost their brakes and just fell off the mountain. When that happened, nobody hurried down into the valley because they knew the driver was dead. They just chalked him off the list for the next day.

After a few days, the two adventurers left the lumber camp and started hitchhiking again. They made it across California and Oregon. But once they reached the Washington State Border, they had a new problem. The Washington Legislature had just enacted a new law that forbade the picking up of hitchhikers. This was due to the ability of Japanese submarines to surface and land agents and saboteurs along the miles of unprotected Washington State coastline.

Still two hundred and fifty miles from Seattle, the pair split up. Homer continued on towards Seattle, while Gene returned to the Greyhound Bus Station in Vancouver, Washington.

I wired my mom for some money to continue on, but she made a mistake and sent it to Vancouver, British Columbia in Canada. I sat at the bus station during daylight hours and slept there at night.

The lady who ran the station was Mrs. Foster. She and her husband gave me ten dollars for a bus ticket on to Seattle. She said, 'You don't ever have to pay me back. All I ask is you pass this favor on to somebody else who needs it.'

The Lord had answered my prayers. And I have done what Mrs. Foster asked me several times. The ticket was six dollars and I was finally able to buy something to eat. My stomach sure appreciated it.

Gene made it to Seattle and found Homer, who was watching for him. Siems Drake Puget Sound Bridge and Iron Company hired him immediately, just as the man in Houston had said. He joined Homer in a barrack, and, after four days, the two left along with twenty or thirty other men on a ship bound for Dutch Harbor.

I had signed on at $405.00 a month, plus overtime. It was fabulous. Some of the people didn't like the cold, but it didn't bother me. I was going to town up there.

We didn't go directly across the Pacific Ocean. Instead, we went up the Inland Waterway along the Canadian Border. It was all so beautiful. The first real settlement we saw was Ketchikan, Alaska. We docked there to take on supplies and more people. The town was built on the side of a mountain, and there was this big sign that could easily be seen from the dock, that said, Blackie's Bar.

After leaving Ketchikan, we headed west into some of the roughest water I've ever experienced. The wind blew so hard you couldn't go on deck, and the swells rocked the boat continuously. I had never drunk champagne before, but a man offered me some and I took it. When we hit that rough water, the champagne started working on me. The ship would come up and then the champagne would come up. I mean it was like that all the way to our next stop at Kodiak Island.

After taking on additional supplies and men at Kodiak, the ship continued on to Dutch Harbor. On the trip, Gene found out most of the men were just "good old boys" like himself and he formed a bond with several of them.

The name Dutch Harbor is applied to that portion of the City of Amaknak Island across from Unalaska. It is still one of the most beautiful places in Alaska and encompasses one-hundred and sixteen square miles of land and ninety-nine miles of water.

The economy has always been dependent on commercial fishing. Unalaska holds a strategic position as the center of a rich fishing area. The Great Circle shipping route from major west coast ports to the Pacific Rim passes within fifty miles of Unalaska and Dutch Harbor and provides a natural protection for fishing vessels.

It was because of Unalaska's military importance that the U.S. Government was expanding its presence in the area.

Arriving in Dutch Harbor, Gene went to work the second day. He worked ten hours, but if the weather was good he would work twelve or more hours. Sometimes, he worked additonal hours at night unloading ships.

The Aleut Indians didn't stevedore. They fished, and that was it. There were also very few women on Dutch Harbor. There were a few White Russians and Aleut indians on nearby Unalaska island, but you had to catch a ferry over. And they had someone watching the civilians and military all the time.

Gene was hired on as a laborer, but after they discovered he had worked as an apprentice pipefitter, he was moved to other jobs with higher pay scales.

Before long, I was building houses, helping on the airstrip, unloading ships and working all the overtime hours I could handle.

CHAPTER II

THE GREAT ADVENTURE

In the cottony light of six a.m. on Wednesday, June 3, 1942, seventeen-year-old Gene Tapia emerged from the dynamite shack on Dutch Harbor, Alaska. He was stretching as he started walking down the sloping path to the mess hall for breakfast. This was one of the rare days when the weather was not foggy or rainy. He could see the bay, the beached ship, the SS Northwestern, which lay grounded near the shore, that was used as a power plant, barracks and mess hall and far out into the Bering Sea.

Tapia had worked overtime as a security guard the previous night and now he was ready to eat and link up with his regular work crew. As a civilian worker, he was allowed to work as much overtime as he wanted. U. S. Army Air Force planes and reinforcements were scheduled to arrive soon to bolster the Aleutian Islands defenses against a Japanese attack, and the airfield had to be ready.

"I looked up in the sky and there were planes everywhere." He continued on the path toward the mess hall, when suddenly, he realized things didn't look right.

Tapia was one of the first people to witness an attack on American soil by a foreign government since the War of 1812. He describes those first few minutes of the attack:

"Down below in the harbor, there was a squadron of Navy PBY flying boats. All of a sudden, the lead plane just peeled off. As I watched, I thought to myself, "The reinforcements have arrived." I didn't know at the time it was a Japanese Zero— until it got closer. One of our PBY's was trying to take off, but it was slow, just like an old seagull. The Zero came down and just splattered it with machine-gun fire. It trembled like a big wounded bird, fell back down, and then run up on a spit of land in Dutch Harbor."

The PBY that Gene watched get shot up was taking off on its daily mail run to Kodiak Island. It was spotted and strafed by Japanese Zeros. The pilot, Lt. Jack Litsey beached the damaged plane. Two other men were killed by bullets and a third, though wounded, died when he jumped out the rear of the plane and drowned just thirty feet from shore.

The planes Gene stood watching were part of a Japanese force of fifteen ships, 200 planes and 5,000 men that had sailed from Saipan on May 29, 1942. Putting out from Guam to join them was another support force. As these ships were heading out into the Pacific, another strike force of two light carriers, two heavy cruisers, two seaplane tenders and four destroyers was already halfway across the Pacific to its targets at Dutch Harbor.

By June 1, the entire strength of the Japanese Combined Fleet was at sea. Its goal was to win control of a tiny Pacific sand and coral atoll, called Midway. So confident had the Japanese Army been that when it left Saipan, it gave instructions to forward all mail to the "Island of The Rising Sun," the name it had chosen for the small island.

Except for the breaking of the Japanese fleet code by American Intelligence on May 28, the attack on Dutch Harbor might not have been discovered for what it was—a feint while the real Japanese task force headed for Midway Island.

Fog and heavy clouds covered much of the Bering Sea on the morning of the attack. This allowed Admiral Takeo Kurita's carriers to make their run eastward to within two hundred miles of Unalaska Island and Dutch Harbor. They were never detected by any of the Navy PBY Catalinas that patrolled from Dutch Harbor. Admiral Robert A. Theobald had a task force of American cruisers, but all his forces were four hundred miles to the southeast because he believed the Japanese would invade Kodiak.

However, the attack didn't go as planned for the Japanese either. Shortly after sunrise, Japanese planes from two carriers, Junyo and Ryujo took off. The Junyo's planes lost their bearings and had to return to refuel. Four dive-bombers and eleven fighters from the Ryujo were able to locate their target, and shortly after six o'clock that morning, they broke through the clouds and bore down on Dutch Harbor.

Within a few seconds after witnessing the attack on the Navy PBY in the harbor, Gene knew they were under attack and ran into a nearby stone guardhouse. "I wasn't where I could get a gun or anything like that. I was just trying to save my hide. There were people outside firing assorted type guns at the planes. They were flying so low the pilots could be seen looking down and grinning. By this time everyone had seen the rising sun on the sides of the Zeros. One of the principal targets was the SS Northwestern that was used by some of the civilians as living quarters. It had been beached by a storm that hit Dutch Harbor earlier, but the Japanese pilots didn't know it was grounded, and made run after run, raking it with machine-gun fire each time."

There were two types of planes that took part in the first day's action. Flying high and level were thirteen "Kate" single-engine bombers. These were really torpedo planes, but each one carried one 550 pound and four 150 pound bombs. Flying low and fast were the Zeros (sometimes called Zekes). Their mission was to protect the bombers and use their machine guns on ground targets. They carried no bombs.

Tapia had a good view of all the action and he was able to watch the planes as they dropped down out of the sky on their bombing runs. His living quarters were blown to pieces on the first raid. In the midst of the attack, Tapia says an unexplained incident occurred. "Fort Mears was the Army base next to the construction site. Someone had ordered the soldiers outside, making sure everybody was accounted for in the ranks. It looked pretty silly. They had those soldiers standing out there and planes were zipping overhead and bullets were whining by."

According to historian Jeff Dickrell, the incident Gene refers to involved a group of new troops that had off-loaded the night before and were not told to take shelter. In the confusion an officer of the 151st Combat Engineers ordered his men to fall into ranks. Eight of his men and seventeen men from the 37th Infantry were killed, and twenty-five men were wounded.

There were also lots of heroic actions.

One of the bravest acts that I saw that day was performed by a Negro cook. This cook came out with a 30-caliber light machine gun and a belt of ammunition. He wrapped a blanket and some towels over his arm and cradled it in the crook of his arm. He fired belt after belt of ammunition. Pretty soon, I remember the barrel was smoking hot.

He'd throw it down, reload another belt and slap it back in the crook of his arm and begin all over again. He didn't have anybody out there with him to help—just him and that 30 caliber. And he was doing a lot of good. About every third round was a tracer. You could see those tracers hitting close to the planes. How he learned to handle a machine gun, I'll never know because on board ship they didn't get that kind of weapons training. But he wasn't the only person firing. Anybody that could get their hands on a gun was throwing lead. There was even a Navy lieutenant firing a tommy gun. There was only one Zero shot down in the first attack and I'm sure this cook was the one that brought it down. I saw it get hit, and afterwards there was a trail of vapor smoke. They said a gasoline line or tank was hit. It didn't ignite, but I believe a round punctured one of the tanks. After being hit, it continued on a glide out into the tundra.

While the Army and Navy units were making preparations should there be a second day of attacks, the civilians had no clear orders. Tapia recognized that being near the military installations was not the best spot to be in case of another attack, and there were other problems. "I won't say it was chaos but avoiding the Japanese pilots wasn't our only problem. Obtaining food was another. All the cooks had joined the bird gang and fled to Mt. Ballyhoo, because they thought we were going to get invaded. In the meantime, we still had to eat."

Unlike the cooks and many other civilian personnel, Tapia thought up his own plan for survival. Before leaving the harbor area for a safer place, he obtained a few cans of sardines, crackers and other canned goods from a big bearded Russian immigrant who ran the commissary. He had made friends with this storekeeper, and was allowed to buy on credit.

After getting the sardines and other canned items, he and another worker named Jim went about 1-½ miles up in the low hills, at the base of Mt. Ballyhoo. In their new position they would have an escape route in case the Japanese armada came sailing into the harbor.

All their plans about survival and getting away from the harbor was one of the best ways to insure their survival, or so they thought. As dawn broke the next day, the two boys were in their new hiding spot on the side of a hill about two miles inland.

They had found a trench that had been dug into the tundra about four feet deep. It was open on both ends, but had a covered spot in the middle. Gene was sure this would afford the two escapees a safe place in case of another air attack.

We were awful glad to find that trench. You couldn't just go out and start digging trenches any place you pleased. The ground had to be heated first and then you dug. You heated and dug some more. The ice had to be melted before you could dig very deep.

The Japanese plans originally called for a mission against a U. S. base on Adak Island. There was no U. S. base on Adak, so the mission was canceled due to bad weather and a second strike was planned against Dutch Harbor.

The Japanese were much better prepared for the second day of bombing. They had taken photos of the base on the raid the previous day, and they also had more aircraft. In addition to the eleven Zero fighters and nine Kate bombers, there were eleven Val bombers. The thirty-one planes arrived over Dutch Harbor at 5:55 p.m.

THE FEEL OF HOT LEAD

What the two boys didn't know was that they were hiding near an ammunition storage area. What made it even worse is the Japanese had already designated the area as a bombing target.

We were walking around outside this trench when we saw a plane coming at us in a sharp dive. We could tell it was headed right for us, and we jumped back inside the trench. But I wasn't quick enough. As I dove down, I felt a stinging in my left rear. A bullet from one of the plane's machine guns had ricocheted off some rocks and hit me in my left buttock.

Cringing in pain and fear inside the trench, Jim and Gene could only gape in horror as the Japanese pilot banked the Zero, then made another dive, this time directly toward their hiding spot. "Jim and I watched as that pretty silver bomb floated down towards us. We looked at each other, but neither of us said a word. We shook hands because we both knew we were goners. But somehow or other, just before it got to us, it skipped over and hit about a hundred and fifty yards away. When the bomb exploded, the earth vibrated like a rubber band, throwing us back and forth across the ditch several times." That was enough. Rather than sit there helpless waiting for another attack, Gene grabbed their food, jumped out of the trench, and, ignoring his wound, ran as fast as he could farther into the hills.

Gene's wandering spirit had taken him to a place where people were shooting at him and all he could hope for was a safe hiding place. Thus, at the age of seventeen, he had become aware that human beings kill other humans. He had been introduced to the anxiety of being shot and watching helplessly as property and lives were destroyed. He had seen the attacking planes, felt a bullet and after the raids, listened to others tell about the horrors of the attack.

Even though he says he felt "entirely inadequate," he was not particularly frightened by the experiences. His fear was "a healthy fear," he said. Throughout the two days of attacks, he maintained his composure and even a certain amount of bravado.

Later that afternoon after the bombers had left, Gene headed back to his construction area. Suddenly, he spotted something shiny and gold near the trail. Walking over, he picked it up and realized it was a piece of metal from the nose cone of one of the bombs.

After I could see it wasn't attached to anything that would blow me to pieces, I picked it up. It was a bright shiny piece of bronze metal that weighed about five or six pounds. Inscribed in a circle on it were the words, 'Made in USA by International Harvester Corporation.'"

Gene took it back to his quarters and showed it to several of his buddies. Word soon got around about the souvenir he had acquired, and some Navy officers came and asked to see it. "They told me they wanted to take it with them and show it to their superiors. I never saw it again. There was no way they were going to let it leak out that an American company was in the business of making bombs for Japan."

Some time during the night of June 4, the Japanese pulled their task force back. Since wounds have a tendency not to heal well in that part of Alaska, Gene's employer arranged passage for him out of Dutch Harbor on a Navy shuttle plane. After a fueling stop on Kodiak Island, he was back in Seattle to wait for his wound to heal.

Gene had found Alaska entirely to his liking. He was accustomed to hard work and strict accountability. He wanted to compete, he said later, in just such an organization as the U. S. Marines, in which the rules were strict, known, and made to be obeyed.

There was a group of Marines that were sitting out in the harbor on the USS President Fillmore. This little band of gunners had some anti-aircraft guns and they kept those Jap pilots away from the docking area because they were right on target with their fire. They saved our bacon there at Dutch Harbor. If they hadn't been throwing flack at them as good as they did, those Japanese would have wrecked the entire harbor."

The stubborn resistance, efficient action and spectacular performance by this group of men convinced Tapia that these were real men and his type of hero. From that point on, becoming a U.S. Marine was his life's goal.

What Gene didn't know was the President Fillmore had a load of 37 mm anti-aircraft guns on board that was enroute to another military installation. When the Japanese planes began to attack, the marines unboxed the guns and sent up a terrific barrage of fire.

Finally, he was given a doctor's clearance to return, but he was notified that the situation in the Aleutian Islands was becoming increasingly dangerous. They expected that all civilians in Dutch Harbor would be sent back home soon because American Intelligence reports indicated the Japanese would mount even heavier attacks against the Aleutians.

THE AKUTAN ZERO

A few days after returning to Dutch Harbor Gene was one of less than a dozen civilians chosen as members of a team to dismantle and return the downed Japanese Zero to Dutch Harbor. According to historian, Dickrell, a Navy PBY while on patrol about a month after the June 3 attack spotted the Zero. It was located nearly fifteen miles away in the tundra. This was the first Japanese Zero ever recovered intact by the U.S. Government. Gene and the civilian work party traveled by boat to the remote region of tundra.

When it went into the tundra's short grass, the pilot apparently thought he would just go in and land. But it didn't happen that way. The wheels couldn't roll in that wiry tundra-grass, and when it hit, it just flipped over. The pilot didn't have a shot in him, instead his neck was broken. I guess he was killed when the plane flipped over with him in it. The plane was in almost perfect condition. The fuselage and tail section was made of laminated bamboo. That's what made it so light. The only damage to it was one bullet hole in the main body. We dismantled it and loaded it on to a barge that had been towed there by some type Navy tug. It was just a flat barge, not any type of LST or other military landing craft. We had to camp out one night in small tents. After we got it loaded on the barge, it was brought back to Dutch Harbor.

According to Tapia, there was a LIFE Magazine Correspondent in the salvage party, and a photo of the downed plane appeared in an issue of LIFE. Dickrell says the plane was shipped to San Diego, California where it was repaired and flown by American test pilots. But it did not have any influence on future American fighters, because they had already been designed.

Gene and Francine had been married for six months, yet he did not call home while he was in the hospital in Seattle. "I didn't get in touch with my family because I didn't want them to think I was in danger and besides, I liked the big money I was making. Why, I was making more money than you could imagine! As I look back, yes, I wish I would have done a lot of things different. I shouldn't have been doing the things I was doing. But what most people might not understand is this, I was drawn into these things. Unless you've felt the pull to adventure, you can't fully grasp what I mean. It wasn't a pull; it was just something in me that I had to respond to. I didn't have a choice."

TWO PHOTOGRAPHS ON FOLLOWING PAGES

"The Akutan Zero," which Gene Tapia helped recover is shown loaded on a barge. This was the first Japanese Zero to be captured intact by American Forces. The plane was taken to San Diego, California, where it was repaired and flown by American test pilots.

Aftermath of the Japanese attack on Dutch Harbor, Alaska, June 3-4, 1942, showing Marines dug into trenches. Smoke is coming from burning gasoline storage tanks in background.

CHAPTER III

THE ALASKAN ADVENTURE ENDS

The jump from twenty five dollars for a week's hard, dirty labor in gulf coast shipyards to six hundred dollars in Dutch Harbor was a staggering amount of money for the young boy. Suddenly, he saw that he and Francine would no longer be faced with an oppressive budget. He could afford more than one pair of dress shoes, and maybe even hire her a maid when he did get back home. Gene Tapia was finally a man, working at a man's job for a man's wage.

He did not know the circumstances or what was happening with any of his family. All of his available time was spent working. When not on his regular job, he worked as a stevedore unloading the endless stream of cargo ships that were bringing in military equipment and supplies. There was only one troubling thing in this place of escape, where the wind blew and it rained constantly. Gene told himself he was happy, for now. But he knew that before long he would have to return to his former role and face his fears.

We had been hearing almost daily rumors that our government thought it was getting too dangerous for civilians in Dutch Harbor and we would be sent back home. About the second week of October, our foreman called a meeting and told us we would be leaving soon. He told us a ship would be in Dutch Harbor in a few days and for us to be ready when it arrived.

Within a week, a Navy transport arrived and all civilians were evacuated from Dutch Harbor. On the way back to Seattle, the ship stopped at Kodiak and several other small ports to pick up cannery workers and transport them back to the Continental United States.

While Gene's first great adventure was over, luck still favored him. During the voyage from Dutch Harbor back to Seattle, Washington, he won over $2,000 in a poker game. Combined with all the job earnings that he had accumulated at Dutch Harbor, he had a small bankroll. When he reached Seattle, the first thing he did was call his family in Mobile, Alabama. The news involving Francine, his wife, was almost unbelievable.

MARY FRANCIS HAYS

Mary Frances Hays young life had been a roller coaster of happiness and sorrow. Until she was seven years old, she lived in a world cushioned by make-believe dreams, and played dolls with her two sisters, Lorraine and Dorothy.

She was born August 13, 1926 in Memphis, Tennessee. At an early age, her family moved 50 miles west to Forrest City, Arkansas, near her paternal grandparents.

Francine was the second of three girls born to Irma Mae Hull and Willie Dyer Hays. Dorothy was three years older, and Irma Lorraine was three years younger. When she was growing up, her family ran a grocery store in downtown Forrest City.

When she was seven, her mother died from peritonitis poisoning during a miscarriage with her fourth child. Now, she would have probably lived, but in 1927, they didn't have the cures we have today. A nurse later told Francine the baby, who was a boy, would have been born perfect.

The story goes that one night after they closed the store, my mother was filling vegetable bins. She asked my father, who was outside drinking a beer, to come inside and help her. He said, 'just a minute.' Rather than wait for him, she picked up a one hundred pound sack of Irish potatoes and dumped them in the bin. A few minutes later she fell over with the cramps. They took her to the Forrest City General Hospital, but it was too late.

She had already lost the baby. The complications set in and I never saw her alive, again. She died at the age of twenty three.

The three children left their home believing they were going to visit their mother in a hospital. Instead, they were taken to a mortuary.

When we first saw momma, Lorraine said, 'look, she's asleep in the cradle. The first thing I did was put my arms under her and try to lift her out of the coffin. When I did her right eye popped open.

My momma was sweet, and very beautiful. She had raven black hair and black eyes. Her skin was smooth, and she had pretty, white teeth. I cried for days afterwards because I loved her so much.

The death of her mother deprived Francine of a "great opportunity" in life, and it along with the physical events that followed, caused an interruption of something vital to her. In figuring out how to replenish herself, the young girl began to develop inner strength.

A few months later, her father closed the store and Francine and her two sisters were sent to live with Aramenta and Robert Hays, their grandmother and grandfather, who lived nearby.

This old couple also had a store, plus a rolling store, that traveled throughout the nearby countryside. The rolling store was a cross between a bus and truck. It was stocked with groceries and hardware and ran daily routes out in St. Francis County.

Francine and her three sisters grew up not having to do housework or cook, but their grandparents were strict.

I was raised with a silver spoon. We had a maid and even a butler that chauffeured us around. We never learned the things most girls do about housekeeping. But we had to behave, and act decently.

Years later, the adult Francine would understand that different persons have different reasons to go to church. But that would be years later. Going to Sunday School at the Forrest City First Baptist Church was what she looked forward to each week.

All three of the Hays girls liked church, and one of the methods of punishment, their grandparents used, was to keep them out of Sunday School.

I don't know if the church was a place of love or security,

but I enjoyed going. My early life was built around being able to attend church on Sunday. It was there that I developed a love for Jesus and faith.

After a few years, Francine's father, Willie Dyer Hays, moved to Mobile, Alabama because there was a big need for workers at Gulf Coast Shipyards, and wages were higher than in rural Arkansas. There was an acute housing shortage in Mobile, but Willie Hays found a widow, Ada Tapia, who had a farm. She allowed him and several other men to build a bunkhouse on the rear of her property. She needed the additional income, and it was a beneficial arrangement for both families.

My grandparents were having some problems with my sister, Dorothy, so it wasn't long after Daddy moved to Mobile that she joined him. In the spring of 1941, my grandmother died. Granddaddy wasn't able to take care of me, so I left Forrest City to join Dorothy. Lorraine had already been sent to live with a family in Lake Village, Arkansas, so I was the only one left.

Fourteen year-old Francine said goodbye to all her family and friends and boarded an eastbound Greyhound bus late one evening. The trip through Memphis, Tennessee to Mobile lasted the entire night.

I thought I was in some kind of English Moors when we arrived in Mobile. We had been traveling through lots of fog and you couldn't see anything out the window. My daddy and sister were waiting to pick me up. Right outside the bus station there were cars just popping up out of nowhere. They were going into and coming out of Bankhead Tunnel, which went under the Mobile River, but at the time it made me shiver.

They walked me around town, and it was all so foggy. I couldn't see the top of the buildings. The streets were brick and cobblestone. It was like a scene from movies, where something scary and spooky is about to happen. It wasn't until I got to Miss Ada Tapia's that I relaxed. She made me feel good the first time I saw her. Less than twelve hours after arriving in Mobile, I met Gene, her youngest son. I thought he was the best looking thing I had ever seen.

A LONG LINE OF HORSE THIEVES

In 1831, Manuel Jose Tapia was working as a stable hand for a wealthy Spanish don in Ecija, Spain. After the wealthy landowner whipped a beautiful white horse, fifteen- year-old Tapia rode off on him. Eluding the police for several days, he finally arrived, exhausted, in Seville.

With the gendarmes right behind, Tapia spotted an American ship that was about to sail. Tying the horse at the foot of the gangplank, he went aboard and related his story to the Captain

As the ship slipped away from its mooring in Seville Harbor, Manuel Jose Tapia was standing on the deck, clutching the bridle of the horse he loved so much. As the ship moved out into the bay, his pursuers had reached the dock. But the boy and the horse he loved so much continued their journey.

Family tradition says that Manuel Tapia arrived first, in Savannah, Georgia, and then came around the tip of Florida to Mobile. After arriving in Mobile, he began to race his horse against local horses. Either he made enemies among the locals, or word got back to Spain as to his whereabouts, and he left Mobile in a hurry. This time he wound up in Montgomery. Later, he returned to Mobile and commanded a small sailing ship that ran the Union blockade during the Civil War. What made this family story about his great grandfather come alive for Gene Tapia a century later was that a descendant of this original Spanish horse lived on their farm.

When I was three years old, I was playing in the sand bed back of our old place where I was raised. This horse, named Prince, used to run and play all the time. One day, old Prince was running wide open as he came around the house and I was sitting in the middle of a sand bed. After spotting me sitting in his path, he jumped. My uncles measured the jump and it was forty feet from where he left the ground to where his hooves touched again.

Gene experienced the first childhood emotional traumas when he was four years old.

There was a lady horse in a pasture next door that became amorous. Old Prince was over there cutting up and showing off and doing his thing on his side of the fence. He thought he could jump anything, but when he tried to leap over the high fence, his front knuckles on his knees hung and he cut a flip. He hit the ground and broke his neck. Old Prince had to be destroyed.

I can remember hearing the shot just like it was yesterday. That was the first real loss I suffered. Right about that time, I developed a thing for adventure. I know that I got it honestly. After I became a grown man I realized I came from a long line of horse thieves.

Gene's parents, Homer Tapia and Ada Johnson both grew up near Montgomery, Alabama. They were married in 1918, and moved to Mobile two years later. They had three children, a daughter, Flidera, (January 30, 1919) and two sons, Homer Jr. (March 31, 1922) and Eugene Henry, born March 16, 1925.

His mother played the dominant role in his emotional development. He describes her as an industrious diplomat. She neither spoiled him nor waited on him as a child. What he did learn from her through her own daily patterns in the home and at work was a sense of responsibility, even when the job was boring.

Gene's father was quite a ladies man and had a way with all the women. After a six-month courtship the two were married. Homer was an excellent mechanic and machinist. By day he worked at the Louisville & Nashville Railroad shops in Mobile as a machinist. In the evenings, he often worked on cars belonging to friends or relatives in the backyard. And he was also an avid reader.

His mother favored his older brother and his father seemed to favor my sister.

It seems like I was just there. At times I felt like if it hadn't been for my sister, life would have been much worse for me. She was my mentor and guardian angel that kept me out of trouble many times.

Being six years younger than his sister and three years younger than his brother, Gene played by himself most of the time until he started school. He was fascinated with pictures and apparently was impressionable as a child. He was very inquisitive with a vivid imagination and learned to read the daily newspaper comic strips by the age of four. It was with the continued reading help from his sister that made him learn and understand words at an early age.

The three Tapia children were all active, lively, and physical youngsters, wholeheartedly engaging in the usual sports. Flidera was a girl with lots of musical talent and very independent mind. Her mother and father arranged for singing and piano classes, so she could develop her talents. She went on to become a talented singer and music teacher, who married and now lives on the west coast.

A rivalry developed between the two boys at an early age. Even though Flidera was inclined to music and arts, she kept a keen eye out for her youngest brother.

One Sunday afternoon, when Gene was about four, the two boys got into a tussling match. Both youngsters, who were dressed in somewhat formal children's attire—shorts and white shirts, wound up on the ground. Later, Gene said his sister, who was only nine or ten-years old at the time, took matters into her own hands, and saved him from getting a whipping.

Home for the Tapia family was a modest two-story frame house on twelve acres. The house sat back off the main road, U.S. Highway 98 that ran from west Mobile to Lucedale, Mississippi. It had been built in 1924 as a barn. There was no inside toilet. The family used a four-hole outhouse.

By 1929, when the Great Depression hit, the house had a living room, two bedrooms, fireplace, and lean-to kitchen on the lower floor. Upstairs there were three bedrooms and room for a bathroom. After 1929, all work on the bathrooms stopped because it was impossible for the Tapia family to get enough money to complete them. All the family took baths in a number three washtub; sister first, then Homer Jr and finally Gene. In the wintertime water was heated in a large reservoir on the wood stove.

It was a happy but working home. Homer worked five days a week at the railroad shop while Ada managed the house and sold milk, eggs and chickens and ducks, and sewed. All members of the family worked. On Saturday, both brothers worked with their father around the house. As a boy, Gene was impressed with his father's mechanical ability, but the two never developed a close bond. One of the reasons stems from an early childhood incident.

POSSUM IN THE HEN HOUSE

Gene loved to hunt. One night when he was six or seven years old, he followed his father over to a neighbor's house to catch an opossum.

Mr. Tapia," come quick," a neighborhood lady screamed

from her fence. "There's a possum in my hen house. Come help me get him out before he kills my chickens."

So my daddy went tearing out over there and, of course, I was right behind him with a little flashlight I'd gotten the previous Christmas. I wanted to help catch that possum. After we got over there, my dad lit a kerosene lantern and the three of us started looking all over that hen house for the possum.

I was looking all around when I noticed the lantern was out. But I kept right on looking and hunting for that rascal because I knew he had to be there somewhere. Finally, I thought I spotted my dad and this lady down on the ground in the corner of the barn. I reached around and took my flashlight out of my back pocket and turned it on. Boy, what a sight. My father and this lady had that big black possum hemmed up in her lap. I could see that my dad was helping her with that possum. But as young as I was, I also could see there was something going on that wasn't right, and I had sense enough not to ever voice it to my mother or anybody else.

That was the second of three childhood events that affected Gene deeply. The third was still about five years away.

The dining room table was the communication hub of the Tapia family. It was where the parents planned the workday, caught up on family news and gossiped. In a family of five, the table was just the right place for the exchange of ideas. Unfortunately, the table wasn't large enough for all the guests who sometime ate around it.

Even though members of his family were not strict religionists, Gene developed a strong sense of morality and responsibility at an early age. He recalls an incident that occurred one Saturday morning when he was five or six years old.

My daddy was paid every two weeks. After cashing his paycheck on Friday, he would pin the money inside his shirt pocket. I was running around the house early the next morning and I spied his shirt hanging across the back of a dining room chair. I knew that he pinned the money in his pocket to keep pickpockets from stealing it.

I unpinned the money and took out a one dollar bill. Then I pinned it back just like he had it. I ran down to the store and bought four cents worth of candy. When I got back to the house, daddy was fussing. He had counted his money and there was only seventy-five dollars. I knew where the other dollar had gone, but he was fuming because he thought the people who cashed his check had shorted him.

Feeling a deep sense of guilt, Gene was unable to own up to his act. Instead of confessing, he went out back of the house, dug a hole and buried the remaining ninety-six cents.

About four or five years later, I was playing where I hid the loot and I noticed a penny lying in some leaves. As I picked it up, I spotted the rest of the change from that dollar I had stolen out of daddy's pocket. All the guilt feeling returned. I was very sorry for what I did.

That actually was one of the best things to ever happen to me, because it taught me a valuable lesson; never to steal.

Gene and his brother had a rivalry when he was growing up. Homer Jr. was an intellectual person and Gene was the physical type who loved to play Tarzan and dream of pirates like Errol Flynn. His early heroes were most of the early cowboy actors, but he also liked the real-life bandits including Bonnie and Clyde, John Dillinger and "Machine Gun" Kelly.

To admire robbers and thieves back in those days wasn't uncommon. What you've got to remember is that the banks were looked at as the villains. They were the ones who foreclosed on family mortgages. Common people didn't have any money in those days. I believe most people looked at these bank robbers as a type of Robin Hood.

I never thought about them killing anyone. I wouldn't have approved of that. What fascinated me was their guts and daring ability.

Gene's family kept as many as fifty dairy cows. As he grew older, his role in the family business increased. By the time he was eleven years old, his arm and leg muscles had developed and he was as strong as his three-year older brother, and less fearful. The two often teased or played pranks on each other.

One day Gene and another boy, Darrell Foster, conspired to drop an egg on Homer's head from the roof of the house. Gene climbed up on the porch while Darrell called Homer outside on the pretext of seeing a strange-looking airplane.

As Homer stepped out the front door, I dropped it. That sucker splattered right on the top of his head and ran all down in his hair. Darrell then said, 'You shouldn't have done that because it will turn his hair gray.'

Boy, was Homer mad! Then the two of them came up with a plan to get even with me.

Homer and Darrell caught Gene and tied him with rope. With his feet and hands tied behind, they carried him next to a group of beehives at the rear of his family's property and poured sweetened water over him.

They left me laying there with those bees buzzing all around me for about three hours with only a pair of shorts on. The entire time I was trying to get loose I was thinking about what I was going to do to them.

After untying myself, I went in and got my Mama's 20 gauge shotgun. My brother and Darrell knew I was serious, and they left the country until I cooled off.

Living on a farm and dairy, the Tapia household had many pets; dogs, cats, and even a bird.

Though the Tapia children worked because of demanding circumstances, their lives were far from joyless. They not only played while working, but they went on a planned vacation each year because their father was employed by the Louisville & Nashville Railroad and was entitled to free coach passes.

We always tried to make a game of work so time would pass quicker. My mother would let us take the car and go swimming in Carrie Lake. The people that ran the lake were neighbors. Occasionally, we gave them chickens so they wouldn't charge us anything to swim.

Mama never did short us. We helped her make the money and she didn't mind giving us a little extra spending money because we had earned it.

In addition, she paid for extras that we needed. I had to ride my bike to school through Crichton, which was a pretty rough neighborhood, and she wanted to be sure I could take care of myself.

An older friend, L. G. Wilson, was attending Littleton's Gym on Conti Street in Mobile. Gene's mother arranged for him to take boxing lessons. Gene was already a good wrestler since he was strong, stout and stocky, but, after a few weeks at Littleton's Gym, his confidence grew.

Gene says he was not a bully, and that he only hated people who tried to bully others.

Because of all the work that continuously needed to be done at home, only one of the boys could leave for an extended time. When the entire family went on vacation, they hired someone to stay on the place.

LIFE OUTSIDE MOBILE

In 1935, Gene's father and sister went to the World's Fair in Chicago.

After my sister returned from Chicago, I became fascinated with all the new sights she talked about. She sat and described to me all the exhibits and new technology she had seen. Seeing and hearing about all the great new sights my sister described increased my desire to get out in the world and see things. It was through her eyes that the world began to open up more and more for me.

I knew right then there was more in this world I wanted to do than clean chickens and milk cows.

The following year, at the age of eleven, the simmering feud between Gene and his father surfaced. It occurred while the family was visiting an aunt in Tampa, Florida.

We had gone to visit my aunt, Mary Alice, who had married a Cuban or Spaniard, who was part-owner in one of the many cigar-making factories in southern Florida. Aunt Alice and her husband had a real nice home in a semi-exclusive neighborhood. He had a new 1935 Ford and furnished all the gas on rides to see all the splendid homes, but spent nothing on meals.

Gene recalls always being hungry, since back home on the dairy farm he always had plenty of milk, eggs, butter, bread, cereal and bananas. After two days, he began to miss all the good food he was accustomed to and became more and more miserable.

On about the third day we finally ran out of boring tours of these lovely homes and headed for the beach. It was a beach of people. They were enjoying themselves swimming and playing, and there were concessions with hot dogs, hot tamales, hamburgers and ice cream. As we rode slowly, I saw a place that rented motorized scooters for fifty cents an hour. My excitement after all the boredom of touring the homes returned. It was very apparent to everyone how much I wanted to rent a scooter.

But Gene's elation soon turned to disappointment.

Young folks back then were supposed to be seen and not heard. As we continued to travel along the beach, it became apparent to me that I wasn't going to get to ride a scooter because my uncle thought it might cost him some money, but I had my own money. Pretty soon, I had to elaborate on how I felt. I announced to all that my brother and I didn't care one bit about looking at those old estates. We wanted to ride a scooter on the beach.

What happened next may have been the final wedge in an already tenuous relationship between Gene and his father.

My father reached across my brother and slapped me so hard I saw stars. He had slapped me for expressing both my brother's and my own thoughts. Deep down, my father was probably of the same opinion, but I wasn't supposed to say anything.

That incident was one of the few times his father ever hit him. Usually his mother took care of the chastisement. Gene hardly spoke a word to anyone for the remainder of the trip, except to say yes ma'am or no ma'am. He stayed quiet and noticeably withdrawn.

Not being one to cry or display emotions, he let his mind automatically flash back to the shameful secret about his father that he had carried around for five years. All of us have some type of personal story we might not want told, but Gene's secret story remained embedded like a black piece of gravel under his skin.

After that trip to Tampa, the relationship with my father went downhill. I never was a snitch or tattletale. I never told anyone, and to think that my daddy would fly off the handle and slap me after I had been so discreet about what happened on the opossum hunt! It probably had a lot to do with us not seeing, eye to eye after that. My father knew very well the condition that existed between us, and I had as little to do with him as possible until his death. I never could trust him after that.

One day Gene's father decided it was time to further his boys' education in self-defense, so he bought a set of boxing gloves. Gene describes the day he set out to teach them how to defend themselves. But by this time, Gene and his brother were being called, "the tough Tapia boys" by the older women in the neighborhood.

The gloves my father had brought home were big ones that looked like pillows. First, he put the gloves on my brother, and the two of them sparred around for awhile. My brother was dressed in new coveralls and tennis shoes.

Mama had bought me a pair of new coveralls, too, but I was dressed in my usual cut-off britches and no shirt. I watched them with disinterest. Finally, Daddy decided my brother could handle himself pretty well. He removed the gloves from my brother, and called me over. I had no idea he was going to give me a lesson because we more or less ignored each other and he spent very little time with me. I guess he didn't want to leave me out so he told me to put them on. He did not want me to be a sissy, he insisted.

My brother was about sixteen at the time, and he stood about three inches taller, but was much slimmer than me, and out weighed me only ten or twelve pounds. Daddy hadn't noticed how I had sprouted and had larger arms than my brother. Playing Tarzan, milking those old cows and other chores had made me pretty strong. So that I wouldn't be at a disadvantage, Daddy got down on his knees.

He said, 'Come on, hit me." I told him again, 'Daddy, I don't want to hit you.' He insisted. Poor old Daddy didn't know what a golden opportunity that he was presenting me. Past memories and the slapping incident entered my mind as I started from my knees with an uppercut. It caught him squarely on the left side of his chin where it joined his neck. His neck was stretched about two inches. His eyes crossed and when he came back to reality, he just said, 'Damn,' removed the gloves and that was the end of the boxing lesson. We were even on one count.

One of the last good moments between Gene and his father happened in the autumn of 1938.

I slept on the second floor of our home. I was right under the tin roof, rain was pattering down and I was sleeping real good. I awoke to find someone caressing my forehead and discovered it was Daddy. I guess he realized how much our relationship had deteriorated and in his way was trying to let me know how much it was getting to him, also.

It was too late. The damage was done. Things of that order never did change. I guess we were both too bull-headed to allow it. We just avoided each other from then on as much as possible. At least, I avoided him.

THE OMEN IS TRUE

Homer Sr. had been sick for two or three days and had been taken to the hospital.

I was in the barn milking one afternoon when I heard the phone ringing up at the house. We had a maid, Madam Belle, but she wouldn't talk on the telephone. When I repeated what was told to me she began to shout. The news was about my Daddy.

'I knew it, I knew it,' Madam Belle shouted. 'I knew it was a bad omen when that bird flew into the roof a little while ago. I knew there was going to be a death.'

As I turned to run back down to the barn to tell my brother, Belle fainted and fell on the yellow linoleum rug in the kitchen next to the table.

Homer Tapia died October 12, 1939, at the age of forty-three. Gene was fourteen.

His brother was a senior in high school, preparing for college. This placed a big burden on Gene because, now, his mother expected more work out of him. However, he says it wasn't the work but the way he was treated that forced him into a painful decision.

No longer did he have Flidera around to help mediate decisions made by his mother or brother that affected him, because she was attending Montevallo college. Gone also, was her beautiful voice and piano playing that added an extra element of life to the entire household.

Something happened, and my father's insurance didn't pay off like it was supposed to. That meant my mother had to make the dairy and poultry business, support the entire family.

Every morning I had to milk cows before I went to school, and in the afternoons I had to kill and dress chickens and ducks and deliver them to customers. I couldn't stand to clean ducks because they had so many pinfeathers and it took forever to get them off. Since my sister wasn't home and my brother always had something to do, most of the extra work fell on me.

But what really ticked me off was the way I was treated. My mother didn't give me the same privileges as she did my brother. One Monday morning I asked to use the car on Saturday night and she said that would be okay. When Saturday came, my brother asked if he could use it to go out on a date, and she said yes.

Gene and Homer fought that evening. Eventually, his mother broke them up, but she took sides with Homer. Gene decided to move out.

That was it, I'd had it. I felt like I was doing more than my share of the work and I really didn't propose to change my way of looking at life. I knew what I wanted and I knew how to get it. I left immediately.

Ellis Wilkins was a few years younger than Gene, and grew up a short distance from the Tapia family.

"Gene was one of the big boys that lived across the street and our paths didn't cross that much as we were growing up," Ellis said. "He always seemed to be involved with cars. Early on when he was a young boy, in his preteens and teens, he had an old stripped down car that didn't have an engine in it. He and his brother Homer would push it up to the top of their land, which sloped down, and then he would coast down and steer it. That went on for a long time. They were sort of into physical fitness. I remember they got up early, took their cold showers and did things that made both of them physical specimens. I really didn't spend much time with Gene during those early years. But he always had access to something on four wheels. Eventually, the stripped down car wasn't stripped down, it had an engine, and he could drive it.

"I remember we were into sandlot football and we played in the Brantley's front yard, which was a football size yard. We would be playing football and Gene would come down the road in his car, wheel up in Brantley's driveway and go for a touchdown right through the middle of the field where we were playing and we would scatter like leaves. That was about as athletic as he got. I knew who he was, but there never was a closeness.

"Indeed, he was a wild Indian. I had some not so kind feeling about him because of one incident. He came flying down Moffett Road in his car almost out of control, to the extent that my Mom and I had to dive into the ditch in front of old man Shreve's house to keep from getting run over by him. I didn't appreciate my Mom being endangered like that."

OUT ON HIS OWN

Even though he was only fourteen years old, he was large for his age. Gene made plans to live on his own.

First, he knew where to rent a room in a boarding house run by some of his friends in downtown Crichton.

Another friend, Grady Mills, who drove a truck for Mobile Cigar and Tobacco Company, had hurt his back and needed a temporary driver.

Gene drove the tobacco truck until Grady Mills' back healed. Then he was job-hunting again. Finding one was no problem for the industrious and headstrong Gene Tapia. He went to work as a lather, installing wooden slats for mortar and brick.

The minimum age to work in an Alabama Shipyard was sixteen, but since Gene was large and muscular, he was able to convince the personnel director for Dilute and Ewing Contractors that he was sixteen.

He went to work on locomotive cranes that were left over from World War I. It was a hot, hard and dirty job, but he prospered. His starting salary was twenty-five cents an hour. Six months later he was given a fifteen-cent an hour raise. After two more months, his pay went to fifty cents an hour. He worked six and seven days a week, sometimes sixteen hours per day.

In a few months I had worked myself up to a special apprentice. I was making so much money I didn't know what to do with it. I purchased a 1929 Ford Model A convertible for thirty-five dollars. I was proud of myself, the car, and being able to live out on my own. Man, I thought I had it made!

Whenever Gene got off work early he usually came to his mother's to eat dinner.

I walked in one night and everybody was in the kitchen. My brother, Homer was on one side of the sink and Dorothy and a good-looking little thing were on the other. I think my mother was washing dishes.

There was a hook in one corner of the ceiling where a stalk of bananas always hung. Gene headed straight for the bananas.

Well, I didn't know who she was, but a firecracker went off inside me. I had one eye on her and one eye on a banana. My older brother and I both grabbed for the same banana. He shouldn't have done that.

Gene and Homer Tapia started fighting over one single banana. Right in the middle of the ruckus, Dorothy Hays turned around and said, "If you two crazy boys will stop fighting, I'll introduce you to my sister."

Gene says, "The fight stopped. Each one of us was holding one part of that banana. After the introduction, we started all over again. I don't know who ever got that banana we were fighting over, but from that night on, I kept my eyes on the banana that had been standing over by the sink."

Most of the time, Gene didn't have to go out of the way to find opportunities or adventure. They came to him. In his particular life, he always had more than enough.

I didn't have a lot of education. But when I saw that little flibbertigibbet, something in me just started going crazy. There was something in me that wanted out. I had a strong body, but a strong will also.

Gene was determined not to let this little girl upset his life. He had things to do. He had a good-paying job at the shipyard, a good car and adventure was calling the young man, but love began to do strange things to him.

I suspect a lot of my friends thought I wasn't acting sane. Of course, I never came right out and said what was bothering me. That wouldn't have been the manly thing.

Gene had the car and money to court Francine, but working sixteen-hour shifts didn't provide a lot of personal time. Whenever he had to work overtime and didn't arrive punctually for their date, Francine sometimes went out with other boys.

After a brief stay in the small house behind Gene's mother's home, Willie Hays moved his two girls to a large house just off Springhill Avenue in Mobile. This caused Gene a lot of grief and emotional concerns, because she began to have a lot more boyfriends. Her daddy's only stipulation was she had to be in by ten o'clock, and since Gene had to work a lot of overtime, she sometimes went out with another boy, which didn't set too well with Gene.

Five days after the bombing of Pearl Harbor, the two slipped across the Alabama and Mississippi Stateline, lied about their age and were married by a Justice of The Peace in Lucedale, Mississippi on December 13, 1941. Gene was sixteen and Francine was fifteen.

CHILDHOOD AND FAMILY PHOTOGRAPHS

Ada Johnson Tapia and Gene during an egg hunt in front of John Foster's barn, 1928.

Ada, Gene, and sister, Flidera after Gene's return from Alaska.

Henry Eugene Tapia after his return from Alaska.

Walter Douglas Cook and Flidera Tapia Cook at their wedding reception.

Francine Hays Tapia and Gene in 1943.

Francine's mother, Irma Mae Hull Hays.

Francine Hays Tapia

CHAPTER IV

THE BIG THEFT

Before he left Mobile, Francine had told Gene she was going to have a baby. Even though she was treated well and enjoyed being with the Tapia family, she decided to have her baby in Memphis, Tennessee, because she had relatives living there. In July 1942, she left Mobile on a Greyhound bus and went to live with her Aunt Catherine and Uncle Jimmy Hull. Gene, being out of touch with his family, was not aware of her plans or of the expected date of the baby's arrival.

She returned to Memphis, her birthplace, while she prepared herself for the birth of her baby. But nothing she had been through in life could prepare her for the next and biggest nightmare any woman would ever have to face—the loss of a child.

On the morning of September 24, 1942, sixteen year-old Francine Hays Tapia laid on her back in a fourth floor hospital bed in St. Joseph Hospital in Memphis, Tennessee. She wore a faded blue hospital gown, and was slipping in and out of consciousness because of the ether administered to her earlier. As she tried to roll over, she caught sight of the plastic IV tubing that ran from the bag of clear fluid above her to her left hand, where adhesive tape held the catheter firmly in her vein. She had shoulder length hair brown hair that fell loosely around her neck. A sharp pain suddenly hit her and she jerked. A senior nurse approached and rubbed her shoulder.

"You're dilating well, it won't be long."

As another contraction began, she closed her eyes and gripped the side railing of the bed, her knuckles whitening as she clinched. Aunt Kitty was sitting in the only chair. Every once in awhile, a woman could be heard crying out in pain, sometimes even screaming. Abruptly the crying or screaming might stop, followed by a brief stillness, and then the sound of a crying baby would be heard. The mood on the fourth floor unit was a mixture of tension, calm, and joy.

Kitty slid her chair close to the bed and started talking in order to get the young girl's mind away from the pains that were getting closer together. This was to be her first baby, and she'd had a normal pregnancy. Once she left the hospital, the two would live continue to live with her relatives until Gene returned. Everything appeared normal as Francine was transferred from her hospital bed to a stretcher, and wheeled into the delivery room.

One of the obstetrical nurses grabbed her loose hanging hair and gathered it under a paper cap. Francine looked at them, biting her lip. The anesthesiologist began to talk to her softly, in an easy, reassuring way. He seemed to be explaining what he was going to do and what she was going to feel.

Francine stared back with confused and imploring eyes, wishing the anesthesiologist hadn't said anything. She had turned her faith towards God, believing He would handle it all.

She heard the cry of her baby, and some words that sounded very distant, as she dropped off to never-never land again. When she came out from under the ether in another few minutes, she was back out in the room, and her aunt was rubbing her forehead.

Instinctively, she groped around the bed, feeling with her hands, searching for the baby she had just given birth to.

A nurse came in and said, "You had a boy."

"Where is he?" Francine asked. "When can I see him?"

"In a little while," the nurse replied. "First, what would you like to name him?"

"I want to name him Larry Eugene Tapia. Now let me see him. I want to hold him," she continued.

The nurse quietly left the room, and the sixteen-year-old mother drifted back into a restless sleep. After a brief period she awoke again. This time more determined, she raised her voice, and, even though it cracked, she knew it could be heard outside in the hallway.

Aunt Kitty, where's my baby? I want to see my baby. My baby, my baby!" she continued, her voice louder and louder.

MISS GEORGIA TANN, THE TENNESSEE TERROR

About this time, Georgia Tann, Assistant superintendent of the Tennessee Children's Home Society in Memphis, arrived in a side parking lot of the hospital in her big blue chauffer-driven Packard automobile. It was nine o'clock in the morning. She climbed out and entered St. Joseph's by a side door. Instead of taking the elevator, she climbed the hospital's rear stairs to the fourth floor. A stocky woman about five feet, four inches, wearing horn-rimmed glasses, she went directly to the maternity wards. For the past twenty years she had visited nursing homes and hospitals. Most of her visits were to remove a baby or child for adoption.

Born July 8, 1891 in Philadelphia, Mississippi, Beulah Georgia Tann was the only daughter of George C. Tann, a lawyer and judge in Neshoba and Newton counties. Growing up, she witnessed child-placement cases in her father's courtroom.

After graduating with a B. A. from Martha Washington College in Abingdon, Virginia, she taught for several years in the Lowndes County, Mississippi School System. She decided to take up law, and eventually passed the Mississippi State Bar Examination. Whether by choice, or because of the custom of very few women practicing law, she did not pursue a career in law.

By the end of World War I she had gone to work at the Children's Home Society in Jackson, Mississippi. There she helped care for orphans, and find homes for children who had been placed with the agency by the courts.

In 1924, she moved to Memphis and assumed a position with the Tennessee Children's home Society. This agency received and boarded children that had been removed from homes in Shelby county and other parts of western Tennessee. It had only been operating for two years, when Georgia Tann was placed in charge of the Aid Division.

During the 1920s and 1930s, many farm families migrated from rural towns in Arkansas, Mississippi, and Tennessee, to

Memphis in search of jobs and new homes. But few were available. These poor families continued to have children, which many of them couldn't take care of. The children of these families soon became the focus of the Shelby County Juvenile Court System.

Her authority and adoption practices had never been questioned by judges in Shelby County, Tennessee, despite the unscrupulous tactics she often employed in removing babies from their parents, even going so far as to tell the mother her baby had died when it hadn't. Today, she was behind on an order. A few weeks earlier she had promised a baby boy to a Jewish couple in Brooklyn, New York. They had promised to pay her ten thousand dollar fee, and now it was time for her to make the delivery. The nationality, parents health or background of the baby was immaterial to her. She had an order to fill. The adoption process couldn't be delayed. Her sources had told her exactly where to find a newborn infant boy to fill the application.

THE BABY IS GONE

Just before lunchtime, a maternity ward nurse entered Francine Tapia's room and went directly to her bed. "You can't see your baby," she said. "He's been taken by Georgia Tann."

There was silence in the room. Neither Francine nor Catherine Hull knew what to say. They were both shocked.

"Who is Georgia Tann?" Francine demanded. "What in the world is she doing with him? What business is it of hers to take my baby? Is there something wrong with him? Are they taking him for tests? What are they doing to him? Where is she taking him? If there's something wrong with him, tell me. Just let me see my baby, please."

"All I can tell you is Georgia Tann has taken your baby and you can't see him," the nurse stated again.

At this bleakest of moments, while Francine was screaming and crying, Kitty, who was sitting on the side of the hospital bed, reached over and hugged her niece, and both mothers wept uncontrollably.

By this time the nurse had turned and walked out the door.

"Don't worry, baby, we'll call your Uncle Jimmy and he'll get to the bottom of this," Aunt Kitty said. "You just wait and see."

James "Jimmy" Hull was a veteran Memphis police officer that knew the layout of Memphis, its politics and social structure. If anyone could unravel what had transpired on the fourth-floor nursery of St. Joseph's, James Hull was the man.

POLITICIAN, EDWARD H. CRUMP

But little did Officer Hull know that he would be powerless in his search. Memphis politics had been under the control of political boss, Edward H. Crump for several decades. He is thought by some to have been responsible for most of the abusive adoptive practices that went on at the Memphis children's Home.

Born in 1874, in Holly Springs, Mississippi, he moved to Memphis in 1894 as a clerk. He managed to court and wed Bessie McClean, the daughter of a wealthy and socially Memphis family. By 1936, he had his own thriving real estate company.

In 1909, he had been elected Mayor. He was reelected, but was forced to resign his office in 1916 by the state legislature for not enforcing Prohibition laws. Less than a year later, he was elected to the office of county trustee. Since this office paid him a percentage of the taxes that he collected, he became one of Memphis' wealthiest men in just a few years.

By the 1930s, Crump's organization had total political control over Memphis, including most of the judges. It was through Crump's influence that a woman with questionable credentials, Camille Kelley, was appointed Juvenile Court judge. With her signing most of the adoption papers, Georgia Tann stole over 5,000 babies.

Officer, Jimmy Hull would discover in the next few days just how close and powerful, the Crump politicians, Judge Camille Kelley and Georgia Tann were.

For many years, mothers, fathers and entire families had been telling the weirdest tales about Georgia Tann and the Tennessee Children's Home Society in Memphis. It was rumored that the local nursing homes were filled with unwed mothers who, year after year, returned and gave birth to children for the market. Others told of children being born to patients at Western State Hospital for the insane with children being given a false background and placed out for adoption. But by far the most repeated tale was that the children were taken from local hospitals like St. Joseph's and exported to New York and California in large numbers for a price.

The Tennessee Children's Home Society was the oldest child-placing agency in the state. It was originally chartered as a private non-profit corporation some twenty years before the enactment of Chapter 120 Public Acts of 1917. This act required the social investigation and approval of such applications for a charter, and the licensing and supervision of such child-placing organizations.

In the early history of social work in Tennessee, some of its board members and staff rendered a fine public service as pioneers in providing care for neglected and homeless children in family homes. Children without responsible parents were not then otherwise provided for except in county almshouses and orphanages.

Professional education or social work was in its infancy, and it was not until the 1940's that social agency boards in Tennessee generally began to recognize and require professional training for staff members. Consequently, it was not until this time that it became apparent that the Tennessee Children's Home Society was lagging behind other private agencies, continuing the use of untrained personnel.

Because Shelby County, Tennessee, had the highest infant death rate of any county in the United States, the U. S. Children's Bureau set up a special study and, in 1937, published a report of its findings. The Beulah Maternity Home was closed and at the same time some of the placement practices of the Tennessee Children's Home Society were questioned.

In 1941, a spacious Memphis mansion, located at 1556 Poplar Avenue was donated to the Memphis Children's Home Society. It was converted into a nursery and receiving home for children. Georgia Tann moved her office into this facility.

Miss Tann, as assistant superintendent of the Tennessee Children's Home Society in charge of the Memphis office, wielded a strong influence not only within that organization but also throughout the state. From 1941 until 1950, she had both strong critics and staunch advocates.

Her critics accused her of the political placement of babies for adoption, unscrupulous tactics in the separation of children from their parents, movement of sick children without due regard for their health, appeals to adoptive parents for financial donations, and the manipulation of the political influence of foster parents through misrepresentation and intimidation.

Her advocates called attention to the satisfaction brought to adoptive parents through the easy procurement of children and the elimination of "red tape" usually delaying adoption procedures.

JUVENILE JUDGE CAMILLE KELLEY

Like Ms. Tann, Camille Kelly had a sterling reputation. A 1948 national poll named her one of the "Six Most Wholesome Women in The World," along with Britain's then-Princess Elizabeth. But she also had a darker side: She supplied Georgia Tann with twenty percent of the children she placed.

Judge Kelly accomplished this by having an informant in the Shelby County Welfare Department. The person would ask parents applying for financial assistance the names and ages of their children, and then this information would be relayed to Judge Kelly. She in turn would order the removal of one or more of the children (usually the youngest) because of a "poor home environment." Next would come a quick court proceeding, as a result of which the child would be declared a ward of the state. Throughout the proceeding, Georgia Tann would be seated in the back of the courtroom.

Camille Kelley was born about one hundred miles northeast of Memphis, in Trenton, Tennessee, during the 1880s. She was the daughter of Dr. And Mrs. J. P. McGee. When she was a small child her family moved to Memphis. Her father was a surgeon at the Memphis Medical College. About the time she started to school, both her parents died, and she went to live with relatives until she finished high school.

She attended college at Jackson, Tennessee, and even considered becoming a doctor. But after the death of her sister, she returned to Memphis and cared for her sister's children until her brother-in-law remarried. By this time, she had decided to give up her medical career, and married Fitzgerald Kelley, a notable Memphis attorney.

Kelley was appointed judge in 1920, the same year women were allowed the right to vote. She went on to begin a career that led her to become one of the most influential women in the state. Many prominent citizens of Memphis who were associated with Camille Kelley and Georgia Tann in the operation of the Memphis home were unwilling to believe reports that had circulated for many years.

It may be hard to imagine today, how two women could terrify poor and lower income families that lived in Memphis between 1930 and 1950, but it was very real. It's also impossible to conceive of the children's sufferings. Born, usually, to uneducated parents, these children might suddenly find themselves with adoptive families who were doctors, actors, or in other professional fields. At best, some of these children were returned several times to Georgia Tann, and they were placed again and again. Others were handed over to Juvenile Courts hundreds of miles from Memphis.

Many families were duped into accepting children that were supposed to be mentally and physically healthy, and be from a good home. Most often the children had a poor home environment, while others received premature babies.

To solicit business outside Tennessee, Georgia Tann distributed booklets to various news agencies. In 1929, a news article appeared in the Memphis, Tennessee newspaper, entitled, A Baby For Christmas. Accompanied by a cute Shirley Temple look-alike girl, the article was picked up by the wire services and ran in newspapers throughout the country.

It wasn't long before her business was booming and she was sending children to cities like Los Angeles and New York, where many wealthy people lived who could pay her price. Since she asked so few questions of prospective parents the demand soon outstripped the supply.

In most cases, if a couple had a special request, Ms. Tann would try to fill it. Finding a baby with blue eyes or black hair was easy. But when she received more difficult orders, such as a child with college-educated parents, or one who's parents were talented—she simply lied. She might pass the child of a poor itinerant couple off as the son of a well-educated college professor. And she wasn't above selling the same baby over and over again if it was returned for medical or other reasons.

A FINE JEWISH BOY

Jeanne and Lester Adelson of New York read one of Ms. Tann's newspaper articles in the summer of 1942. After contacting her Memphis office and answering a few questions by mail, the couple was told it would be no problem to find them a fine young Jewish boy, but the cost would be $10,000.

By nightfall, Francine's eyes were almost closed because she had cried so much. But even as she lay in a depressed condition, Georgia Tann's adoption plan for the newborn baby was in progress.

On the morning of September 24, 1942, Lester Adelson, a buyer for Macy's of New York, had left La Guardia Airport on a two-week buying trip to South America. His wife, Jeanne Adelson, was relaxing at home. Shortly after noon the telephone rang in the Adelson apartment.

"Hello, is this Mrs. Adelson?"

"Yes, it is."

"This is Georgia Tann of the Memphis, Tennessee, Children's Home. How are you today, Mrs. Adelson?"

"I am just fine Miss Tann. My husband left this morning on a trip to South America and I was just getting ready to have some lunch."

"Well, Mrs. Adelson, I have some good news for you. We think we have located a beautiful baby for you."

Shock and disbelief almost overwhelmed the young woman at first, but then a tide of joy poured upward from deep within her. Jeanne Adelson could not have any children, so she and Lester had chosen to adopt. Since it was very hard to adopt a child, they had contacted Georgia Tann and after filling out an application, were put on a waiting list.

The way the Adelson family learned about Georgia Tann's adoption agency is unknown, but in order to drum up business, Ms. Tann distributed booklets featuring pictures of her Memphis home, a former mansion on Poplar Avenue.

She also had a reporter friend write an article entitled, A Baby For Christmas, for a Memphis newspaper. Accompanied by pictures of an adorable, Shirley Temple-like child, the article was picked up by the wire services and printed in newspapers across the country, where couples seeking to adopt could see it.

There was silence on the telephone as tears rolled down Jeanne Adelson's cheeks.

"Did you hear me Mrs. Adelson? There is a fine beautiful boy available now but you must hurry."

"Oh, thank you Miss Tann, but, but, my husband's not here and he won't be back for two weeks. Will that be soon enough? Can you send us a picture?"

"Oh no, this baby's mother and father were killed in an automobile accident and you must pick him up within twenty four hours."

"Oh, how wonderful, but can't you keep him until my husband returns?"

"I am sorry, but because of the circumstances, you must pick him up tomorrow. It won't be necessary for your husband to be present because the application with his name on it has been approved.

"You need to be in my office by nine o'clock tomorrow morning if you want the baby. We couldn't possibly hold him any longer."

"Oh Miss Tann, can you tell me a little about him?"

"There really isn't much to tell. As I told you, his parents were killed in an automobile accident and several other couples want him.

"If you can't be here or have decided you don't want a baby, then we must see that he goes to another couple."

"Miss Tann, we do want him. I will be there. Is there anything else I need to know?"

"Only the fee. Remember to bring the $10,000 fee in cash."

Jeanne Adelson felt a big lump rise in her throat. While they weren't a poor couple, raising that much money by herself in only a few hours seemed impossible. But because of her and Lester's desire to have their own son, she felt compelled to at least try.

"I...I'll be there Miss Tann......with the money."

"Thank you so much, now remember, be in my office by nine tomorrow morning."

MIDNIGHT FLIGHT TO MEMPHIS

It had taken Jeanne Adelson all evening to raise the money. But with the aid of friends, their lawyer, and two different bankers, she raised the $10,000.

Back in her apartment, she began calling the airlines. Since this was wartime, most flights had limited seating. Finally, a ticket agent at Trans World Airlines told her she could make connections in St. Louis, Missouri and arrive in Memphis before 8:00 a.m. the next morning.

Jeanne had stuffed the $10,000 in the bottom of her handbag. The DC-3 twin-engine propeller plane stopped in Pittsburgh, Pennsylvania; Cincinnati, Ohio; and Louisville, Kentucky, before touching down at St. Louis. Not once did she close her eyes or relinquish her grip on the handbag. After changing planes in St. Louis, she arrived at the Memphis airport shortly after eight. Immediately, she caught a taxi and told the driver to take her to 1556 Poplar Avenue, which was the address Georgia Tann had given her.

The meeting for Jeanne Adelson with Georgia Tann and her new adoptive son lasted only a few minutes. Again, it was stated, the baby's parents had been killed in a car wreck. Within an hour the trio was standing before Shelby County Juvenile Court Judge Camille Kelly.

After Judge Kelly exacted her court proceedings, Jeanne Adelson had what she had always wanted, a wonderful little Jewish boy. The woman from New York wasted no time in Memphis. After calling several friends back home, she headed for the airport, the same day, and the long return flight.

But the young mother's joy was about to turn into major anxiety.

Once onboard the plane, the two-day old infant suddenly had an asthma attack. This was very frightening, but both mother and son were able to get through it and made it back to New York without any further incidents. The next morning after arriving home, her husband called from Buenos Aires, Brazil. He cut short his buying trip and was back in New York, about ten days later.

THE RETURN HOME

As soon as he arrived back in Seattle, Washington, Gene contacted his mother, Ada Tapia, he learned that their son had been stolen, September 24, 1942 from St. Joseph's Hospital in Memphis by the infamous baby merchant, Georgia Tann.

When my Mama told me what happened, I didn't know what to do. I just wanted to get back and see Francine. The best and quickest way was a train across the northern part of the country. It was so pretty coming across Montana and some of the other states. I believe I changed trains somewhere in Minnesota. I know it was very cold. When we got to Chicago, I got off the train during a stop and slipped on the icy platform and hurt my back.

One November night Francine and her Aunt Kitty Hull were sitting in the living room. Kitty was crocheting or sewing while Francine was reading a magazine when the telephone rang. 'It's for you, Francine,'" Kitty said.

"For me?" Francine asked.

"Yes, it's Gene."

After he called and told me he was on his way I was so happy. I was elated to know that he was on the way home, even though it would take him several days. We still loved each other.

I knew my reputation as a father and husband had hit a low point with Francine's family, but I couldn't resist the call to adventure. After a few days with Francine's family, I didn't know what to do or which way to turn.

Her Uncle Jimmy, who was a policeman, had better tools to help find the baby than anyone else, so I gave up. The guilt was like a poison in my soul. I accepted full responsibility for the loss of our baby. If I had been at the hospital, minding the store, it wouldn't have happened.

Both families were aware of the war that was raging in both Europe and the Pacific and pretty soon Gene would turn eighteen, and would have to register for the draft.

The couple moved out of Catherine and Jimmy Hull's house and rented an apartment on Peabody Avenue not far from where Francine had lived for the past three months.

"It was like an efficiency apartment across from my grandmother's," Francine said. "I will never forget it. We were just half grown kids. Right after Gene came home it snowed. He had the flu and a bad sore throat, but we still went out and played in it. From the time he came home, all we did was act like we were still kids."

"We spent the winter of 1942 in Memphis, while he worked as a pipefitter for Grinnell Sprinkler, under Mr. Scotty Goodwine. But all the time he had one eye on the clock, because we both knew in May of 1943, he would receive a notice from his draft board calling him into the military."

The couple returned to Mobile in January 1943 and moved back in with his mother. As Gene reentered his local society, thoughts of his youth came back to his mind

When I was about seven years old, my cousin found some quail eggs over in Baldwin County. He brought them to my mother and she placed them in an incubator. Out of about nine eggs, four of them hatched. We kept them in the house and I tried to act like a mother quail, but three of them died. But one little fellow survived, and what a tough little bird he was.

That quail was the spunkiest animal you ever saw. The entire family learned so much from that little bird. We didn't wear shoes at the time, and he'd run up and 'zap,' he'd peck my toe. I'd kick him gently off, and he'd be right back, pecking again. After he got tired, I would pick him up and rub and pet him and before long, he would be asleep in my lap.

Cheepie loved my sister and thought the sun rose and set in her just like I did. He would get up on a long buffet and just prance back and forth in front of the mirror, admiring himself.

One day he followed us out the door, and the screen door slammed on his middle toe and cut it off. But that didn't slow him down. When my Mama went to town, he would sit on the back seat of the car, and if somebody tried to get in, he'd fly into them, trying to guard that car.

He had the run of the neighborhood and did what he pleased. He would fly up and down the street, and once in a while a neighbor would call us and we would go get him. What he loved most was tantalizing the neighborhood cats.

He would lay out in the sand bed flipping his wings in the sand. This was his way of getting the mites off. All those old neighbor cats wanted Cheepie. Once they started stalking him, he would lay still and watch and wait until they got a few feet from him.

Then, 'zoom,' he'd take off. Usually that old cat would jump and cut a flip in mid-air, but they never caught him. Sometimes he would fly past them a couple more times, just to tease them.

We were on a two-party telephone system. Our phone had two rings while the neighbor's only rung once. If two rings came up, Cheepie would fly to the back screen door and whistle. If we were working down at the barn and heard him whistling, we high-tailed it into the house because we knew someone was calling.

One year my daddy entered a liars contest at the Alabama Deep Sea Fishing Rodeo on Dauphin Island, Alabama, and won the contest, but the stories he told about Cheepie were true.

He lived four years, which is pretty old for a quail. One day we painted the house and were using turpentine or mineral spirits and the fumes from it was too much for him. I missed that little rascal for a long time, and I still think about him.

When Gene was about ten years old, his family rode a steam locomotive from Mobile to Montgomery, Alabama and visited some of his mother's family, the Gordons. They were met by a member of the Gordon family who drove them in a motorized milk wagon to Zack Gordon Sr.'s home. The Gordons owned two dairies. One was run by Zack Sr., a great uncle and the other by his son, Zack Jr. Both were located in Hope Hull, Alabama about four miles from each other.

The highlight of my day was getting up at 4:30 in the morning and going into Montgomery on the delivery wagon. My uncle Zack bottled chocolate milk, and I just loved it. He'd let me drink it until I thought I would pop.

Uncle Zack loved to bird hunt. He and I would get on horses and go out with the dogs and kill a mess of quail. He smoked a pipe and put something in it called Deer Tongue. When we were out hunting, he'd pick a mess of this Deer Tongue and take it home. After it dried, he'd mix it into his tobacco and it was the most aromatic smelling mixture I ever smelled.

After one hunting experience, Gene and his Uncle Zack developed a close relationship.

We went 'coon hunting one night. The dogs had struck a scent and Uncle Zack was way up ahead of me. We only had one lantern, and as I jumped on a log, my foot slipped. I got tangled in something I thought was vine, so I kicked it. But it wasn't a vine. I had kicked a snake in the mouth and he had bitten me on my left foot. The fangs went through my canvas shoe.

Uncle Zack made me sit down and take off my shoe. There were two wide marks where he had struck me. He gave me his knife and I cut an X over each one of the bites. He mashed each cut until it bled. He made me sit on that log in the pitch-black darkness until it quit hurting so much. Finally, I put my shoe back on and we continued 'coon hunting. The wound never gave me too much trouble, but that experience taught me I didn't need to go coon hunting where I couldn't see.

GREETING FROM UNCLE SAM

After returning to Mobile from Dutch Harbor, Gene was able to get his old job at the Gulf Shipyard. He worked twelve and sixteen hour shifts until he received his draft notice to report for a physical in June.

We lived there on my mother's place and I helped do things because help was hard to find. I knew I was going to be drafted, but I wasn't worried about Francine being taken care of. My mother loved that little girl better than she did me. But she mentored her too. When we first got married, Francine didn't know how to boil water without burning it. She taught her how to cook and to this day, I'm still receiving my mother's cooking because she learned my mother's ways and recipes.

Gene received a notice to report to his local draft board and was sent to Ft. McClellan in north central Alabama for a physical. While at Ft. McClellan, officials attempted to put Gene in the Army, but he refused, saying he wanted to be a marine.

I told them I was going to be a marine. They sent me to a Marine colonel and after sizing me up, he said he didn't see any way I could become a marine because I didn't have a high school diploma. After telling him of my experiences in Dutch Harbor and the admiration I had for those marines, the recruiter changed his mind.

Gene was allowed to return home for five days. After that he

Gene signed up for the marines on June 4, 1943, but was allowed to return to Mobile for four days. "I bid my family and my lovely wife, adieu and headed for San Diego, California on a train. It was two and a half years before I saw them again."

was put on a train headed for San Diego, California.

After a four-day train ride, he arrived in San Diego. There were military vehicles parked right near the tracks and men were climbing in them. These were mostly open-bodied trucks with no tarps or tops in case of rain. MP's were yelling and as soon as one truck was filled with recruits, it pulled out and another took its place in line.

What really caught my attention was the way most of them were dressed. Some wore fancy shoes, while others' skin was so white it didn't look like they had ever been in the sun. Some had sparrow-like legs, while others looked like real hoodlums.

I already had my suitcase anticipating a command to move out. One boy who wore glasses was bending down to tie one of his shoes. "You there," shouted an MP. "What's the matter? Don't you understand what I said? Move it!

I laughed and thought, boy, I am really going to enjoy this.

CHAPTER V

586TH PLATOON OF THE UNITED STATES MARINES, 1943

As they bounced along the streets in the overcrowded truck, Gene was a steadying influence to the other recruits, helping them stand the shock of their new life and what they were seeing as they arrived at Boot Camp, San Diego.

I was more prepared for boot camp than most of the fellows there, because I had come from and seen a lot more rough and tumble things than most of them had. A lot of them came in from big cities, and they'd never been exposed to any training or discipline. A lot of them were still Mama's boys and a few of them were dressed like thugs.

After getting a GI haircut, the new recruits learned how to shower, do their business and shave in five minutes. The next thing in the mornings was calisthenics, and then breakfast.

A lot of them didn't know how to march. They didn't know their left foot from the right. A lot were just unadaptable at becoming good marines. But our three instructors, Sergeant Wagner, Corporal Hurley and PFC Jackson were fine marines. They tried to take all the vim and vinegar out of everyone. You bet we had the rug pulled out from under us, but after they took the starch out of us they built us back like Marines.

There was a war going on. The Marine Corps needed replacements in a hurry. The normal ten-week boot camp training period had been cut to six or seven weeks just before Tapia's company was formed.

After four weeks into the training, the platoon began to get synchronized. They had completed bayonet and judo training, and learned to do whatever they were told.

I had been doing things like that all his life and loved it. A lot of those fellows couldn't summon up enough courage to do things like that. But near the end of training, they really taught you what to do. They marched you down to a brick wall; you kept right on marching, trying to walk right on through that brick wall no matter what. They knew that later on we would be told to take a hill or something. If that hill wasn't necessary, they wouldn't tell you to take it. We'd march into that wall until the instructor was satisfied that we could do it.

We had some big boys. I was about a hundred and seventy pounds, and some of these big boys would try to throw their weight around. But I never liked bullies. It sure was embarrassing to those big fellows when a hundred and seventy pound fellow like me would put them in their place.

As basic training graduation drew near, we were taken to a base movie theater. All those burr-headed kids who'd been disgraced by cutting off all those golden locks and taking the starch out of them were becoming men. One night we were coming back from the movies, and I knew the platoon had shaped up and come together. PFC Jackson was in charge. As our platoon was marching, he started off the cadence, and then he stopped. We marched all the way back to our barracks with everyone in step. They were strutting like a bunch of showoffs.

When one foot hit the ground, everybody's feet hit it. Everybody, including our Sergeant, recognized that the platoon had come together.

Right after that, my platoon was given the first liberty pass. I didn't know how to act in San Diego. I knew I had to fulfill the Marine image. A lot of them that had been overseas had come back and still wanted to sow their wild oats. But I didn't do too much. If a sailor came along and needed taming, we'd oblige him.

There was this swabby that was stinking drunk. He just wanted to fight somebody, and I happened to be in front of him. I let that fellow swing at me for fifteen minutes and he never connected. I didn't want to hit him and he just kept swinging at me until he fell out.

One week later, basic training ended. Most of the marines in Tapia's company were put on transports and sent to the South Pacific. In addition to making excellent scores throughout training, Tapia scored 348 points out of a possible 350 in the M-1 rifle competition. This qualified him to attend additional training at the Marine Scout Sniper School if he chose. It was not mandatory, but Gene jumped at the opportunity.

SCOUT SNIPER SCHOOL

I knew that only fifty percent of the men who became scout snipers returned home. But that didn't matter to me. I had slipped around as a boy and shot squirrels, and couldn't believe it would be much different.

The next two months, we underwent scout sniper training at Green's Farm, a large farm northeast of San Diego. They only allowed the two highest scoring men to volunteer for scout sniper training. But the whole thing was enjoyable. Now, it was hard, but I soon found out those instructors would help you if they saw you really wanted to learn. Everything they taught us was right up my alley. When my instructors saw how good I could shoot, they really took to me. They even prepared me to join the Marine Corps Rifle Team, which competed worldwide.

Gene never competed with the team in an actual contest, but he did practice with them. Being with some of the world's best marksmen made a lasting impression on the eighteen-year-old

Alabama farm boy. It served to heighten his interest in the training he was receiving.

If you couldn't sneak up on your opponents without being discovered, you didn't get to go on liberty. You had an objective and you crawled around toward the target without being spotted. If you could crawl in and hit the target with one shot, you advanced faster.

Gene advanced rapidly. Six weeks was all it took for him to complete the schooling.

The only thing bad about it was I always had skinned knees and elbows from crawling so much.

They taught us how to become invisible. We learned to read maps and the compass and how to travel twenty miles by going from point to point. We called it snooping and pooping. I spent more time on my hands and knees staring rattlesnakes eyeball to eyeball than I did my feet. But you couldn't jump when you came across one. You had to back off easily and go around that sneaky fellow, because if the officers, who were watching through binoculars saw you, you didn't get a night off that week.

The company's routine was to train eight days on and four off. If one marine failed, the entire platoon failed.

While most men struggled, Gene says he actually thrived on the rigorous training. Out of twenty-eight men who started the training, only eight graduated.

It was so interesting. All of it! And they kept you so busy. We didn't have time to think about anything else. You knew you had to be good to survive. You learned the know-how to help your buddy and rely on him, too. We learned not to go in there expecting to do it all yourself. We were taught over and over again that if a marine fell, someone would take over. If my captain fell, the next man would take over. And we had versatility enough to do this. We were taught to take care of ourselves, and that's why the Marines were so successful at what they did.

Completing the course meant qualifying again with a rifle. For long distances, Model 1903 Springfield's with scopes were usually preferred. There were a lot of men that could hit the target when it was just one thousand yards away, but there were very few that could hit it at 1,100 yards. But I had learned about windage, and it just came natural for me.

Near the end of training his company had been in the field eleven days and were given four days off.

They put us on a bus and took us to Los Angeles for liberty. There was an old Marine Raider named, Carlton "Red" Hill, that I really respected. He taught us a lot of marching songs, but mostly we sang these songs coming back on the bus after we'd been on the town for a while. Those old songs were pretty bawdy, but then again, the Marines weren't a sissy organization.

Going on liberty and looking at all those women was like being let out of a cage. As we were coming back to the base late one evening, we passed two women riding bicycles. One of them reminded me of Sally Hendrick, an attractive girl that lived in the neighborhood back in Mobile.

Uncle Aaron Wilkins had killed a three or four foot rattlesnake and had it mounted and placed it inside his Gulf Service Station on Moffett Road. His boy, Ellis Wilkins, rigged an air hose to the snake's tail. They had a button on the hose and when you pressed the button, that snake would start hissing.

One day, Sally had a flat tire on her bicycle, and she came pushing it into the station. Now, this girl was really good looking. She had long legs and was developed to a "T." All the boys tried to go out with her, but they never got to first base.

Just about the time she got her tire aired up, Ellis pushed the button on that snake and it began to hiss and wiggle around. Sally turned and when she finally saw that thing, she froze. But as soon as she stopped shaking and realized the snake wasn't alive, she grabbed a big stick and took out after them.

There had been a lot of snickering by the boys that were hiding inside, but when they saw her pick up that piece of two by four, they headed out the back door and into the woods.

MARINE RAIDER TRAINING

As graduation neared, his instructors told him that he might qualify for Marine Raider School because he was one of the top two men in his class.

Going to raider school was an option, not mandatory. But man, what marine wouldn't want to go to raider school? I would have given my right testicle for the opportunity. The Raiders had the reputation of being the toughest bunch of fighting men in the world.

After graduation from scout sniper school, he was sent back to San Diego, but this time to Camp Pendleton. On one side of the camp were Marine paratroopers. On the other side was a company of British commandos.

We trained to go in on the beaches, reconnoiter and then get the hell back out without being seen. But we learned just about everything, including the use of dynamite, and more judo. We had lots of forced marches that lasted from sixteen to twenty-four hours. The sixty and sixty-five-mile marches would be fast and quick. We didn't carry any heavy weapons, just Tommy guns and Reising guns. A Reising gun was flimsy, but it threw a lot of .45 caliber bullets. And it spewed them out fast.

One of the best gunnery sergeants I ever saw was Sergeant Forte. He was only about five feet, six inches tall, and a veteran of the Spanish Civil War. He enlisted in the Marines in 1935 as an armorer. He took an interest in me and taught me so much.

Anyone who ever believed the Raiders thought about heroics in advance was deceiving himself. We thoroughly enjoyed what we were trained to do. We were like a bunch of monkeys that had just been turned out of a cage. If we hadn't enjoyed the intensity and pressure, we wouldn't have lasted through the first week of the training.

The training was so rigid, and I had so much instilled within me that it's still with me until this day. The key was 'we.' It was a 'we deal.' We were all together. You talk about gung-ho. We were an outfit that really took care of each other. It wasn't just me. There were hundreds more just like me. It's just that I got to do a lot more than most people because I volunteered for everything.

Yes, I got scared but it's not a good idea to get scared because you lose your cool. If you overcome your fear, then you're more than likely to survive and get that other fellow before he gets you. The Raiders were the most synchronized fighting outfit in the world—highly trained, expert shots with no weak persons. They weeded them out to begin with.

To make it as a Raider, you had to believe you were the fastest and best. It was something that we ate and slept. You had to live it twenty-four hours a day.

If the officers saw you had weaknesses and weren't interested in being a first-class killer, zoom, you were gone. I was just a country boy. I didn't have much education, but I had a lot of good sharp common sense. I'd always hunted and shot things all my life. My mother taught me real early to be a crack shot and I couldn't see my mother outdoing me. My dad taught me a lot of things also. He taught me to always cover the ground where you stood. It was a no-no to run. I might have been a lot better off and a lot smoother if I had learned to run away from something, but the best thing in a ticklish situation is to run into it and get in the first punch.

Gene had been a rebel during his youth. But the Marines supplied the ingredients he needed to overcome that.

I was assigned to Company C of the Third Marine Raiders. The Company Commander was James Roosevelt, son of President Franklin D. Roosevelt. Just before we left San Diego, his mother, Eleanor Roosevelt came for a visit. She didn't like what she saw. She said the Raiders were too cruel and vicious. She said we should be banned from society and penned up for six months after the war in order to adjust to a normal life. She was probably right. But I didn't have any use for her after her visit. Later on, she caused the Raiders to be disbanded and her son removed from the dangerous outfit.

The Marines had a secret. They knew how to train all the fellows and what they needed to learn to do their job. Once a marine, always a marine. If a bunch of marines were to walk by right now, I'd take notice. It just makes my heart feel good to know I'm a Marine.

DESTINATION: SOUTH PACIFIC

The Marines in the Pacific needed men. By mid-December, 1943, Tapia had excelled in all the training the Marines were able to dish out. Two weeks before completing Raider School, he received his orders. He was to be a Marine Raider replacement. His assignment would be with the Third Marine Division.

This Division had some of the most seasoned veterans of any Marine group. They had taken part in many South Pacific campaigns. As Gene was completing Raider School, many of the men he would fight alongside were taking part in the Battle of Bougainville, one of the Solomon Islands.

For many men it might have been bad news, but not for Gene. He had completed schools in bayonet, hand grenade, demolitions, all types of rifles, machine guns and mortars, rubber boats, defense against chemical attacks, scouting, patrolling and field fortifications. Now he was prepared to take his place as a member of the roughest, toughest fighting organization in the world.

I was living my dream.

In December 1943, Tapia boarded a ship in Port Angeles, California: destination; Noumea, New Caledonia. He spent Christmas on board ship.

Joining up with the Second Marine Brigade, the Third Marines were called upon to man the island's defenses and carry out its intensive training plan. As their skills increased in jungle fighting amid incessant rain, they learned to use ropes to scale the steep mountain walls. This training would be needed on Guam and other islands.

One of the first Marines Gene admired on New Caledonia was a fellow Raider named, "Red" Hill, the same man who had helped train him in Scout Sniper School.

Sergeant Red Hill was a first class anything-he-wanted-to-be. He had dropped from being an officer all the way down to the brig. He just couldn't stand prosperity or promotions. It just wasn't in him to stay straight. They'd given him a battlefield commission because he had been in all the Marine fire fights and skirmishes up until that time. Two days after getting that commission, he busted another officer in the mouth and they threw him in the brig.

He was a first class killer. He practiced on us and taught us how to be vicious. Officers carried a riding crop, and Red had one of those. But Red's crop had a six or eight inch stiletto hidden in it. He would twist the handle, and instead of a riding crop, he had a spear. One day he got drunk and accidentally stuck one of our men in the knee with it. He misjudged, and stuck a marine named Harry Stuper with it. Even though he lacked certain finesse, Red was my kind of hero. He was the kind of marine I would prefer to have backing me in a battle.

While on New Caledonia, Gene learned about the Leper Colony on the island.

Quite often we patrolled through the area, but we never stopped. That was a no-no. I remember seeing an old man on the opposite side of the island that had Mumu. The proper name for it is Elephantiasis, where the testicles swell. This man's were as big as watermelons and he pushed them along in a cart.

One thing I recall about downtown Noumea was the Pink House. This was a house of prostitution. I never partook of these ladies services who worked there, but the line of servicemen extended outside for half a city block. I think it was two-dollars for two minutes.

Gene stayed on Noumea only three weeks. After an intensive daily training in jungle warfare, the Third Marine Amphibious Scout Company he was assigned to received orders to pack their gear.

CHAPTER VI

GUADALCANAL

    While myself and other members of my scout company had been training in jungle tactics, our superiors were studying and analyzing the situation on Guadalcanal, another one of the Solomon Islands. The Marines had already secured Coconut Grove, the main beach area around Henderson Field, but the thousands of Japanese left on the island were causing perplexing problems. They had fled the low areas and moved into the higher elevations. Jungle warfare was the only way to complete the victory on Guadalcanal. The Third Marine Division were selected for the job.

    When the troop ship left Noumea, I knew only that we were headed to another island.

    We were never told in advance where we were going. We only knew there would be fighting. I had no idea we were going to Guadalcanal until we rounded Cape Esperance and I saw the harbor and Henderson Field. All around the harbor area were beached Japanese and American ships.

Attrition was beginning to take its toll among the Japanese forces on Guadalcanal. Their destroyers continued to rush in reinforcements every night, but Marines, with the aid of heavy artillery, were able to push their perimeter farther west and prevent a new Japanese beachhead at Koli. But the Joint Chiefs of Staff in Washington had discovered the determination of the Japanese soldier on Guadalcanal. It was going to be hard to defeat them militarily. The apparent American naval victory in November 1942 ended a major buildup in either supplies or troops, but Japanese supplies still continued to arrive.

We were told that our mission would be to locate and destroy the enemy and train for future missions without doing anything foolish to ourselves or other marines.

Even a half world away from his family, the world still made sense to me. On board the troop ship to Guadalcanal, I learned I had become a father. A baby girl, named Shaaron, had been born December 31, 1943. While I had wanted another son to compensate for my guilt over the loss of the one that was stolen in Memphis, I felt overjoyed after receiving the news of Sharon's birth.

At nineteen years old, I was living my dream. I had only heard mention of dengue fever, malaria, jungle rot, the dangers of coral cuts, or any of a dozen other tropical diseases that would plague me later on.

Guadalcanal was the most beautiful island I ever saw. There were 200-foot waterfalls with water so clear you could spot fish forty feet down in the pools. The plant and animal life fascinated me also. I had never seen so many coconut palms, mangroves, breadfruit trees, bananas, papaya, orchids and beautiful birds. There were parakeets, parrots and flamingoes and all kinds of amazing multicolored birds big as American turkeys, as well as furry animals and iguanas.

Once, while looking at a particularly beautiful waterfall, there appeared a rainbow in the clear water as it cascaded down into the deep pool below. Suddenly, the water became alive with music. I was transported back to some of my earlier years when I used to hear my sister playing the piano in our home. As the water came off the top, it seemed like notes of music fell with it all the way to the bottom.

We often experienced hard times, but late in the afternoon when the house was quiet, and everyone was either sitting around or listening to the radio, my sister would practice her piano lessons. She had a beautiful voice. In addition to playing classical music, she would take little ditties that rhymed and make a simply tune out of them. Nobody could bring back sweet memories of home like my sister.

That was one of the few times I was able to stand in the jungle, surrounded by Japs, and experience any of my childhood pleasures.

But just as in every earthly paradise there are elements that Gene was about to discover that weren't so good.

Whenever we were out trying to round up Japanese stragglers, everything in the jungle would be quiet. Sometimes, you'd hear this crunch, crunch, crunch. Hearing any kind of sound would make you tighten up and start looking around. You were expecting something to pop out of the bushes any minute. You'd try to become as invisible as possible and melt into the jungle, but as the crunch sound got louder and louder you'd almost get scared out of your wits. Then pretty soon along came acres and acres of land crabs eating everything they came across. If you didn't get out of their way, you were a goner. They ate everything in their path.

Being in the jungle was really strenuous. You were hit by the heat, mosquitoes, leeches, and dense undergrowth of vines with hooks that would tear a chunk out of your arm, if you rubbed against it just right. There were ridges along the top of the island, and between those and the beaches, it was all jungle. After a heavy rain or late in the afternoon when the wind was quiet, there was a dead smell from all the decaying matter. After wading through a stream, you'd suddenly feel a sting, and there would be this creature on your leg full of blood.

At night we had swarms and swarms of mosquitoes and biting insects. They'd get in your mouth, ears and eyes. We had some stuff that was issued to us, but I think the bugs ate it for dessert after feasting on our bodies. The best remedy for the insects was mud—if you could stand it. This mud had a distinct, damp, musty and powerful smell. We got used to covering ourselves with this mud because it was the most effective insect repellant on the island.

Living conditions on Guadalcanal were never pleasant.

You did not grow accustomed to the noise. The sounds were constant. There were always bird and animal sounds day and night. The jungle at night was solid blackness. Some of the trees grew to over 100 feet in height. All light from the nighttime sky was shut out, whether the moon was shining or not. The enlisted men lived in small, hot tents when we weren't out patrolling or scouting. Food wasn't all that good.

Had Tapia's family known some of his actual missions, they would certainly have worried. Almost immediately after landing, he began to take part in scouting operations. By his own admission, he either volunteered or was chosen for nearly every mission because of his foolhardy attitude and proficiency with a Browning automatic rifle, or BAR.

A STRANGE LOOKING ENEMY

The Third Amphibious Scout Company was told they would leave on a three or four day scouting mission the following morning. Its mission was to round up Japanese stragglers and clear out snipers that were reported to be in the center of the island. Something that happened during this mission caused him to experience real fear for the first time.

The soldiers had little to fear from predatory animals. Because there was so little open grassland, there were no large grazing animals. The only exception were tame water buffalo belonging to the natives. The hordes of insects supported an array of bird life, including some colonies of large bats. Snakes were rarely encountered, and the only apparent water threat came from crocodiles and sharks.

Japanese snipers were one of the marines worst fears. They were dreaded because they never knew where their fire was coming from. If a marine could determine the direction of the sound, then the entire tree or grove could be sprayed. Most of the time, a forward patrol would spread out and move on, allowing a rear unit to deal with the sniper. Whatever their position, a sniper's main role was to slow down the American troops. A patrol might bypass the sniper rather than be pinned down on their scouting mission.

We got up about 4:00 a.m. and had our usual breakfast of powdered eggs and cream of wheat. But I didn't eat much of the cream of wheat because it always had black specks that I knew were weevils floating in it. We got our gear and were ushered into waiting trucks. We were taken about five miles to the Piti River. After wading across the river, the platoon assembled on the opposite bank.

Hour after hour was spent going through the almost impenetrable jungle undergrowth in a linear, or single-file column. There were no landmarks, but trails that we sometimes had to use because of the impassibility of the vines, and undergrowth. We crept, crawled and waited motionless while a guard or point man was sent out to check on something. When all the birds quit singing and cackling, you knew something was up.

There was a hush over the jungle and the entire platoon stopped. Pretty soon the platoon moved on, but since I was acting as the rear guard, I didn't know it. Visibility was less than a few yards, and the man ahead of me, Art Rogers of Mississippi had gotten out of eye-contact from me. He was supposed to tell me when we pulled out. The next thing I knew, I was all by myself. Just me, the jungle and a bunch of mad Japanese who'd like to cut my throat. Pretty soon I realized what had happened. It was up to me to find my platoon and catch up.

Concealment was easy, all you had to do was stand still. I had become thoroughly skilled in jungle movement, but so had the Japanese. I knew I had to avoid all trails and slip through the jungle as quietly and quickly as possible without being spotted. The idea of being captured wasn't an option. It didn't exist in the Raider Code.

One thing you always avoided was getting out in the open when there were palm trees around. These were a favorite hiding spot for Japanese snipers. They liked to pick you off. Suddenly, as I came to a clearing, I saw a palm that didn't look right. Some of the fronds were missing in the top. Fear never hit me, but for a few seconds I wasn't sure what to do. If I tried to move and there was a sniper in it, he might see me. And as close as I was to the tree, he wouldn't miss. I decided to try to sneak up on him, so I crawled a little bit here and a little bit there, each time keeping some bushes between us. About every fourth of fifth step, I would sink down in soft mud. When I would pull one of my boots out, it made a whoosh sound. Finally, I made it near the base of the tree without being spotted. My plan was to get directly under and look up through the branches. My first instincts were to let loose with a burst from my BAR, but that wasn't what I had been trained to do. If I fired, the entire area would know where I was and my platoon would be in jeopardy. Somehow I managed to control my emotions.

Suddenly, it seemed like the entire top of the tree exploded and this huge six or seven feet Iguana lizard came flying down the trunk, headfirst. After hitting the ground, that thing started scratching and tearing up leaves and limbs and just knocking them everywhere. Finally, it stopped, looked at me and flicked its tongue out a couple times. The hackles on its back were all raised up. After staring at me for a few seconds, it circled the tree two or three more times, then scooted back up the trunk and into the branches where it disappeared.

I had just stood there watching this big green monster of a lizard almost run over me. It all happened so fast I wasn't able to do anything. I can only believe it was a female who had a nest in the top of the tree and was warning me to stay away from her eggs.

After that experience, I was able to find my platoon and we completed the mission without further incident. They didn't even know they had left me. But I sure let Mr. Rogers know what I thought about him."

All the major fighting had been done near the coast, the major mountain peaks had not had a lot of military significance. The jungle-covered mountains were left to the various tribes of native peoples. It was into the caves along the ridges that the Japanese had retreated. This area between the beaches and mountaintops was rugged, precipitous, and lacked water. The area between Lunga Point and Mount Austen was heavily fortified by Japanese hidden in caves.

SHORTLAND ISLAND MISSION

In addition to being an excellent BAR man, Gene was also a good swimmer. Soon after arriving on Guadalcanal, he was told he was being attached to an eleven-man intelligence squad and they would leave the next morning on a submarine for a secret mission.

Allied Intelligence had reported that the Japanese were stepping up their resupply voyages into the Shortland Islands, one of a group of islands in the Northern Solomons. Several battalions plus artillery were suspected of being on the islands. Admiral Kelly Turner, commander of the naval and amphibious forces on Guadalcanal, needed to know the exact strength of the enemy on the islands because of a planned invasion.

The mission was critical. If there were heavy fortifications and large numbers of Japanese forces on the island, the Allies would not invade. If there were only a small number, then the Marines would prepare for an invasion.

They picked me to go on this mission because of my ability with a BAR. Since we didn't carry any light machine guns on our missions, a BAR was the next best thing. Any time there was a mission, it seemed like they wanted me because they knew I could back them up in case we were attacked from the rear.

In close-range fighting the BAR was a poor choice of weapons, because they were too large. But in terms of sheer firepower, they were second only to a machine gun. It was in reality a light machine gun that held a twenty-round clip of .30 caliber rifle ammunition and could be fired from the shoulder. Not every few marines was capable of carrying the twenty-pound weapon and lugging along ammunition, also.

In the Marines, you always had a buddy. The two of you looked out for each other. If one of you got in trouble, you knew there was somebody nearby to help you out. My buddy was a boy from Tyler, Texas, named Robert O. Bruce. There was myself, Robert O and nine others. I don't remember all the other men, but there was a Lieutenant Oscar Salgo, Sergeants Ed Cole and Charles Reed, and Corporal Paul Crokie.

We boarded a submarine about seven o'clock in the morning. They never told us the name of the sub because of security reasons. It was real tight quarters. We had brought all our equipment plus two rubber rafts. The crew aboard the submarine were nice to us and fed us well. Once we neared the island, the submarine surfaced a few miles out and we went ashore in two rubber dinghies. The plan was to go in and reconnoiter the island and rendezvous with the sub the following night.

Our job wasn't to go in and raise cane and chop down everyone we could find. We were to go in, reconnoiter the island and get out without being discovered. But if we were trapped, we would make the best of it, even though we knew none of us would survive.

The idea of being taken prisoner was never considered. If we had to get into a firefight, we wouldn't leave alive. That's the way the Raiders operated. There never were over eleven men on a patrol. Most patrols operated with four to six men. The more men you had, the more chances something could go wrong.

We inflated two rafts with a little hand pump on the deck of the sub and put all our gear in it before sliding it into the water. All the men jumped in the water, and pulled themselves into it. Each man had a small paddle, that he used very gently and quietly, so as not to make any noise. Both teams stayed together and landed on a small sandy beach near the east end. After wiping out our tracks with palm fronds, we pulled the rafts into a little canyon and deflated them. We knew we were going to spend the rest of the night and the next day, so we hid them in some underbrush in a small canyon.

The scouting party had landed in the planned location. All members had to climb an almost vertical bank to reach the top. Surrounding the canyon walls were lots of low, thick, scrubby underbrush and trees.

After scouting around, we discovered there was an estimated 15,000-25,000 Japanese on the island. We found out later the Marines wanted to invade the island, but they had been misled. Had our side attacked this well-fortified island, we would have lost a lot of men.

We spent the day hidden from view of Japanese scouting parties. We came across several quite suddenly. Even on this island, they were camouflaged and hard to see until they all seemed to pop up out of the brush only yards away. At times it was scary and confusing: they seemed to be all around us. But in spite of the uncertainty about getting off the island, we were able to make detailed maps of their strength and positions. After gathering what we felt was as much as possible, it was imperative we get that information back to Marine headquarters on Guadalcanal.

That night, we inflated the rafts and headed back out, being sure to avoid the coral reefs that would have either cut the raft or capsized them. It was rough going, because we had to row quietly, but with the incoming swells, it took at least thirty minutes to clear the reef. After paddling around for several hours, we never made connections with the submarine and had to come back and spend another day on the island.

The tide had pushed us away from our original hiding spot, so we had to locate another one. This time the scrubby area we chose to hide in this time was less than an acre in size. The low underbrush was mostly made up of ironwood trees. They were only three or four feet high and thick and matted. After hiding the rafts for a second time, we discovered that a Japanese regiment had set up a base camp and our entire patrol was encircled by enemy troops.

That next day was pretty tense. They were so close we could hear them during roll call. If somebody had coughed or hiccupped, none of us would have made it back. But there would have been one hell of a fight.

The next night, we put the rafts back in the water and paddled back out. Every man still had his small wooden paddle and we dipped together.

Finally, our party made connections with the submarine. We found out later there had been a Japanese patrol boat in operation the night before. By midmorning the next day, the sub was back at its dock on Guadalcanal.

We were immediately taken to Intelligence and debriefed. Based on our observations and scouting reports, the invasion of this island was postponed. It would have been too costly because of the number of men we would have lost. The only landing area on it was so small that the Japanese gunners would have picked them off before they could have established a beachhead.

Instead of invading it, the Navy surrounded it with patrol boats to keep supplies from reaching their men. I don't know how the poor fellows survived. I guess they ate coconuts until they starved to death or the war ended.

On Guadalcanal, it wasn't just the Marines that were against the Japanese who were left on the island, it was the natives also. They hunted the Japanese down and killed them because they had taken their food and shelter and raped many of the women. All younger men had been forced to flee into the hills rather than meet death or slavery at the hands of the Japanese. As we moved into the more mountainous terrain and remote jungle areas, the natives volunteered as guides and trackers.

Many islands in the South Pacific were populated by Polynesians, but natives on Guadalcanal were of Melanesian descent. This war came without warning to them and concerned issues they did not understand. With only a few notable exceptions, few had a personal stake in the outcome of the war. Although Guadalcanal was a huge island, people who lived neared the coast experienced the most fighting. Individuals and families who lived inland might only see aircraft and patrols. Most of those who were driven inland by the fighting rejected the Japanese because of the treatment they received at their hands, which included theft, forced labor, and rape of the women.

The native villages were real neat. Each village consisted of six to ten thatched houses built of poles. They were gatherers, not farmers, but every village grew their own yams. They moved the entire village several times a year, based on the type fruit that was in season.

Their hair was very bushy, but most of the children had orange colored hair. As a child, they had been dipped headfirst into a vat of hot lye solution. The medicine man or leaders of the tribe picked the little kids up by their heels and dipped them headfirst down to their ears into this solution. It killed the lice, but it caused the hair to be permanently colored.

They were big strong people who didn't wear anything but cut-off green shorts or grass skirts. The women didn't wear tops and she usually had a youngster on her hip that might be sucking on one of her breasts. They didn't think anything about it. This was the way they lived, and the Americans were welcome.

They'd burn something every night to keep the swarms of mosquitoes away, and the smell this gave off permeated everything. Sometimes, it could be detected as far as a mile away.

Only the fisherman lived right down on the beach. The other natives lived up near the center of the island where it was mountainous. The higher up you went, the cooler it got, and there was always a breeze that blew in off the Pacific. If it quit blowing, look out, because a hurricane or bad weather was coming.

Once you got down in the jungle, there was no wind. It was just sulky, nasty and clammy. You had to chop your own paths because everything grew so fast. There was a road that went around the island. It was like a tunnel because all the tree limbs overlapped it.

THE BOY GROWS UP

After a few months, Gene had learned the real meaning of jungle warfare. He had battled an unseen enemy in strange, densely wooded territory amid rain, mud, sweltering heat and clouds of insects. He had found the Japanese to be crafty, determined fighters. He respected them, but he wasn't afraid.

This was the real South Pacific of mud, where the beautiful green of the jungle dripped with infected water and crocodiles.

Guadalcanal was the worst of all tropical islands. There were scores of sunken ships in Ironbottom Sound that oozed oil and other contaminants, and there were also sharks and salt water crocodiles which had developed a taste for the human flesh they found on board the sunken ships.

Even though his unit was still rounding up Japanese stragglers, preparations for the next operation had already begun.

Training was vigorous. We reviewed and practiced all our jungle fighting in some of the densest jungle you can imagine. There were places so thick we had to hack our way through with machetes.

Food wasn't all that good. We usually tried to supplement our C-rations by gathering bananas, coconuts, papaya and breadfruit when the enemy wasn't around. The clear pools were plentiful with fish. But they wouldn't bite a hook. The only way we could catch them was to take a grenade, and, after popping the cap, hold it about two seconds and let it drop. The ten-second timer would usually go off about where the fish was, and he would float belly up to the top."

While there was plenty of water on Guadalcanal and it rained everyday, the water contained parasites. The Americans could not drink it unless they added an atropine and water purifier tablets. There was some type of larvae in the water that was a carrier of malaria. Drinking it caused a bad sickness.

When we went on these two or three day patrols, we would try to get a couple slices of bacon and a few potatoes from the mess hall. We usually got to take a break about noon and eat. If the platoon leader didn't think we were close to any Japanese, he would allow us to cook. It's an art to building a small fire, especially if the wood is wet. After I got the fire going, I'd put some bacon in my mess kit. That made a little grease, and then I'd put in the potatoes. It wasn't too bad because we usually had our C-rations, too.

The water wasn't any good to drink, but we learned how to cut open a green coconut and get the water out of it. And there were papaya that had a lot of juice and a type of cactus, whose leaves contained water.

But one of the worst things was camping out at night. It rained every night. The platoon would stop just before dark and guards were posted. We tried to get set up before it got real dark. If you chose a low spot to sleep in and it rained, you got soaked. The water would just run down on you, and the next morning your skin would look like a dried prune. Sometimes, you'd be lying there listening to the sounds of birds or animals, not being able to sleep and your mind would drift back to other times.

The whole thing was kind of ticklish. There were all kinds of sounds, strange animals and always the land crabs. The bad thing about the land crabs at night was you didn't know which way to run. Eventually, we were able to detect the difference between animals and humans walking in the jungle. One of our sergeants walked through to train us to tell the difference in human sounds. These patrols were sometimes nightmarish. A constant danger to the marines were small pockets of Japanese who would sneak in at night and cut the throats of sleeping marines, then slip back into the jungle before they were discovered. We didn't have many night skirmishes because it was too dark to see anything.

Members of my company made friends with the 19th Marine Seabee Company. They were composed of older construction workers and engineers. As a rule, they had better and more plentiful food. Whenever we were in base camp, I tried to eat at their mess hall.

These men weren't trained as much for combat as we were, but they were just as tough. We respected and depended on each other. Whenever they'd go into the Japanese infested areas with a bulldozer, some of us would go along to help protect them. I saw a bulldozer operator raise the blade on his machine and plow right into a Japanese pill-box.

While most of the time we were either hunting Japanese stragglers or training, there was one strange incident that was never explained to me.

One day I saw a group of four men surveying. They had instruments like they were taking measurements for some type of construction project. There was an American, a Dutchman, New Zealander and an Australian. When I started to ask questions about where they came from, no one knew. Nobody that I know of ever officially declared that they were on the island.

One day they didn't show up and then nobody could prove they were ever actually there. But I saw them and so did many others. To this day, I've never been able to find out what they were doing there. I speculate they were German agents who were picked up by a Japanese sub.

In late January 1944, the Marine garrison on Guadalcanal was entrusted with the safety of Henderson Field and rounding up Japanese stragglers still on the island. As other Third Marine veterans returned to Guadalcanal from Bougainville in February and March 1944, emphasis was placed on whipping the entire Third Division back into shape for the next operation.

By this time, I acting as an instructor to other marines. While many of the men who returned from Bougainville had seen lots of action, they had not received the extensive scout sniper and Raider training that I had undergone in California.

You got to understand that marines had to be ready for anything. All the marines who returned from Bouganville had seen action on the beaches, but many of them hadn't received the training I had. Once you were in the line of Japanese gunfire, you learned respect for those fellows. When bullets began whizzing around, you had to be smart to survive. A dead marine was of no use to his family or us.

Some of the marines were thrown in the brig. It was usually because they had hit an officer or something like that. Because he was in the brig didn't mean his training ceased. When the proper time came, he was sent on a mission with the rest of us. His training had to continue. He needed to be able to keep himself alive and work alongside his buddies.

The composition of the forces on Guadalcanal was made up of the Third Marine Raider Battalion, 10th and 11th Marine Defense Battalions, and a portion of the Army 43rd Infantry

Division, 35th Navy Seabees, several small artillery groups, and a small mixed Naval boat pool. By late February, Henderson Field was home to nearly 180 aircraft.

It was in this mixture of troops and personnel that Gene worked and trained. In addition to being an explosive expert, he was an excellent swimmer. While on Guadalcanal, he took part in several scouting operations to other Japanese held islands. Gene and Robert O Bruce teamed up as swimmers. Each one acted as the other's left or right hand. Since they had to have a dark complexion so they could not be seen at night, both lay out in the sun to get dark tans. No swimmer could have red or blonde hair because it would be easily spotted at night.

Sometimes we would go on a submarine, but most of the time, they would put us on an LST or some other type landing craft that could get us within three miles of the shore. Robert and I were like twins. We stayed together on the missions and never got out of each other's sight. We would swim in with just a kabar knife and flashlight. We had to pick our location by the contour and silhouettes of the island.

All these islands have coral reefs, and I cut myself many times. I still experience pain from cuts I received scouting these islands. After we scouted the beach, we'd either signal by flashlight for the main party to come on shore, or, if we thought it was heavily defended, we'd swim back out and hope we could find the boat or sub.

On one mission, Gene and Robert swam ashore and had just reached the beach. Suddenly, one of them saw a figure hiding behind a large log nearby. We didn't have to tell each other which direction we were going. It was instinctive. Robert went around the log on the left side and I went right. As I crawled around the end of that big log, I raised my knife. There was the man! As I was about to plunge my kabar knife into that Japanese soldier, I heard this quiet voice, 'Is that you, Taps?'

It was Robert O. Bruce; he had come around the other end of that big tree trunk. What we had thought was the silhouette of a soldier was just a limb sticking up with a leaf still on it.

Before all the Japanese were evacuated from Guadalcanal, Japan had suffered her most humiliating defeat. Of the 38,000 troops sent in to fight on the "Island of Death," 24,000 never left. The number who died of diseases and starvation outnumbered those killed in battle.

SHIFTING BATTLE FRONT

By the latter part of May 1944, the Marine Raiders had been disbanded. Gene was reassigned to the Third Amphibious Reconnaissance Company. His company and a Dog Corps began conducting full-scale practice landings under naval and aerial bombardment of beaches at Cape Esperance on Guadalcanal.

We were either training or out on missions hunting stragglers. But near the end of May, our training really intensified. We began preparations for what we knew would be another major amphibious landing. The only thing different in our training was house-to-house combat.

By this time, it was more like a game. We were pitting our game against theirs. We knew that we had the best team. A marine just knows he's the best in the world. You knew within reason you were going to get shot somewhere, but you didn't think about getting clipped.

I could not stand cook or mess details. If I knew my name was on some camp detail, and something else was going on, I would volunteer for it, no matter how dangerous it might be.

They knew I had been a Raider and a sniper, and I did my job and I was what they needed, therefore I got picked a lot. And by this time, I had earned a lot of respect from the officers. If I had a little more education, I would have become an officer.

We had this young lieutenant fresh from the States on a training program. He knew what he was doing, but he'd never been in combat. He began to tell us how our squad should handle a line of enemy barbed wire.

Back on the farm, I had several bulls run me into barbed wire. You just had to know how to handle it to keep from getting all cut up. He asked for a volunteer to lie across that wire while the rest of the platoon crossed over on his back.

Well, old stupid Gene just had to volunteer. I dove into that barbed wire. My rifle was between my body and the wire and my butt was up in the air, while all ten men in the squad crossed over. After the last man was across, I just rolled off that wire with very few cuts on me. From then on I had a lot of respect from all the men and officers.

A REQUEST FROM THE HOMEFRONT

I did not write many letters because I didn't want to worry the folks back home and besides, most of the time I was just too busy. It was after a long mission or when we were heading for another battle that I thought most about home. Once, I was summoned to the chaplain's quarters because Francine had written a letter to my commanding officer.

Out there, we didn't have time to think. We stayed out in the jungle for three to four days, then when we'd get back, we were tired. It was usually dark when we returned and all we had to write by was a small candle. We had no pens, and I would have to scrounge around to even borrow a pencil. It wasn't because I didn't care about my family. We had a job to do, and, by golly, I was going to see that I did my share. But as soon as the chaplain let me go, I went straight to my tent and wrote that letter.

"For me and the family, the waiting with no word from him was agonizing after not hearing from him for almost a year," said Francine. "Everything was running well at home. Mr. John Diering took care of everything around the place, while Gene's mother worked most of the day at her four restaurants. Lenora Jane, Gene's grandmother, who we called "Gangy" and I pretty much ran the house. By this time, Shaaron was walking and getting into everything. The days were always busy, but I missed Gene. The last thing I did before going to sleep every night was ask God to bring him back safely.

"I didn't write Gene's commanding officer because I wanted to get him in trouble. We wanted to know what was happening with him. We all loved him and cared about him. I don't think we had gotten but one letter from him since he had left for boot camp. We didn't know if he was dead or what. But most of all, he was my husband and I can't tell you how worried I was about him."

Members of Third Marine Division Jungle-Fighting on Guadalcanal

CHAPTER VII

INVASION OF GUAM

After completing more extensive training, the Third Marines were told to get ready. It was time to move. What Gene or the rest of the division didn't know was that the next field of action wouldn't be mopping up operations. It would be a full-blown invasion involving thousands of troops.

On June 7, 1944, Gene and members of the Third Marine Division and other elements of Task Force 53 left Guadalcanal, still not knowing their ultimate destination, and headed for staging areas in the Marshall Islands.

We left early in the morning with all our gear packed. We had everything but ammunition. That was passed out on the ship. We wore boondock shoes and dungarees and helmets. That helmet served so many purposes. You could pour water in it, take a bath out of it, and make stew in it. Of course it would be smoked up, so you'd have to rub sand over it to get the blackness off.

The actual invasion was to be the island of Guam, but after a two-day delay, parts of the task force were ordered to standby on several small islands until the invasion was rescheduled. After practicing amphibious assaults on Kwajalien and Eniwetok islands, portions of the task force sailed for the Marianas and the planned attack on the Island of Saipan. Gene and most of the Third Marine Division remained on board ship as a reserve force.

W-day for the liberation of Guam had originally been set for three days following the assault on Saipan, presumably, June 15. But the order canceling W-day was received on June 16.

When it became apparent there would be an indeterminate delay, the major landing force of which Gene was a part stayed near Eniwetok. The Division had long been ready to fight, and this delay only created tension.

We had been cooped up on that ship for over three weeks, and of course we didn't know where we were going. We exercised every day, but it wasn't like being on the ground and running. We were getting soft. Our ship had to anchor two or three miles off the shore and we got in landing craft and went to the island almost daily. Once we got to the beach, we started swimming and playing on some of the sandy islets around the l lagoon.

DANGER IN THE SEA

You could look down through this beautiful clear water and see the coral and brightly-colored fish. It reminded me of what I thought waters in the Garden of Paradise must be like. We found some big rocks out in the center of this inlet. The tops of them were about a foot below the surface of the water. We all took turns climbing up on these big mossy rocks and diving off. They made excellent diving platforms.

We noticed the incoming tide was very swift. You could almost see the level of the water rising. About the time the tide started coming in one day, it was time for us to leave. One of our platoon sergeants, Horst "Tony" Schramm, was still swimming.

We didn't know it at the time, but those rocks we had been diving off were giant clams. As Tony swam by one of them, his arm slipped into its mouth and it clamped shut. There he was with an arm stuck in this giant clam, and the tide was rising fast.

He began to tell us, 'Hey, fellas, my arm is caught and I can't get it out.'

Some of us dove back into the water and began inspecting the big rock and discovered what it really was. We had heard of those things, but no one had told us they were on any of these islands.

The tide was rising, and Pony was running out of arm and air. He was keeping his head up, but he was losing to the incoming tide. We took turns diving down and chipping away at the shell with our kabar knives, but still we could not get his arm out. We either had to chip the shell out around his arm and free it, or cut his arm off.

'Whoooosh,' Tony said after we finally chipped his arm free and he was able to get a deep breath of air. 'That was a close one.'

The Third Marines remained on Eniwetok for nearly two more weeks. All told, Gene and the other members of the Third Marines spent forty days on the transport. It wasn't until July 21, 1944, that the task force stormed the beaches at Guam and established the planned beachhead

"We knew by this time we were going to a real firefight. I liked to lay out on the deck of the troop ship as much as possible because it was hot down below. Marines who couldn't stand the rolling and tossing of the ship were constantly throwing up."

The island of Guam came into the possession of the United States in 1898. It is the largest, most populated and southernmost of the Marianas Islands. Thirty-two miles long and four to eight miles wide, it covers an area of about 220 miles.

Prior to the war, Guam had very little value, either economically or as a military base. Though it did have a small harbor, it was not suitable for any large-scale shipping operations or fleet anchorage.

The Japanese only required four hours on December 8, 1941, to attack and seize it. The labor and expense it cost them to defend it was considerably more.

Topographically, the northern half of Guam is formed by a broad plateau sloping upward from an altitude of about one hundred feet at the lowlands between Agana and Yona, to an elevation of six hundred feet at the end of Ritidian Point. In the southern half of the island, broken country arises from the central lowlands. A prominent range paralleling the west coast from

Agana to Port Ajayan forms the backbone of Guam. In little more than a mile inland from Apra Harbor, this range rises to Mt. Alutom, Mt. Chachao, and Mt. Tenjo, all about one thousand feet in height.

The sections of the island that are of volcanic origin are covered with sword grass, cogon grass and low bushes. The coral lime areas support dense tropical underbrush and large trees.

For seventeen days, naval gunfire and aerial bombardment from Task Force 53 had pounded the island. The destruction to the beaches and landscape was tortuous. An hour before the transports dispatched the troops, the shelling stopped.

Lt. Gen. Roy S. Geiger, Third Amphibious Corps commander, issued a statement to the marines as they left the troop transports at 0830, July 21, 1944: "The eyes of a nation watch you as you go into battle to liberate this former American bastion from the enemy. The honor which has been bestowed upon you is a signal one. Make no mistake; it will be a tough, bitter fight against a wily, stubborn foe who will doggedly defend Guam against this invasion. May the glorious tradition of the Marine esprit de corps spur you to victory. You have been honored."

We were already out on deck, preparing to get into the LST's, as the ship's gigantic guns rose and resumed firing, this time at targets farther inland. I adjusted my field pack and held tightly to my Browning automatic rifle as I climbed down the rope ladder into the landing craft. Soon, we joined dozens of others headed for the beach.

The fight was underway. Guam was the next island in the Allied plan that would eventually reach the homeland of Japan. The battle and outcome were now in the hands of the United States Marines.

We came ashore on two thousand yards of beach between Asan Point and Adelup Point, called Beach Blue As soon as we landed on the beach, we started digging a foxhole. That first night was miserable. Mortar shells and cannon fire fell everywhere, all night long. And then there was the rain. It poured on us. The foxholes filled up with water, but you couldn't get out because if you did, you'd get blown away.

The next morning wasn't any better. We had to claw our way across that beach and up into some hills three or four hundred yards inland. There were fortified caves hidden in these hills that our bombing hadn't touched. The Japs in these caves laid down a crossfire that raked our lines continuously.

From the beginning of the battle for Guam, caves became the individual battlegrounds for hundreds of skirmishes. Lying in wait in hundreds of sheltered caves and wooded folds of reverse slopes, the Japanese had survived the American Navy's initial shelling and had guns and mortars perched above the Third Marine Division.

The Third Amphibious Scout Company countered this with our training, speed, coordination and the will to win. You took a machine gun and kept enough fire on each cave until you could advance some troops on that cave. Each cave was a separate combat firefight. We had to take them cave-by-cave and hill-by-hill. And there was always fire coming at you from other caves.

If we could have gotten the leaders of all the countries involved in those cave battles, the war would have ended right then.

You had to attack them with either flame throwers or depth charges. We had a dog platoon that was attached to us. Some of the bravest acts I ever witnessed were performed by these dog-men. Those men and their dogs saved many lives.

It was rough going. You couldn't defend yourself; because you never knew which way the bullet was coming from. Those dogs were invaluable. By watching the dog's actions, the handler could tell when the dog was onto a Japanese, because the Japanese had a different smell from Americans. The handler was always in a precarious position, because he was up ahead of us with the dog. They were always in grave danger because the Japanese snipers fired on them first.

It was my job to scout and reconnoiter behind enemy lines. Attached to the platoon were Nisei—Japanese-Americans, who broadcasted to the Japanese in an attempt to coax them into surrendering.

We had captured a group of barracks to the right of where we landed that had been used by the enemy. They left a lot of documents, and it was our job to go through them and learn what we could. The information we learned told us about their troop strength, number of Japanese on the island, and the layout of their artillery.

RESCUE OF THE 27TH ARMY DIVISION

While we were deciphering all this information and relaying it back to headquarters, the U.S. Army's 27th Division, which had made it ashore, became pinned down. They weren't as adept at this type fighting as we were. They had come within range of several Japanese in caves. Boy, they had them targeted. They weren't able to move forward or backward.

The 27th Division was caught out in an open area. Between the division and the hills was a large open plain. Holed up in caves in the cliffs were enemy snipers.

The Army believed in laying back and letting their artillery take care of things. That's good, but in this situation, the artillery wasn't doing any good against the Japanese in those caves.

After about four hours, the situation had worsened. More Japanese were firing on them. If one of those fellows blinked an eye, he drew sniper fire. We were the only marines in the area, so they sent word for our squad to go up and clean those snipers out and allow the 27th to move forward.

From inside their caves in the hills, the Japanese were able to watch our squad as we worked our way across an open field towards the cliffs. Now, the Japanese snipers had a new target and they redirected their fire right on us.

We were sneaking up on these caves, and wham, one of our dog men got it. The bullet went right through his heart. He was gone instantly. I felt so sorry for that old Doberman dog after his handler got hit. They were attached. They ate together. They slept together. They went everywhere together. They were a pair. When his handler got killed, it was like he died, also. It just shattered his spirit. But I can tell you, we did locate that sniper and he didn't shoot anybody else.

Going up against a seemingly insurmountable invisible enemy, we pushed forward and upward. First we fired, and then we ducked and tried to make themselves invisible.

We worked our way around to the left side of the caves. Robert O. Bruce was the grenade man and I was the BAR man. After pulling the pin on one of those pineapples, he would hold it for two or three seconds, and then throw it in the mouth of the cave. As soon as the thing went off, I'd jump up and spray the twenty rounds from my BAR into it.

We repeated this operation three or four times at each cave. Each time after firing, I would duck back down and slip in another twenty round clip while Robert tossed them fellows another pineapple. It wasn't long before they stopped firing.

Finally, the 27th Army Division was able to move out.

Eventually, we became so adept at clearing out Japanese caves with our system; we were assigned an extra ammo and grenade carrier who followed us at a distance.

After Gene and his squad eliminated the snipers, the 27th went on to become involved in the bloody battle of Sugar Loaf Hill, one of the bloodiest and costliest battles on Guam. By the end of the second day, casualties were high for both sides. The combined total by midnight, July 22, reached 815 killed, wounded or missing. The Third Marines had paid dearly for the small, yet strategic amount of ground they occupied.

The terrain of the island continued to favor the enemy. Because of the enemy's advantage on the hills where they had artillery, the Marines were subject to a fusillade of fire. Eventually, the Marines were able to capture Piti Navy Yard and the small offshore island of Cabras.

A seemingly unending flow of reinforcements into the Japanese positions on the Third Marine's left flank meant that the main enemy troop strength lay north and east of the Third Scout Company lines.

There was only a few hundred yards of beach. When you got away from that, you were in the hills and caves. The terrain would not allow us to move rapidly, and this allowed them to bring in reinforcements against us. This was some rough fighting, but the Marines hadn't come there to just sit and wait. We hated sitting around. They weren't going to stop us. Yes, we met resistance, but we overcame it. We fought snipers in trees, ravines, and we fought them in caves. Wherever we found them, we fought. There were a few times we had to back up and take cover, but we came to win. We killed a lot of Japanese soldiers, but we lost a lot of good marines.

It was necessary to call in artillery and air strikes in close support of an attack. The supporting planes used rockets, and the attack was usually successful. Over 200 Japanese dead were counted in one spot. After two days of fighting, the Third

Marines were able to capture some high ground that had been a thorn in the side of the whole division since W-day."

BATTLE OF SUGAR LOAF HILL

Because of the 9,000-yard battle line frontage the division was severely overextended with practically no reserves available. Only one depleted battalion, the First Battalion, Third Marines, was in reserve. One of the largest and costliest battles fought on Guam began on July 25. As Gene and the Third division moved inland, they came to the Fonte-Mt. Tenjo Road. Gene refers to the highest area as Sugar Loaf Hill because so many men died on it. The enemy had heavily fortified the long plateau and a long battle ensued.

The Battle for Sugar Loaf Hill came about three days after we had rescued the 27th Army Division. That was a bad, bad experience. It was pretty raunchy. There were caves and tunnels honeycombed into the mountain. At one time this had been a Japanese headquarters area.

Shortly after midnight, on the morning of July 26th, artillery and mortar fire began raining down on the Third Marines. Our entire Scout Platoon were attacked and forced to withdraw. Unless you've experienced hand-to-hand fighting, I can only say, it's death for the loser. Fifteen Japanese were killed in a wild bayonet charge by the Second Battalion. A combat post was overrun, and there was activity all along the line. About 1:30 a.m., on the morning of July 26, the Japanese launched several small attacks all along the Marines' front line. The attackers were well armed and equipped, with even demolition charges, which they rolled down the steep slopes.

After not having slept for five nights, you might think we would be sleepy. But it was hard to sleep. Those jokers were constantly firing on us. In a situation like that, nature has a way of looking out for you. You develop a fatalistic type attitude. You just don't care. You know what you've got to do and you do it. You don't think. If a man were to think in those kind of situations, he would either kill himself or go crazy.

In the morning darkness, just before dawn, it sounded like all hell had broken loose. First, there were mortars and grenades. Then there was wild screaming. It was part of an attack to drive us back from the beachhead. Flares lit up the sky and everybody was firing. But our machine guns cut them down. They never reached us.

Other Marine Battalions weren't as lucky. Company B of the First Battalion lost thirty-two of their fifty men. Tanks parked in the rear of the lines began mowing down the Japanese troops as they broke through the line. One report described the Japanese as a horde of ants. A few made it through the line. The Mortar Platoon of the First Marines was practically wiped out.

We had lots of casualties, but the Marines held their position. The next day we traced the breakthrough by the line of dead bodies. First, you would see a Japanese laying there, then a marine, and then more bodies. All that next day we mopped up small units that got stranded behind our lines.

According to a report issued by the Twenty-first Marines, many of the enemy were drunk. A number of canteens found on the enemy dead contained liquor, and empty sake bottles were found near the front lines. An estimated 3,200 Japanese died that night, according to Third Marine records.

You couldn't get any rest at night. Just about the time you got dug in good, you would begin to hear the loud shrieks that were typical of Banzai charges. And if it got quiet, then you worried about them infiltrating the lines and cutting your throat. The Japanese didn't mind dying. His mentality was if he died for the Emperor, he immediately went to heaven. They would come in and try to get you, knowing they were going to die.

After most of the heavy fighting stopped, and we started to the top, there were dead bodies everywhere. Most were Japanese but there were many Americans, as well as cattle and other animals. The fighting had been going on for nearly two days when we made our way up to the high areas. The stench of the bodies was almost unbearable. And the flies! There were millions and millions of flies swarming over the bodies. Scrambling to the top, we realized that these flies were almost as much of a threat as the enemy snipers.

The next day a strange thing happened. I guess nature has a way of balancing itself out because when we were coming down, millions of frogs, that looked just like our toads, appeared and were eating the flies. I actually saw lines of frogs on one side of a body, while there would be two or three sitting on top of it. They would zap, zap, zap with their tongues at these flies. It wouldn't be but a few minutes and each frog would be big and swollen from eating so many of those flies. Then he would jump or fall off, and two or three more would climb on to take his place.

We buried our dead right away, but they brought in some Seabees with bulldozers and dug trenches and buried the Japanese. Weeks later, after the island had been called secure, Admiral Nimitz, who was head of the Pacific Fleet, decided he wanted to set up his headquarters right on the top of that hill because it was one of the highest points on the island. The only problem with establishing a headquarters building was the hundreds of Japanese bodies we had buried in the side of the mountain.

To solve this problem, the United States hired the Chamorro natives to dig up the Japanese bodies. After they were disinterred, they were hauled away to another burial site in Marine trucks. This high spot where Admiral Nimitz eventually set up his headquarters is often referred to as Nimitz' Hill.

When Admiral Nimitz decided he wanted to establish his headquarters on Guam, he wanted it so he could see the Pacific Ocean on both sides of the island. The only suitable place to put his headquarters was right on top of Sugar Loaf Hill.

I'm sure they picked the best spot on Guam for his headquarters but the job of digging those bodies up and hauling them out of there by the truckload and taking them to a different area was very precarious. There were still Japanese stragglers on the island. When the Japanese found out that our government had hired the natives to dig up their dead, they became increasingly hostile toward the natives and started ambushing them. Like we weren't having enough problems saving our own necks, now we had to protect the natives, too.

THE FATE OF JESUS CHAMACHO

During the reburial work, I made friends with one of the Chamorro natives. His name was Jesus (pronounced Hay-souz) Chamacho, but we called him Jesus Chamorro, because he was a native. This little fellow was about nineteen or twenty years old and only stood about five feet eight inches, and weighed less than one hundred thirty pounds, but he was a live wire. And he could speak pretty good English, better than most Chamorros.

There were blood and guts and dead bodies being dug up by the truckloads and hauled away to another burial ground. Now, you can just imagine what we had to go through watching all this and guarding the natives from snipers, too. If the natives picked up a body by the leg or arm, it would usually wind up coming off. The smell permeated our bodies, clothing and everything. You never get used to that kind of thing. So who could blame us when we took a drink of some Japanese Sake? Every once in a while, the natives would find a bottle of untapped Sake in a cave or somewhere. Jesus liked me and a few other fellows, so whenever a bottle of Sake was uncovered, he would have the natives hide it for us.

Jesus was a good fellow. He was likeable and was able to keep the other Chamorros working. Now, it wasn't like they were digging up these bodies for nothing. No, the United States Government was paying them outrageous prices.

We had been digging the bodies up for several weeks and were within three or four days of completing the job. Jesus found a U.S. Marine's .30-caliber carbine, and he began to inspect it. He thought if he took the clip out it wouldn't shoot. He was looking down the barrel when the round that was left in the chamber went off and blew the side of his head off. There was another friend of mine that had gotten killed. He was our favorite of all the Chamorro workers, but that was his fate.

As long as I remained on Guam, I had intestinal problems from drinking water. Even though I attempted to purify each canteen full, dysentery and other stomach problems were always with me.

Those frogs were so numerous they fell in the streams, wells and contaminated all the water. From then on, we had to purify all the water before we could drink it. One day right after we had left Sugar Loaf I filled my canteen from a beautiful clear stream. I dropped two purifying tablets in it and continue on patrol. About a hundred feet upstream, there was a Japanese body laying in the water.

Whenever possible, I would drink the water from green coconuts rather than using my canteen water.

Coconuts were a main source of food for the Chamorros. It was fine to eat the meat, but if you drank the juice of a mature coconut, you were very subject to getting the skeets. You had to drink it before it became oily in the coconut. If you looked at it and it was oily looking on top, you didn't drink it. If you did you were going to have a bad case of diarrhea. The natives taught us what stage coconuts to get. And you had to be awful careful walking under coconut trees, because coconuts fell all the time. When you were out in the jungle and one fell, you would always jump, because you didn't know whether someone was getting ready to chop your head off or what.

By this time Robert O. Bruce and myself were pretty good at cave warfare. On Sugar Loaf, we killed the Japs who swarmed out of the caves and sealed the remainder inside by blowing up the entrances.

There wasn't anything secure on Guam. There were hundreds of caves that still had Japanese hiding inside just waiting for an American to walk into his rifle sights. While we were guarding those natives, Robert and I would leave some of the guards in the native village and we would go out exploring.

Probing around in a cave that had only been blown half-shut, we discovered it was full of Sake wine.

Boy, how can I describe the elation we felt? We didn't know you were supposed to drink it slow. I don't know how much we had put away before a firefight broke out between the Marines we had left guarding the natives and a group of Japanese soldiers. They had come out of some caves below us and were going to kill and destroy the entire native village. By that time, old Bruce and I thought we could whip the world.

Intoxicated from drinking a half-case of wine, I got to laughing and tumbled down the edge of the cliff. Instead of falling backward, I fell forward, right down near the fighting.

Man, I told you that the Captain must have enlisted a lot of angels to protect me. And this was one of those times. I didn't fall all the way down into the Japanese soldiers. I somehow managed to stop about halfway. There were some small trees and rocks, and the Japs couldn't see me. Later, I was able to climb back up. Old Bruce was laughing his head off. But by the time got back to the top, I had sobered up.

Fortunately, for us, the Japanese squadron retreated without attempting to destroy the native village. By this time, the two of us realized what a precarious situation we were in and made our way back through the coconut trees and jungle to the village and squad. We remained in the village, which was surrounded by banana, papaya and coconut groves. We had fresh fruit to eat and a gabled bamboo house to sleep in. It was a welcome departure from the foxhole life.

For the next few days, Robert, myself, and a fellow marine with a flamethrower went back to cleaning out caves.

In making this sweep through the caves, we learned there was a Japanese General hiding out with an entire battalion in the area. If we didn't get fire back from a cave, we would crawl down inside and try to discover something that would help us pinpoint their layout.

We were down in one cave that must have been a Headquarters Company. There were a lot of papers, boxes and other stuff laying around. We both chose some things to bring out to the light and examine. He took a little mahogany box and I brought out a leather saddlebag, the type you drape over the rear fender of a motorcycle.

We were both very careful to open these two things because of booby traps, but when I opened one of the flaps on the saddle bag, it was full of money. It was packed with wads and wads of currency. For a few seconds, I thought I was a millionaire. Then as I began to unfold it, I realized it was Island, or Japanese Occupational Currency. All of it wasn't worth one American dime.

But old Bruce's little mahogany box was filled with pearl handled Hari-Kari knives. There must have been fifty of them. He had a small fortune and I had a saddlebag filled with worthless paper currency. I threw my millions away and he sold most of his knives for $50 each.

We learned from some of the natives there was a Japanese lady operating in the area, that was leader of a gang. I don't know if you would call her a geisha or not, but she was definitely a business lady. She was the leader of a gang of Japanese cutthroats who raided the native villages and plundered everything valuable. They lived in the jungle, and would come out on forays to pillage these poor natives.

One day we cornered this Queen Bee and all her gang. They were in hiding in a cave with all their stolen merchandise. We brought in a Nisei, who broadcast to them, but they refused to give up. They didn't believe the Japanese had been overrun and wouldn't surrender. The war ended for them that day, right in their hideout. They didn't have any more use for all their stolen loot after the fight.

The Japanese also used dogs to help locate the American troops. As the number of Japanese units dwindled, these war dogs were turned loose. There was a group of war dogs that we ran into. The leader came running and snarling at me. I believe he was a large cur with a curled tail. I waited until the last minute, hoping he would turn away, but I had to shoot him with my .45 pistol. That was the first time I ever shot a dog. But it was either he or I. He belonged to a small force of Japanese soldiers that we ran into later.

Life was never boring, but miserable, yes. We were dispatched in advance for scouting and guiding. Sometimes it rained all day. The rain would pour, and then stop for a while, and then another downpour would come. Having no shelters, we had to sleep in the open or find an abandoned cave.

Often we had to march or go to another area without advance notice. All of us were exhausted beyond our expectations. Along some marches our artillery guns, which were normally towed by trucks with tracks, had to be pulled by men.

It was never quiet at night. My squad was usually on patrol or on outpost guard duty. There were continuous explosions and shots in the jungle all around us. And you would hear marines cry out in pain.

After two weeks of heavy fighting, the initial phase of the operation was over. While awaiting orders to jump off on the second phase, the Third Marines sent out patrols to find and knock out bands of Japanese who still formed pockets of resistance.

Meanwhile, the Third Marines, though badly depleted in strength, prepared to drive north for the capture of Agana, the capital of Guam. Agana was once a thriving town of 12,000, but it had been reduced to rubble by Naval artillery and aerial bombardment. As members of the Third Marines stood on the newly won high ground above the city, they watched as the Japanese performed a full-dress ceremony. Decked in full dress whites, the Japanese marched through the streets with drawn samurai swords. It was an impressive sight, but before the marines could bring artillery to bear on them, they had dispersed.

As the Marines entered the capital city, all the houses had been reduced to ruin. But there were still snipers. The roads leading into the city were mined and there were many casualties by the advance units. We were sent out every evening after the regular units were dug in to determine the strength and position of the enemy in preparation for the next day's battles. Though opposition was usually light, the heavy jungle terrain required strenuous effort.

THE ONLY MECHANIZED BATTLE ON GUAM

The last major action on Guam was the battle of Finegayan Village that began on August 3. At nine o'clock in the morning, B Company of the Ninth Marines encountered a company of Japanese as they were leaving the town. With the aid of two tanks and a rifle company, B Company overran it and killed over one hundred of the enemy.

About two miles west of Finegayan Village, in some rugged terrain, Japanese machine gunners and riflemen had taken cover in ravines, ditches and heavy brush. After some delay, an attack was launched and the position was captured, but American casualties were heavy.

That afternoon, an armored column consisting of the Third Tank Battalion, the Third Amphibious Reconnaissance Company, and a Company of the 21st Marines assembled a mile and a half south of Finegayan and moved north. After passing through the village, the First Battalion was hit by a concentration of firepower, consisting of 75-millimeter guns, automatic weapons, and tanks that came at them from three sides.

This was a tough battle. The artillery and mortar fire was just tearing our positions up. We were up against a tough enemy after leaving Agana.

We were probing at the time. They wanted to build an airfield on the upper end of Guam to take care of the B-29's, so we were sent to check the area out. They had a 75-millimeter on the road we were on. Behind us was our own halftrack with a 75-millimeter and .50 caliber machine gun.

Strange things happen to save your life. Greg Perrault, driver of the halftrack crossed his legs up underneath him in a Buddha-style sitting position every time he stopped. During this battle, a shell came through the front and went right under him. He was sitting on his legs, and it just scorched his butt, then went on in the rear and exploded. Had he been sitting upright, it would have taken his bottom half off, but he survived. The gunner on the 75-millimeter was killed.

The halftrack and truck was destroyed, one tank was damaged, and an officer and twelve men were lost. However, the Marines knocked out two 75-millimeter guns, one tank, and several machine guns and killed scores of Japanese. Even though the advantage had been with the Japanese, the fierceness and firepower displayed by the Marines made the difference.

Later, it was learned a battalion of Japanese Special Landing Forces called Imperial Marines carried out this attack. That was the first and only mechanized battle the Third Marines encountered, and it raged furiously for two hours.

We only ran up against the Japanese Marines once or twice. And those fellows were tough. Most of them were larger than the average Japanese soldier, and they weren't afraid to fight. We could always tell when we ran up against a company of them because of the resistance they gave us. I had a lot of respect for them as a fighter.

On August 10, the Third Marines reached the northernmost spot on Guam, Ritidian Point. This was the final day of organized resistance. The Marines combed the beaches and heavily wooded areas along the north shore. We discovered and eliminated small groups of Japanese hiding in caves and on the fringes of the jungle.

The Third Marines had met the last of concentrated Japanese forces, but the enemy was far from wiped out. Aggressive patrolling and mopping up operations continued for much longer. In twenty-one days, the Third Marine Division buried 3,264 Japanese and an estimated 2,000 bodies remained in the jungle. Cost of the operation to the Third Marines was 3,626 casualties, including 619 killed in action.

Calling the island secure was something the politicians needed back home. Believe me, there was still a war going on as far as we were concerned. Advance throughout the island was hampered by opposition from pockets of Japanese that were still holed up in caves. We still patrolled, and some of it was in dense undergrowth. It wasn't just in the large battles that we lost men. A jungle sniper could kill you graveyard dead.

Anytime you are hunting a fellow and he is concealed, he has a good chance of getting you first. Those Japanese snipers were excellent at camouflage. We've been out in palm groves and thought we had looked at every palm tree, then zap, one of our buddies got it. But when he made that shot, it was probably his last, because we chewed him up pretty bad. A lot of them would be tied to tops of trees and after he was shot, he would just be dangling up there.

Wandering enemy groups were constantly being engaged. There were still areas the Marines had not reached, either because there were no roads into the area or the Japanese had shifted their base camps.

After the battle for Ritidian Point, we spent a few days clearing out additional stragglers in caves and patrolling in Agana.

THERE'S MY MAN

It was still my job to take car of the Tapia household," said Francine. By now Shaaron, our baby was beginning to crawl about the house. As she grew, I would show her the picture of Gene in his marine uniform and say, 'That's your daddy.' The Tapia home was almost like a public meeting place because so many family members and friends were always stopping by.

"The first step Shaaron ever took was at my sister's in Fairhope, Alabama. Dorothy had been asking me to bring her over, so one day Shaaron and I went over. While we were there, my sister wanted to go to the movie.

"Prior to the feature movie, news and short serials were often shown instead of cartoons. Movietone News was a regular war film documentary that depicted American soldiers and sailors in actual combat. Each film was produced by the United States Department of Defense to help gain support for the war effort among civilians.

"Dorothy and I were sitting there watching this film of Marines cleaning out caves on Guam. Suddenly, there was Gene. I saw him and I knew he was alive.

"I sat through eleven more showings over the next two days just to see my husband in action. I was so happy. There he was, right in front of me. I was happy, proud and crying, all at the same time."

TOKYO ROSE

After we returned to Agana, we were able to relax a little. We had a lot of enterprising people. One of them was a radioman that had rigged a radio up on a Jeep. We could pick up Tokyo Rose. She was in Tokyo, but I thought she was in the Philippines. She would say some of the darndest things on these nightly broadcasts, talking about what was happening in those islands.

A lot of times she was accurate about her locations. One night she said the Third Marines had lost hundreds of men and had been pushed off Guam. Well, there I was sitting in Agana on an ammo box when she came out with that. That sure was news to me and my buddies.

Hell, the Third Marines knew before they got to Guam they weren't going to be pushed off. But we all got a big laugh out of it. She played a lot of American songs and tried to lower our morale by putting us down and saying things that weren't true. But if it hadn't been for Tokyo Rose we wouldn't have had anything to look forward to. She shouldn't have been arrested. They should have given her a medal because she really boosted our morale."

On one of our patrols on the outskirts of Agana, Robert and I stumbled upon a wooden keg of liquor, the natives called Aggie. This would be similar to the homemade moonshine liquor so common in the southern United States. After testing it, we hauled it back to camp.

There were a lot of loop-legged marines that night. The officers were wondering what in the world was going on, but as soon as they found out we had a keg of whiskey in camp, they joined in the party.

Guam was a lot hillier than Guadalcanal with ravines, gullies and caves. After leaving Agana, the company headed inland. One day we were up on a plateau where a group of marines had set up a pair of .40 millimeter Bouffer Anti-Aircraft guns.

A Captain Turner from Texas was in charge. Suddenly rocks began exploding around us. We were under direct fire from a Japanese .77 millimeter, about a half-mile away on the opposite hill. I mean he was splattering rocks within a few feet of where we were. He had us zeroed in with his sights. It was just a matter of two or three more shells and we were goners.

All of a sudden I locked up and just started shaking like I had the St. Vitus Dance. It was just uncontrollable. I sat there shaking because I knew I was going to get it.

But Captain Turner grabbed one of those Bouffer's and put a five round clip in it and started firing back. Evidently he got the Japanese gunner because he quit firing at us. What Captain Turner did was very brave. A couple more rounds and that fellow would have gotten me.

Our job was to act as forward artillery observers. As we continued along the plateau on a little path, we could see below us for several hundred yards. Off to our right, we saw a company of marines coming. Off to our left came a column of Japanese. Both were on the same trail and headed directly toward each other. There was no way we could warn our troops because it would have alerted the enemy to our position.

As soon as they rounded a bend, each started firing at the other. In a few minutes, each side started looking for a way out of the skirmish. There was a lot of firing, but I don't think either side had any casualties. Pretty soon, both sides disappeared back into the jungle and found a way around each other.

JUNGLE DISEASES

For the first week on Guam, most of the marines in the invasion force did not get to take their boots off. This caused severe cases of athlete's foot and jungle rot.

A lot of times it would be four days before you could take your boots off. You would get your feet wet, then you would walk them dry. Maybe this would happen several times before you were able to put on fresh socks. There was no way anyone avoided getting a fungus or jungle rot.

If it reached a point where you couldn't walk, you went to a corpsman and he put some acid on your feet, and then you'd go back to action. But the coral cuts I received swimming were much worse because it is an organism. The cuts I received from as far back as Guadalcanal still plague me.

I contracted dengue fever about five weeks after arriving on Guam. This is a viral infection that attacks the muscle and joints with fever and chills.

I don't want anyone to think the Marines didn't care about their men. We were in a war with an enemy on a jungle island and there was no medicine or doctors to care for you.

While on patrol I picked up a fever that wouldn't go down. I thought it was malaria, but I couldn't shake it. I went to the medic at base camp. There was no field hospital or doctor in that area. The fever got worse and Atrabrine didn't help.

With no medical facilities to treat me, I had to battle the disease through the forces of my own body and one other marine as I lay in a jungle bed.

After we moved past Agana, the capital of Guam, I began to feel real bad. I had already had several bouts with malaria so I thought I was coming down with it again. They treated me with tablets, but for two weeks, I almost died. I hovered right on the borderline. I have never had anything affect me like that. I had a high fever, chills, listlessness, no energy, and at times I was out of this world. I can't describe all the ailments and how it affected me, but I thought it was my time.

And it might have been time for me to go. The Captain has looked over me so much and it was the only reason I survived. And I couldn't have survived if it hadn't been for a little angel named Roland F. Smith. My regular partner, Robert O. Bruce had been wounded and had his own problems. But Roland liked me and was more or less my little sidekick at the time. We were still in combat, and he made sure I had a little something to eat. I was more or less knocked out for two or more weeks. If an enemy soldier had come up, I couldn't have defended myself. Roland Smith really took good care of me.

Even though all my muscles and joints continued to ache, I got back on regular patrols with my company after two weeks. I was reunited with Sergeant Ed Cole.

By this time we were able to set up little camps at night. One night Sergeant Cole decided he was going to set up a hammock with mosquito netting on the fringe of the camp. He strung that thing between two trees and began to brag about how he was going to get a good night's sleep because he wouldn't have to listen to our snoring.

We had been sitting around listening to Tokyo Rose on the squadron radio when, about nine o'clock, Sergeant Cole decided to hit the sack. Just as he started to climb into the hammock, a Japanese machine-gunner cut loose and the mosquito netting was cut to shreds. From then on Sergeant Cole loved his foxhole and never complained about our snoring.

A SURPRISE VISITOR

As the island became more and more secure, Navy personnel established a base camp called Camp Dealy near Talofofo Bay. Patrols continued to operate throughout the island. Organizations not participating in the patrols began schooling in weapons and other operations at Camp Dealy. The camp also served as a rest and relaxation area for submariners in that part of the Pacific.

Even around camp, Japanese stragglers were prevalent. Two months after the island was considered secure, marines would be found next morning with their throats cut.

We had continuous patrols around the Camp. On the way back one day, I cut this stalk of half-ripe bananas. Another marine was carrying my BAR because I couldn't see too well with the bananas on my shoulder. As we entered the camp area, I spotted this Navy officer in dress whites. Here we were worn out, just coming out of the jungle and to see somebody dressed like that was stupid.

Somebody called at me and said there was a fellow that wanted to see me. This well dressed, immaculate fellow with a little nice, go-to-hell cap on was walking toward me. There were stragglers all around us and they would just love to get their hands on someone like that. But as he got closer, I saw that it was my brother.

Homer Tapia was stationed on a submarine that had put into Guam. For the next two weeks, I was able to visit the Camp Dealy Officer's Club.

By this time, we had been on Guam for nearly two months. Things were quiet around Camp Dealy. Myself and some of my buddies continued to be friends with some Seabees and through their efforts had managed to get some timber and build a small wooden clubhouse near their base camp.

Robert O. Bruce and I continued to scout and gather information about the location and number of Japanese left on the island. By this time, the Chamorros were happy to help because they were forced to feed the enemy at gunpoint. Despite the increasing number of Japanese killed or wounded by the dozens of daily patrols, the Marines and natives were still being harassed by remnants of those Japanese forces still remaining even though small boatloads were escaping to the nearby island of Rota, the last Japanese held island in the Marianas. Periodically, they would sneak back and attack a Marine outpost.

We made contact with some natives and they told us all the Japanese had gone to the northern end of the island. We came back to base camp and relayed the information to Intelligence.

This was near the end of October. On October 23, orders were issued for a complete mop-up of the remainder of the enemy left on Guam. The entire Division assembled and began to make a sweep across the island to its northernmost point, which was Ritidian Point.

Some of these caves were almost perpendicular. There might be little hand trails up to them, but the only way to get them out was with flame throwers and the method Robert O. Bruce and I used.

As we got near the end of the island, I spotted a Japanese dressed in a white uniform on a ledge above us. I guess he must have been a sailor. We had our Nisei announce over loud speakers that if they would come out and surrender within a certain time, we would not harm them. Leaflets were also dropped. Most of those remaining were Imperial Marines from Rota and they would not surrender. That meant we had to do what we as marines were trained to do.

By the tenth of November, the sweep had been completed and we were back at base camp. Unit commanders began to prepare the Marines for future missions.

By this time, life had become more bearable for marines of the Third Division. The Red Cross and Salvation Army had moved in and set up canteens. Now, we were able to buy pork and beans, and Chesterfield cigarettes.

The best people were the Salvation Army. They gave us soap, toothpaste, shaving gear and whatever they had available. The

Red Cross brought in the Hollywood Canteen with its singers and dancers. Bob Hope was there along with Betty Hutton, Ginger Rogers and Hedy Lamarr. Hedy was the most beautiful woman I had ever seen. She didn't wear makeup. It was all natural beauty.

As the action wound down, I found a family of natives that washed uniforms for other marines. I washed my dungarees, but I wasn't too good at washing and ironing my khakis. I inquired around and found out there was a Chamorro woman, named Julia (pronounced Hoo-lea), who might take care of my clothing problem. She lived about seven or eight miles away, so I made a contract with her to take care of my khakis. I made a trip about once a week to her village on a road the Seabees had built to pick up clean clothes and leave my dirty ones.

She may have been washing clothes for Japanese soldiers, but I never saw any on my trips to her house. Her village was located in a deep valley surrounded by hills. It had not been bombed, because it couldn't be seen from the air. The trees and undergrowth were so thick you had to know exactly where it was located to find it.

Her house was made of thatched palm fronds and near a beautiful, clear rippling river. The size was about twelve by twenty-five feet and large enough for the three or four other people that lived with her. The wind always blew and it was a real homey place in which to live.

This family was able to live off the land. They grew papayas, coconuts, bananas, yams, breadfruit, and other vegetables, and raised hogs. By the time I came along, they were allowed to draw staples from the American supply depot set up on the island.

Julia hinted more than once that she also had Japanese friends that she tried to help. Not all Japanese treated the natives bad, so I'm sure they helped them with food and things like that. They were good people, so they were probably just helping the starving Japanese survive.

A stream dropped off the hillside right back of the house. Julia had a large iron wash pot that she would build a fire under it and boil the clothes. She used irons that had been heated in a fire. Those people didn't have matches, so they used a little bow with a string to start a fire. They would get out there and start twirling the stick in a little pile of palm fronds, and in just a few seconds they had smoke, and then fire. It was a beautiful little valley. I guess you could say it was like a Little Paradise.

TWO FACE TO FACE ENCOUNTERS

Even though the action had slowed down, there were still hundreds of Japanese stragglers on the island. In the shallows out near the reef there were lots of holes where crabs and lobsters would sometimes get trapped when the tide went out. One morning about daybreak, I was out scrounging in one of these tidal holes and I saw this funny looking marine. I noticed he acted strange, because as I started walking toward him, he would walk away. When I looked at him, he would turn and look at me. This went on for about fifteen minutes. Pretty soon, each of us recognized the other. He saw I was a Marine and I saw he was a Japanese. I only had my kabar knife, and since we were hunting something to eat and not each other, we both let it go at that.

When there wasn't anything to volunteer for, I would take my BAR, or borrow a .30-caliber carbine and hunt stragglers single-handedly in the surrounding jungle and hills. I called it squirrel hunting.

Returning from one of these hunts empty handed, I came upon a water buffalo. We eyed each other for about ten minutes and the buffalo went back to eating. After getting close enough to pet him, I climbed on his back and rode him into camp. Afterwards, when I ran into him again, I would jump on his back and ride him back to camp. I learned later the animal belonged a native family.

On another day, I had gone out into the jungle planning to gather coconuts. This time I only had my kabar knife.

I heard a noise in the undergrowth and I began to sneak up towards it. Pretty soon I saw a Japanese officer crawling along. My first impulse was to jump up and capture him. But then I saw that he had a long officer's sword. The longer I looked at his sword, the shorter my knife appeared. So I backed away and ran back to camp to get my rifle.

A group of us came back, and we had him hemmed up in a little ravine, but that same fellow, Art Rogers, the one that left me stranded when the patrol moved forward on Guadalcanal, let him get away.

TERROR IN THE SEA

One day the entire Reconnaissance Company as practicing amphibious landings near Piti Bay. By that time I was a platoon sergeant. We were all out in the bay swimming and just having a good time. I had just gotten back into a rubber raft when I noticed something swimming around my men.

I froze.

My hands gripped the handles on the side of the inside of the raft and I couldn't move. All I could do was watch this big monster shark swimming all around the people in my platoon. I was speechless, I couldn't talk, and I was shocked beyond anything I've ever known.

That was as bad as any nightmare I've ever had. I didn't want to spook my men, because if they started splashing around, the shark might attack. He eventually disappeared and that was the end of the story. I don't think any of the thirty or more men were aware of him, and I never told any of them. I can't explain why it happened, but it did. That has been an experience that has lived with me all my life. I still have a fear of swimming in the ocean.

PHOTOGRAPHS ON GUAM

First Photo Page
Top photo: Pfc. Charles Christian on Guam

Lower photo: Seven Members of The Third Marine Amphibious Reconnaissance Company on Guam
Back row: Gene Tapia, Pfc. Rice, Robert O. Bruce, Sgt. Ed Cole.
Front row: Hank Sukup, Pfc. Laurat, Pfc. Dinkens

Second Photo Page
A member of the Third Marines goes after a Japanese sniper in Agana, Guam

CHAPTER VIII

IWO JIMA, THE SULPHUR ISLAND

The United States and the allied forces were moving ever closer to the Japanese homeland. Bombers were taking off daily from Saipan, Tinian and Guam, but a base closer to Japan was needed.

Located at the south end of a chain of small volcanic islands, and 700 miles north of Guam was a tiny volcanic island known as Iwo Jima. The capture of this island meant planes could bomb Tokyo and other cities twenty-four hours a day. Since it was only 670 miles south of Tokyo, planes could carry a much heavier bomb load. The decision was made for it to be taken by the U.S. Marines.

For marines who fought on Iwo Jima, they may have doubted if anyone ever lived there except under compulsion, but strangely enough, Japanese civilians lived on the island for many years.

Until 115 years ago, the entire group of Volcano Islands was uninhabited. In 1887, the mayor of Tokyo visited Iwo Jima, and four years later the tiny group of islands was declared a part of the Imperial Empire.

A few permanent settlers arrived right after 1900, but it wasn't until 1902 that forty-four Japanese families were moved to the island. Cotton, sugar cane, and a small sulphur plant were its only assets.

Iwo's shape has been compared to a pork chop, an ice cream cone and South America. It is five miles long and two and one-half miles at its widest part. Known as Sulphur Island, it was almost a barren wasteland. It supported very few trees and only scrubby growth, most occurring near the base of Mount Suribachi, at the southwest end of the island.

Mount Suribachi is an inactive volcano, 550 feet high with very steep sides and a deep funnel shaped crater. Its surface is mostly rock and black volcanic sand. Two beaches run from the base of Suribachi. Both are protected by rows of rocky terraces up to twelve feet high. These escarpments slope upward and inward to a plateau where the Japanese had constructed an airfield. On all sides were a mass of gullies, rocky outcroppings and ditches.

Because of the layout and terrain, the Japanese defenders had excellent observation points over the land they intended to hold. From the many ridges and hilly areas, they could direct mortar and artillery fire throughout the entire island and watch every move of the Marines as they hit the beaches.

The beaches along the southern half of the island are mostly black volcanic sand, so soft it made the use of wheeled vehicles during the beachhead almost impossible.

The assault on Iwo Jima, which lay midway between the Japanese homeland and the Marianas Islands, was delayed for nearly a month because the Pacific Fleet had been providing air cover for the invasions in the Philippines.

Three Marine divisions had rehearsed for the Iwo Jima assault. The Marine commander, Gen. Holland Smith, predicted it would be "the toughest place we have had to take." The invasion was assigned to the Third, Fourth, and Fifth Marine Divisions. While the men had been briefed on the exacting task ahead of them, there was no way they could know about the extensive network of underground trenches and tunnels.

Over 20,000 Japanese veterans defended the island. Tokyo Rose boasted that Iwo Jima's defenders were "packed full of fighting spirit." As the American aerial bombardment began, the Japanese took cover in their deep tunnels and fortified themselves with "courageous battle vows" as they waited for the Americans to land.

By the second week of February 1945, a quarter million U.S. Marines, soldiers, sailors and airmen were ready to take Iwo Jima from its defenders. More than nine hundred ships were assembled at Saipan and Tinian. Sixteen carriers and eight battleships with their usual escort of cruisers and destroyers set out ahead of the amphibious force to deliver the first blows.

We knew in advance we were going to a heavily defended island, but we didn't know where. Being young, and just a nineteen year-old, it didn't much matter.

We didn't have too much time to think about what was going on at home. We always stayed busy. We were always practicing and training. What we did know is we were going to an island that was supposed to be impregnable. At night, lying on the deck of the troop transport was about the only time you had to think. The ship would be pitching and rolling and you'd just be looking up at the stars.

About the only thing to interrupt your thoughts were the flying fish. Those fellows would sail up out of the water and glide on the wind, sometimes up to a half-mile. Sometimes, we'd see sharks and porpoises, but not all that much.

Now, that was the time you thought about your family. There were enemy submarines all around us but we couldn't see them, and it seemed like the fighting and war was a long ways off. But the question always came, would this be the end? Would there ever be a time in my life when I would get back to Mobile to my family, wife and daughter I had never seen.

And my son. I never had seen him. God, I wish things could have been different! It was times like these when my mind could go back to earlier and easier times in my life, because it was the only time I wasn't thinking or planning on the next battle.

I credited my being on that transport headed for the most costly battle in the Pacific to something within myself, "an adventuresome spirit."

Tapia and other members of the Third Marine Division who had embarked at Guam on February 16 and 17, 1944, were aware not only of the strategic importance of their mission but also of the expected difficulty of their action.

No one underestimated the battle we were going into, nor did we have the slightest doubt about its outcome. We had been given lectures with models of the island, the plan of action and the capabilities of the Japanese troops.

Because of the small beach size, the Fourth and Fifth Marine Divisions were to land first with the Third Division in Expeditionary Reserve. The Third remained on its transports about fifty miles south of Iwo.

If at all possible, the Third Division would be held back because they had tentatively been assigned for an invasion of Sakishima Gunto, an island located between Okinawa and Formosa.

All three divisions had trained diligently for months in preparation for the task. The Fourth Division was to turn left after establishing a beachhead and spread out in the direction of Mount Suribachi. The Fifth Division would turn right along the beach. It was to be the Third Division's job, if they were sent in, to hit the beach and continue inland, sweeping through the center of the island, wiping out pillboxes, the Japanese in concrete bunkers, and mortar and artillery positions.

WELCOME TO HELL

The assault on Iwo began February 19. The savage bombardment that preceded the landing was monumental and accurate, yet the invading forces were disappointed that its effectiveness had been limited. The Marines, under Major General Harry Smith, had requested ten days of preliminary bombardment but got only three.

Commanding the Japanese defense was Lieutenant General Kuribayashi Tadamichi, who had plenty of time to stiffen and complete the island's defenses. By February 19, the island contained concealed concrete bunkers and pillboxes linked by a network of tunnels, only a portion of which could have been destroyed even if all the bombardment in the world were brought to bear.

General Tadamichi's goal was to buy time for his troops and the Japanese homeland. The night before the invasion, he told his troops, "I pray for a heroic fight." The Japanese gave that and much more.

The landing craft headed toward the black beaches on a sunny morning. The Navy Underwater Demolition teams had cleared all underwater mines. The LST's and other landing craft that shuttled the Fourth and Fifth Marines had an easy trip to the beaches.

Once Headquarters Command received the message of the extremely high casualty rate experienced by the Fourth and Fifth Marines, there was no alternative but to order the Third Marines ashore the second day.

Early in the evening of February 20, Gene and other Third Marine units began climbing down the cargo nets into landing craft. However, after meeting a control boat, most of the Third Marines were returned to the troop ship. The designated beach landing area was too crowded with other boats and equipment.

Right after noon on February 21, our battalion boarded the landing craft again. This time we landed on Beaches Yellow 1 and Yellow 2. A massive yet precise, rolling barrage led the landing and stayed about 200 yards ahead of us. Each unit had its own artillery spotters and could order additional tightly controlled strikes from the destroyers and other craft offshore.

As I said, we didn't have time to think and we never thought we might get killed but if you can picture us coming ashore on that black sand and seeing a tank roll over a Marine uniform with a man in it and you don't know if he's dead or alive—that will keep you from doing a lot of things. That scene where the rushing waves of the Pacific met the black sand will remain forever in my mind. It was the most godforsaken place I had even seen. It was like something that had been spewed up from hell.

Men, tanks and jeeps quickly congested the steep sloping cinder beaches. Wheeled vehicles like jeeps were immobilized at the edge of the surf. The powerful waves then washed them broadside, and they became stuck between water and land. Soon the beach resembled a salvage yard of scrapped vehicles.

The Third Division went straight inland with plans to sweep through the middle of the island. The Fifth Marines had gone left toward Mount Suribachi, while the Fourth Marines turned right and headed toward a line of cliffs.

The Japanese had consulted with their German allies about the Normandy Invasion, and did not contest the American landing force as it reached the beaches. They chose to fight a "cornered rat defense" and let the invaders come to them so they could bleed them to death.

We had made it to the beach, but it was brutal. Almost as soon as we landed, it began to rain. During the night we were shelled by enemy artillery, rocket and mortar fire. It was a practice that would continue practically every night.

This island was made up of coarse volcanic sand in the low areas and near the beach. Underneath it was warm, smoldering sulphur. After you dug down into it, you could feel the burning heat. But with all the shelling and artillery from both sides, it was like the island would be blown apart. Mount Suribachi was off to our left and it was just a big black mound. It kind of reminded me of someone's baldhead. There were no bushes or trees left on the island. The shelling had blown them all off.

We couldn't get out of our foxhole. We couldn't even stick our heads out. We were getting food and water, but if you got out during the day, a sniper would have gotten you before you made it three feet. Here again is where the helmet came in handy. If you had to pee, you did it in the helmet, and then threw it out. I saw a lot of good men die because they didn't follow advice. You never knew when you were in someone's rifle sights.

Almost every square yard of the island had been surveyed by the Japanese forces for prearranged zones of fire. With the use of underground telephone lines laid in advance, fire control was simple. A marine remaining very long in one spot was certain to be hit by a barrage of enemy mortar and artillery fire that continued day and night.

General Tadamichi had waited until the beaches were clogged and the American troops had moved inland. Now, his gunners could not miss. There were more than 30,000 American troops on Iwo Jima after the second day. General Schmidt wanted the Japanese to attack. But the Japanese commander wanted the bloodbath to come on his terms.

In four days of fighting, most of the Third Division had moved less than one-mile.

Every time we gained a few feet we were told to hold it at all costs. At night there were flares constantly and so much noise and screaming from Banzai attacks, and also from our own men who had been hit. We were shooting, battling, stabbing, and I even saw some marines using shovels to fight with. That's how close and intense it got.

When captured, it would make the bombardment of Japan easier and quicker because the B-29 Superfortresses would be able to cut down on their fuel loads, allowing them to carry three times as many bombs as they now carried from Guam.

Although tactical maneuvering of elements on Iwo appeared to be almost a physical impossibility, due to the limited area, hazardous and uneven terrain and extremely strong Japanese defenses, members of the Third Marines can be credited with employing to the fullest extent ingenious tactics to repel costly frontal assaults.

In support of the assault battalions, all artillery and naval gunfire which the division commander could control was used against the Japanese defenses.

There were three Japanese airfields on Iwo Jima. The largest, Motoyama Airfield No. 1, was just inland from where we landed. The first American airplane, a B-29 named, "Dinah Might" landed on this narrow strip of land.

The day after I arrived this B-29 came in like a wounded bird. One of his engines was out and smoking. The propellers were feathered. He made a belly landing, then flipped around on the sand. But the crew got out okay. We learned later he had been shot up over Tokyo and couldn't make it back to his base on Saipan.

That was the dammedest thing I ever saw. There were Japanese pillboxes and machine guns within a few hundred yards of where he stopped. We found out later he had one of two choices: either ditch in the ocean or try to land on the short airstrip.

The pilot didn't appear hurt, but some of the crewmen had to be pulled out. I don't know what their condition was. Mechanics were able to scavenge parts off the plane.

A total of 852 forced landings were made on Iwo Jima by planes returning from their bomb runs over Japan. That meant up to 1,700 pilots and co-pilots plus at least 6,800 more crewmen were possibly saved. Some of the planes were repaired and used later. Those that were damaged too badly were scrapped and parts were scavenged from them.

My memory recall for most of the war is excellent, but I cannot recall a lot of incidents that occurred during the first few days of the invasion on Iwo Jima.

Nature has a way of protecting us. When terrible events happen like on Iwo Jima, it blocks them out. The B-29 landing was one of the few things that I have an emotional connection with. I know it must have been even worse than I can remember, but it seems my emotions can't reach down to those first few days of murderous carnage.

The raising of the American flag on Mount Suribachi, the morning of February 23 by members of the 28th Marines, was one event I will never forget. The mountain was like a tall building. Inside was a honeycomb of caves covered with thick concrete walls. At its base were huge guns. Higher up were mortars, machine guns and riflemen. The Marines paid heavily for it.

A 40-man detachment led by 1st Lieutenant H. G. Schreier was the first to scale to the top of the volcano. As they climbed over the rim of the crater, they were challenged by the last Japanese survivors on the opposite edge, and a heated battle ensued. A marine found a piece of wood and tied a small American flag to it that he had brought with him.

First, they had a small personal flag on a stick that belonged to one of the officers. It was so small you could only see it with binoculars. A few minutes later, a larger regimental flag was substituted. About this time journalist Joseph Rosenthal of the Associated Press spotted it, and realizing what a good human interest story this would make, asked if they could do it again, but with a larger flag.

The last flag, the one Rosenthal snapped the famous shot of, was off a navy ship. They sent out and got it off one of the small navy ships unloading supplies near the beachhead. A four man patrol brought it and a piece of pipe back up the mountain and then the two other Marines jumped in to help when they got back to the top with it."

At 10:20 hours, February 23, 1945, Private First Class Ira Hayes USMC, Private First Class Franklin Sousley USMC,

Sergeant Michael Strank USMC, Private First Class Rene Gagnon USMC, Corporal Harlon Block USMC and Pharmacist Mate Second Class John Bradley USN secured the large flag on top of Mount Suribachi.

As men on the ships saw the flag go up, they let loose with whistles, sirens, foghorns and guns. There was cheering all along the beaches, and suddenly there was a brief moment of elation.

For the first time in the long war, the American flag was now flying over Japanese territory.

"Seeing that flag on Suribachi insures a Marine Corps for the next five hundred years," said James Forrestal, secretary of the Navy, who witnessed the flag on board a ship.

Three of the six men who helped raise the flag died on Iwo. Two others were injured.

Rosenthal was awarded a Pulitzer Prize for taking the photograph. While it was a Hollywood style manipulation of what really happened, Gene said the Fifth Marines did have to scratch, crawl and battle three days before they reached the summit of Mount Suribachi.

It was still crowded along the beach area, and the allies had a large ammunition storage depot near the landing area. The night after the flag was raised on Mount Suribachi, Japanese gunners zeroed in on it. The Fifth Marines held it, and isolated it from the rest of the island.

It was a glorious moment. But we still had a lot of fighting left. That night the Japanese landed a mortar shell in our main ammo dump. There was tons of ammunition stored right out in the open. When it went off, red, yellow and green pyrotechnics lit up the sky for hours. It was scary. One shell would set off another one, and things just kept blowing up. We realized we were a long way from securing the island.

GENERAL GRAVES B. ERSKINE

Leading the Third Marine Division was Major General Graves B. Erskine. He had taken command in October 1944.

General Erskine was an old military man that loved to employ rolling artillery barrages. He decided to take a group of us right through the middle of the island. He believed in using a lot of artillery. He ordered them to lay down a barrage as we advanced, but somebody didn't know exactly where our front line was. Instead of starting right in front of us, it started in our rear. That rolling barrage of artillery shells came right across our lines. It was friendly fire, but it was terrible and deadly to many marines.

There was a big marine next to me in a foxhole. One of those phosphorus shells came in. I don't know whose it was, but when it exploded, a chunk of it went down his left side. It's a terrible thing to sit there and listen to a man beg you to shoot him. This phosphorus burned right through him. Pretty soon, he quit hollering.

We had tons and tons of explosives rolling over us and many of them were phosphorus. More than once I heard good men beg and plead, 'please shoot me, please shoot me.' A lot of things happen in circumstances like that and you can't explain what happened or why it happened, you just have to blot it out and go on. I'm very sorry that's the way it was, but I guess that's the way things happen.

When a shell exploded near you, it kind of demoralized you. We had been trained and been shot at, but you never got used to stuff like that. You just had to reach and get something inside you. If we were told to take a hill, and we knew we were going to be killed, we still went out to take that hill.

One of the problems the Marines faced was the strong fortifications the Japanese had constructed. The 75 and 105 millimeter artillery was too light to damage it. Eventually, 155 howitzers were brought on the island, and these were minimally effective.

I guess I needed the excitement to survive. I was always curious and volunteered, even under combat conditions that existed on Iwo Jima. Over time, I developed a fatalistic attitude after becoming accustomed to the fighting and everything we was exposed to. But I never cracked. For those who did, I didn't downgrade them.

A lot of men had to be shipped back to Guam. If a fellow cracked up, I don't say he was yellow. He had stood just as much as his system could stand. After that, he reached his breaking point. Maybe he went through shell shock, or something else, but he wasn't yellow.

I don't believe there was a marine on Iwo Jima that didn't get hit. As we lost men, we had replacements come in and take their place. Some of them were green and didn't know what to do. It didn't take them long to learn. Once they got shot at, they learned quickly to keep that head and butt down.

Sometimes they might take men away from the front line and send him a couple hundred yards to the rear, but it was just as dangerous there. It didn't do any good. You were exposed to constant bombardment and rifle fire. There was no way you could sleep.

As soon as the airfields were secure, the wounded were airlifted back to Guam, a five-hour flight. Twenty-three doctors and eight hundred corpsman were killed or wounded. The flight nurses who worked the flights sometimes were on duty for seventy-two hours without a break. Sometimes all they could do was comfort the casualties.

While the Japanese Navy contributed little to the battle, fifty Kamikaze pilots attacked warships anchored near Iwo. American planes and Navy gunners downed all fifty but not before they sank the escort carrier Bismarck Sea and damaged the carrier Saratoga.

One thing that crossed my mind during the rolling barrage when shells were landing close by was the politicians. I wished so many times that all those politicians and leaders from both sides could have been in the foxholes with us. If they could have been shot at, had grenades popping around them and seen other men cut in half, they would have found a way to end the war quick.

There weren't many atheists at a time like that. I'm not hardhearted, but I'm a lot more religious than most people might think. I know there's a Captain upstairs. He's good and just. I'm hoping He doesn't have a book on all the things I've done and return them to me, because I couldn't stand it.

If an atheist did get out there, he didn't stay that way long. When the shelling and all the shooting started, he called on someone. That included me. I've sat in many foxholes and just shook as those bombs and mortars went off. Anytime I saw something move above my foxhole, I shot it. It was a terrible time. We lost a lot of good marines that way, but you had to be sure and protect yourself.

No mention of Japanese rockets are made in military records, but the Japanese employed thousands of small rockets made of bamboo and plywood and weighing up to 500 pounds. You never heard a sound when they lit them off. Then as it was coming in, you would hear a little squeal, and you would hit the deck and wait for the boom.

Several days after we arrived, we captured one of the launchers. It wasn't anything but a bunch of posts and wood sticking up at an angle. There was always a big squeal as it took off, then about fifty seconds of silence before the big explosion. It was weird!

Most American troops never saw a live Japanese soldier. They were dug into caves and only at night did they come out in an organized attack or as prowling wolves. These stealthy raiders exacted a fearsome toll on the Third Marines.

I was assigned to a Reconnaissance Company of the Headquarters Battalion, Third Marines. Part of our job was to protect the Mortar and Rocket Companies from sneak attacks.

By this time, we had been on the island several days, and there wasn't a spot on it that hadn't been hit by some artillery or mortar shell. And there wasn't a marine who didn't suffer some type wound. I still carry shrapnel in my body that I received on Iwo Jima.

Nights were usually cold and misty. Usually several marines huddled in their foxholes in field jackets and ponchos in an effort to ward off the cold. Most units were decimated and dragging. By this time, the attack force had sustained 16,000 casualties. It was fourteen days from the time I arrived on Iwo Jima before I was able to take a bath.

We had moved into some cliffs above the Motoyama Airfield No. 1, and had found a covered area where we could not be seen by the Japanese. A buddy took turns standing guard while each one used our helmet for a quick 'whore's bath.' After the quick bath, we rinsed off with a canteen of water.

We had to take many detours around Japanese positions because the entire island contained enemy pillboxes, bunkers and caves that were linked by tunnels. We were on top of the island and the Japanese were under it. We had to always watch our backs because those caves had several openings.

Estimates of the number of Japanese positions ranged as high as 1,500 with multiple entrances. As we flushed out one group, others would start firing from another position. Later, we discovered one cave system that was 800 yards in length with fourteen exits.

Many times, we were momentarily halted, but after reorganizing and calling in mortar and artillery, we would mount a bayonet and grenade charge.

There were times we couldn't take a position as it was planned. But we always held what we had gained. And that's when it was bad. Shells and mortars would start bursting all around, and the shrapnel would be everywhere. After that, we knew there was a Banzai attack coming.

The Motoyama Airfield No. 2 was nearly in the middle of the island. Its runways lay across the Third Division's line of action. It provided a perfect field of fire for the Japanese machine guns and 75-millimeter antitank guns.

We were observing a group of Japanese that had a 75-millimeter or howitzer when we saw a Jeep coming along with a colonel riding in the back. The Japanese gunner hit the Jeep, knocking it over. The driver wasn't hurt, but the officer never knew what hit him. His head was blown off.

According to Third Marine records, there were 800 Japanese pillboxes in an area 1,000 yards long by 200 deep along this front.

By the first week of March, many battalions were beginning to feel the loss of experienced men. Many units were now below their assigned operating strength.

There were tanks on the island with flame throwers, but sometimes there was a lack of communication between the tank commander and the infantry. There was also a lack of coordination. Very often the tanks would barrel up behind a unit, firing its machine gun, often into American troops.

SUICIDE MISSION

There were only four of us chosen for this mission: Sergeant Ed Cole, Robert O. Bruce, myself and one other marine. All four of us were nuts. It was stupidity. As I look back, it was a suicide mission. Our job was to go the two and one-half miles to the cliffs at the far end of the island near Kitano Point and report on Japanese activity.

What lay between us and Kitano Point were Japanese gunners, snipers, artillery, and worst of all, minefields. The entire distance would be over open terrain. All trees had been blown away by the weeks of shelling by both sides. We had to locate the main body of Japanese troops. Headquarters wanted to know where they had gone. There was nothing to hide in. But there were shell holes and rocks that had been blown out of the ground. But those fellows were still dug in. After all our shelling, some of those caves hadn't been damaged.

It was very ticklish. Knowing this area had been mined and having to dodge Japanese lead at the same time was ooohhhh, very ticklish. There were several things that got to me, and that was one of them. Boy, you've never experienced anything until you realize you are in the sights of a 20-millimeter gun that's dug in on the side of a hill. That 20-millimeter is a wicked weapon. When it hits you or the ground, it explodes.

We never knew whether the next step was going to be our last, or when we would get hit—that's how bad it was. Having to crawl so easy through the mines didn't allow us to protect ourselves from all the bullets.

We had more than the Japanese to worry about. American planes from carriers were constantly flying overhead. When the pilots weren't firing on the Japanese, they were directing fire from Navy destroyers offshore. And there was artillery and mortar from American guns hitting all around. To protect us from 'friendly-fire,' we had been given three cloth panels to display in case they did come under fire. The panels were about four feet by three feet, each. The center one was red with a big blue L on it. One of them was black and white, and I think the other one had an insignia of the Third Marines on it.

A lot of our planes flew over, some of them were real low. Sometimes we could see the pilot looking us over. When we would see one of our planes begin to make a run on us we'd hold those panels up in a hurry. It was real ticklish, but we had to go. That was our orders. We had to reconnoiter the cliff area. If it hadn't been for the Captain and his angels, I don't know what would have happened to Old Gene that day and many other days.

It required four hours of slipping, crawling and dodging bullets and mines to cover the two and one-half miles to the cliffs. After scouting the target area, we sat down and watched a mass suicide ritual.

We saw these people jumping off the cliffs. They had on dress white uniforms and were just diving over the side to the rocks and coral reefs below. It was awful watching them sail through the air before they splattered on the bottom. Those big black rocks at the base of the cliff were covered with bodies in white uniforms.

As we watched in surprise as the Japanese dove from the cliffs, an American destroyer began shelling our position. We had seen this destroyer about a thousand yards out, but we didn't pay him attention. But when I saw some of those five and six-inch guns swing around towards us, I smelled a rat. We weren't in a good position to display the panels and I guess he didn't get the word that we were on patrol in that area. He turned the ship broadside and began firing on us. None of us were seriously injured, but we got all scratched up from rocks that hit us from his shells. After realizing we were his target, it didn't take long for us to string out those panels. After a few more rounds, he stopped firing at us.

After gathering the information we needed, our party made a reverse route back through the 20-millimeter guns, machine-gunners, snipers, artillery, friendly fire, and mine fields and gave our report.

On March 9, members of A Company, Third Marines, successfully reached the northern beaches near Kitano Point. It had taken the Marines nineteen days to traverse the five-mile long island, but the battle was still far from over.

By this time, we had lost our sense of chivalry. We were just a kind of killer. Something like a fox let loose in a hen house.

After the main body of the Third Marines reached the cliffs at Kitano Point, word was sent from headquarters that my scout company should take some prisoners for the benefit of the news media.

We had to go in there and capture some of the Japanese alive for a publicity shoot. We knew where there was a large group hiding out in a big cave. We had some Nisei with us to interpret. They used portable battery-powered sound amplifiers that were carried like a backpack to get the message to them. Eventually, the Nisei were able to talk two or three into coming out. They were told exactly what spot to go to.

We had a guy in our outfit called Peep Sight Barnett because of squinty eyes. One of these Japanese came up behind us to surrender. Peep Sight became spooked and put a couple rounds in the seat of his britches. This caused the rest of them to run back into the cave. We were told to stay there until more came out because they wanted pictures to show back home.

That night, the Japanese mounted an attack.

First, they screamed and hollered, trying to demoralize us. They came in shifts. The first group would get within throwing distance and fall in a hole. As the second wave came in, he would pop the cap on a grenade and throw it. They did that until they ran out of men or we killed them all.

Sulphur smoke added an eerie quality to the night. One night, we received a report of a Japanese counterattack in our zone of action. Another battalion on our right flank also reported similar activity along its front. A gap of some 100 yards existed between the two battalions. The Japanese were apparently going to try some infiltration behind our Division lines.

Sometime after midnight an estimated two hundred Japanese began infiltrating the gap between the two outfits. A real tough battle broke out with illuminating shells mortar shells lighting up the entire area. They were repulsed after an hour and a half of close and bitter fighting. The next morning we had lost some good men, but there were enemy bodies lying all over the ground. The next day, we reorganized and set up new defenses.

When the attack was resumed on the next night, we were more prepared. Realizing the seriousness of the situation, General Erskine called for artillery and naval gunfire to support us. It was one of the most terrific barrages I experienced. It rained rocks, dirt, and sulphur for over an hour, as the big shells exploded. Quite often, you would see a body flung a long way in the air. What the artillery didn't get, the machine gunners did.

NO MORE PRISONERS

One of our fellow marines, was a sandy-haired Minnesotan named Jamison. He had been reported missing the next morning. The Japanese had captured him during their attack.

After the Banzai charge, members of our company were warned by the Nisei that the Japanese were saying they were going to blow the entire hill away.

Well, that was a pretty good size hill, and we didn't believe anything like that. That night about eleven o'clock, I was still awake. Those jokers had been having roll call about every hour. We knew they were up to something.

There was no warning, just a huge orange flash that knocked me eight or ten feet into the air. As I went up I saw big guns, rifles, machinery and bodies just floating above me in space. The Japanese had detonated at least a five hundred pound bomb in the network of caves under our scout company. All the Japanese who had refused to surrender were blown to pieces. Body parts were scattered everywhere.

Three days after the explosion, we wormed our way into this massive cave system. Down near the bottom, we found one of our men, Jamison, who had been tortured to death.

No amount of threatening from any officer could make us take prisoners after that.

Up until this point, we were exposed to a Japanese Banzai attack at least once a night. I might not have seen one, but I could hear their yelling and then firing by our troops. It was routine; every night they came. There were lots of good men we lost. One of them was a boy named Jim Trimble. He was about six feet, one inch with blonde hair. He reminded me of Adonis, the Greek god. He was a fine looking fellow who had a bright future ahead of him. He had a contract with the Washington Senators to play major league baseball with them after the war was over. But Jim didn't make it through the big explosion that blew the hilltop away. We lost him on that hill along with many other of my buddies.

Flamethrowers were a vital part of the cave operations, but the men who carried them were extremely vulnerable.

A flame thrower shoots napalm, a jelly-like substance that ignites as soon as it hits the air. One of our men was spraying a cave on the side of a cliff and some of the napalm hit the rocks and bounced back and obliterated him. He was gone up in flames in just a minute. Like dog-men, they were the first to be shot by a Japanese sniper.

There was still a Japanese stronghold near Motoyama Airfield No. 3. The Third Marines had become bogged down. General Erskine Graves ordered one of the few battalion size night attacks in the history of the Pacific War. In the predawn hours of March 7, the Marines launched an attack on a hill containing numerous caves that overlooked the airfield and plains. Cushman's Pocket as it was called could not be taken by a frontal attack. A flanking movement to capture Hill 362, which jutted up and behind Cushman's Pocket was planned.

The pre-dawn attack was to take place at 0500. The Twenty-first Marines were to be at the forefront of the attack, while the Ninth was ordered to advance two hundred yards away during darkness as a diversionary tactic.

Every precaution was used to maintain secrecy, including radio silence.

Harassing white phosphorus and other illuminating flares were kept up through the night. A concentration of white phosphorus flares began to cover Hill 363, five minutes before the attack.

The marines were ordered to move as quietly as possible with no firing until the attack was discovered by the enemy.

Foggy, rainy weather, combined with sulphur smoke hampered visibility, but this proved to be more of an asset than a liability. The Ninth Marines were ordered to take the hill, while other battalions were ordered to hold their position and wait for attack orders.

While it was still dark, the Ninth advanced two hundred yards without detection, and without firing a shot. They were told to push on another hundred yards. At the first light of day, the Ninth, which by this time was inside the enemy lines, was hit by annihilating fire from all sides. All hell had broken loose and the Ninth was right in the middle.

But the Ninth had caught the enemy by surprise and took a heavy toll of the Japanese by using flame throwers and small arms fire. With the Japanese reeling, members of the 3rd Battalion were able to advance towards Hill 362.

Right after the early morning fight, Hill 362 was reported to have been taken. However, because of the similarity of Hills 331 and 362, and the inaccuracy of some maps, Lt. Colonel Boehm's driving 3rd Battalion had captured Hill 331, the wrong hill.

Order for the continuation of the battle was issued via radio from Lt. Boehm. After a ten-minute artillery barrage, the battalion resumed its fight to capture Hill 362.

Meanwhile, other members of the Ninth Marines had suffered heavy casualties and was unable to advance. Other battalions were also shot up.

F Company, Ninth, was trapped in a region of craggy and bare, rocky ridges. In what seemed to be a futile fight for existence, Lt. Wilcie O'Bannon, in a desperate effort, led what was left of his company out of the enemy's strongpoint. His company was depleted to a mere handful of troops, and total withdrawal was impossible. Had the Japanese realized the plight of the few men left, they could easily have wiped out the remainder of the company.

Tanks were ordered in to relieve F Company and other units that were pinned down. As the tanks approached, O'Bannon used his radio to direct fire on enemy positions which he could see. But after a short period, his radio fell silent.

The tanks reached O'Bannon's position, and amid heavy enemy fire were able to pull four of his men though escape hatches into the tanks.

Members of the Fifth Marine Division, who were to serve as backups, had failed to clear the high ground commanding the field of action.

For other marines, the going was equally as hard and bloody. Consequently, it took several hours for the assault platoons to send out enough patrols to clean out the enemy pockets. Evacuation of the wounded and resupplying of the front lines was out of the question. Confronted with the situation, B Company was forced to pull back to a better defensive position, but they had to leave twenty-four dead and many wounded until darkness fell.

But the next morning the Marines held the high terrain and being able to look down on the enemy rather than being under his continual observation was a big morale booster to the Third Marines.

I can't say enough about brave Navy Medical Corpsmen. I've seen many of these young men removing a wounded marine under direct fire. During this particular battle, they would come to the aid of someone wounded, and would get pinned down and be forced to defend themselves and the one they had come to rescue. Casualties among those men were high. But I never saw any braver group than the Navy Corpsmen.

The Division had little time to rest. The attack was continued and by this time, each regiment had at least one tank. But there was still bitter, even though disorganized resistance. Progress was slow because of the rocky outcroppings and maze of buttes.

One tank was destroyed by the Japanese, who fired air bursts over it, dispersing the infantry, and then under cover of the smoke, attacked it with Molotov cocktails and satchel charges. However, the pockets of Japanese resistance was shrinking, as their caves and hiding places were destroyed one by one.

A good concept of this battle is contained in a report by Lt. Colonel Cushman, Commanding Officer of the 2nd Battalion.

"We beat against this position for eight continuous days, using every supporting weapon. When relieved, we had destroyed all anti-tank fire in our zone of action and had eliminated 250 yards of the resistance. The core-main objective of the sector-still remained. The battalion was exhausted. Almost all leaders were gone and the battalion numbered about 400, including 350 replacements.

"It is evident that the first phase had taken the skilled leaders and the 'drive' out of the battalion. The second phase was a continuous assault for the infantry, and we lacked skilled troops. Supporting troops were again superb and accounted for our limited gains-some four hundred yards in eight days.

"The enemy position was a maze of caves, pillboxes, emplaced tanks, stone walls and trenches. Only those immediately in front of the troops could be located and, because the Japanese used smokeless powder, some of these were not known. Out of these positions (by later count), we knew roughly twenty of thirty of them."

After this battle, the large bodies of Japanese soldiers were dwindling. There still remained several thousand in the underground caves scattered throughout the island.

March 12 was the beginning of final mopping-up operations on the island as organized resistance elsewhere in the Third Division's zone of action was reduced to sporadic outbursts. Continuing their advance to the west, stubborn resistance was still encountered near a crest overlooking the sea coast. Tanks were eventually brought in, knocking out numerous emplacements. Where firing continued from caves, they were simply blown shut. Often the big guns from destroyers were employed to seal up the mouth of those caves.

Organized resistance on Iwo Jima was declared at an end on March 16-D-Day plus 26.

They announced it was over, but the job was far from complete. My scout company continued carried out mopping up operations throughout the island. There were still thousands of Japanese in holes, bunkers, and caves. There was no way to tell how many were still in hiding. For most of them, it was also their final resting place. You would walk past an area they had called secure, and the next thing you knew, your buddy had been hit.

We stayed on patrol daily. When we found a cave that had been by-passed, we blasted the entrance closed. Many caves had held as many as two hundred Japanese, most of whom had been laborers. The few that did get out were starving and wounded.

As soon as the first airfield was secure in late February, planes from Guam flew in hourly to bring medical supplies and ferry the wounded out. The off-duty pilots had set up a small group of tents in the center of the island away from the enemy lines.

In the predawn of March 26, between 200-300 Japanese troops crept out of caves and caught a group of pilots who were sleeping above ground in tents. They attacked and killed forty four airmen and nine marines. Another forty six marines were injured. There were 212 Japanese killed and eighteen captured.

THE BIG TWO-O

Gene celebrated his twentieth birthday on March 16, 1945, the same day Major General Harry Schmidt, commander of the landing force, pronounced Iwo Jima secure.

The Third Reconnaissance Company left Iwo Jima on March 27 and headed back to Guam. After thirty-four days, the Japanese had lost 22,000 with only a handful who surrendered. The American casualty list was 24,000. More than 6,000 died on the volcanic island. The cost for every square mile of sand on the island was 700 American lives. It was an experience the survivors would never forget.

"Only the accumulated praise of time will pay proper tribute to our dead," said Major General Erskine. "Long after those who lament their immediate loss are themselves dead, these men will be mourned by the Nation.

"They are the Nation's loss!

"There is talk of great history, of the greatest fight in our history, of unheard of sacrifice and unheard of courage. These phrases are correct, but they are prematurely employed.

"Victory was never in doubt. Its cost was.

"Let the world count our crosses!

"Let them count them over and over. Then when they understand the significance of the fighting for Iwo Jima, let them wonder how few there are. We understand and we wonder-we who are separated from our death by a few feet of earth; from death by inches and fractions of an inch.

"All were beat up. Many were physical wrecks because of the constant bombardment and fighting.

"The cost to us in quality, one who did not fight side by side with those who fell can never understand."

THE WAR'S END

We had a four or five day boat ride back to Guam. It gave us time to rehash what we had seen happen. As it sunk in, it almost overwhelmed me. To think about all my buddies that weren't going back with me. I tried to get over the horror and desolation and the waste of life that had transpired right before my eyes. You always admire heroics, whether it's Japanese or American, and there were a lot of heroes. But most of the heroes are still over there. I saw many Japanese heroics as well, including a Japanese sergeant who attacked a tank with just a land mine.

One of our tanks was shooting shells into his troops who were holed up in caves. The caves were about one hundred yards from the tank and our position. He came running out with just a land mine on a piece of rope. His goal was to place the mine under the track of the tank so they couldn't maneuver into position to fire on his troops. The tank's machine gunner let him get within twenty-five yards before he cut loose and chopped him down.

Maybe it was things like this, and having survived that turned my thoughts to home. I know I haven't talked about home, but unless you've experienced war, you don't understand what's it like and how your mind operates. On Iwo Jima, survival wasn't even in my mind. We were doing the job we were trained to do. Day and night our minds were filled with the stench of war. The families back home were never included in any of our battle plans. That's the way it had to be. Things like that are going to change a person. But I knew the job wasn't over. Going on to Japan had changed from a desire to an obsession.

It required thirty-six days of intense fighting to capture Iwo. It required trained leaders, riflemen, artillery and all the forces the U.S. Marines could muster. There was no trickery, no fancy maneuvering—just a solid line of marines driving forward against an unseen foe dug deep into the volcanic landscape.

Myself, as well as most men of the Third Amphibious Reconnaissance Company, returned from Iwo Jima with just his weapon, mess kit and the clothes on his back. Tired and battered by the campaign, we were given a week to rest, because we were beat out. We were more or less physical and emotional wrecks because you can't endure a constant bombardment for that long without being used up.

Our outfit was assigned a new area, this time inland from the beach. It was only partially completed, and much of our time was spent finishing construction on it. The First and Sixth Marines had landed on Okinawa in the Ryukyu Islands the first week of April and some of the Third Division on Guam were rushed in as reinforcements. But my company was so weather-beaten and combat-fatigued that we were not chosen to go.

There were still hundreds of Japanese, both in groups and as individuals fighting on Guam. In early April, it was back to jungle warfare and clearing out caves. In eight days, fourteen Japanese were killed and a few captured. This was not the end of the Japanese on Guam, because another 500 would surrender in the next few months.

Monsoon rains plagued the Division as their training pace picked up.

After Iwo Jima, it was time to prepare for the next battle. Even though we weren't told directly, the Third Marines were scheduled to leave Guam for the invasion of Japan in early September.

We knew we were preparing for the big battle. By this time, I would have killed a songbird or anything else over there because of the losses of buddies and what I had been through on Iwo Jima. We knew it was going to be tough on Japan, but I didn't care. I was so incensed by this time at what I had seen and been through that I wanted to eliminate them. And most of my buddies felt the same way. Men who we trained after coming back from Iwo Jima didn't feel that way. They didn't have the intense feeling we had. We noticed that because we had to train them and we tried to instill some of that killer instinct into them. It was something a human being doesn't acquire naturally. It has to be driven into you.

After several months of simulated beach landings and intensive training the Third Marines were back at full strength and ready. After reviewing the troops on Guam the last week of July, Admiral R. A. Spruance, commander of the Fifth Fleet, said, "That is the finest group of men I have had the pleasure of reviewing. The Third Marine Division is truly ready for combat."

On August 6, 1945, a new type of weapon, the atomic bomb, was used. B-29 Captain Paul Tibbets and his crew aboard the Enola Gay had dropped it over the city of Hiroshima. There were over 130,000 people killed, injured or missing after the blast. And nearly ninety percent of the town was leveled.

Three days later, a second atomic bomb was dropped on Nagasaki. An estimated 75,000 people were killed or wounded and more than one third of the city was devastated.

On August 10, just as the Third Division completed its graduation exercises for battalion landing teams in preparation for the invasion of Japan, word came of this second devastating bomb that had wrecked the entire city.

On the night of August 15, I was heading back to my tent from Camp Dealy, when all of a sudden I began to hear the most god-awful sounds. It was like a huge celebration. Torches had been lit, horns and sirens were going off, ship's whistles were blowing and marines were out in the streets. I didn't know if we were having an air raid or what. I asked somebody what the celebration was all about and I was told the war was over.

Japan had surrendered.

Throughout the ranks, men celebrated the victory. Cans of hot beer were broken out. Groups of Marines staged several mini-battles with rifle, machine gun and mortar fire.

When I realized I wasn't going to get to go on to Japan and work those fellows over, I went into my tent and cried like a baby. Somebody had pulled the rug out from under me. I had so much steam in me that needed venting. But I wasn't the only one that felt that way. There were a lot of us who were sad. We had trained and trained and fought battle after battle, believing we were going on to fight that one big battle. Now there wouldn't be any more battles."

A FORK IN THE ROAD

As soon as official word was received on the surrender, the Third Marines relaxed and shifted to a revised schedule. In place of the daily field problems and exercises, conditioning hikes and weapons schools classes started. Emphasis was placed on occupation of a foreign country, mob control and information on Japan.

General Erskine decided to inaugurate a special educational program for all Marines. A program to enlist Marines to continue their education was offered. Classes were started that allowed men to work toward a high school diploma. The classes used both officers and enlisted men as instructors. Each morning thousands of men lined the dusty roads leading to the makeshift classrooms. But some of us weren't satisfied to sit in one place. As soon as the thrill of victory wore off, they began to wonder what their next move would be. The only possible battle I might be involved in hinged on one thing, Treachery! If any Japanese garrison or outpost chose not to surrender and go down in an act of defiance, then my battalion would be needed.

As the Allies began to move into Japan, China and other occupied territories, Gene had to accept the inevitable. It was the end of one conflict and the beginning of another for him.

Marines were given points based on the number of months and campaigns they had served. Men who had completed twenty-seven months or three campaigns left for the United

States. Gene did not have enough points to leave with the first group.

All the scouting and patrols didn't seem to count when it came to points. About a month and a half after the war ended, they decided I had enough points to come home.

I traveled from Guam to Honolulu, Hawaii, on a small Landing Ship Transport. It had a full cargo of marines headed for the United States. The ship was full, and the supplies were short. It had an abundance of flour, powdered milk and eggs, onions and mutton.

I never could stand mutton, so rather than starve to death I volunteered to work in the kitchen. I buddied up with those cooks and they let me make anything I wanted on the grill. I had dried eggs, cinnamon toast and milk for breakfast and onion sandwiches and cinnamon toast for lunch. Walloping those pots and pans was better that just sitting around.

Once the ship arrived in Honolulu, we weren't allowed liberty. But with all my abilities and skills as a Raider, there wasn't a fence in Hawaii that could hold me.

Some of us intended to see Hawaii, and we did. The Shore Patrol could tell we had been in combat and they looked the other way. We had been out of the picture so long, we didn't know how to raise Cain.

I did see downtown Honolulu, and it was beautiful. But it was nothing but a gyp joint. The merchants ripped off all the soldiers, sailors and marines that passed through. But there were some small islands offshore that were different, and we had a good time on them.

Shore leave was short for us. After only three days we were back on board ship. Our destination was San Diego, California, USA. This time it was a decent ship with plenty of food.

After a short stay in San Diego, I was transferred by train to Camp LeJeune, North Carolina.

Gene was enroute to North Carolina, when the Third Marine Division was disbanded. On December 28, 1945, in a dispatch to the Marine Commandant in Washington, D.C., Brigadier General William E. Riley officially declared the Division inactive. The deeds of heroism performed by members of the Division at Guadalcanal, Bougainville, Guam and Iwo Jima passed quietly into the history books as Gene slept on the train bound for North Carolina.

January 8, 1946, Francine Tapia stood in a line with over a dozen other wives waiting to get a glimpse of her husband, whom she hadn't seen in two and one-half years.

As she was escorted into the Welcome Center at Camp LeJeune, North Carolina, all she could think about was how good it was going to feel when Gene wrapped his big, strong arms around her.

She didn't have long to wait.

About five-fifteen that evening, I ran in there and saw the most beautiful woman I'd ever seen.

"I had no idea he would ever live to get back, and here was the most precious thing I had ever known," Francine said. "Many times I thought he would be brought back in a bag. But thank God, they didn't."

After spending the night on base in a special dormitory the Marines called, "The Honeymoon Suite", Gene and Francine prepared to leave the base early next morning.

I had received my orders. I had been released from active military duty, and was transferred to the Marine Reserves in Mobile, Alabama.

DON'T MAKE A RAIDER MAD

"Even though Gene was leaving Camp LeJeune and the active Marine Corps, he gave a display of his skills to a group of young show-off Marine recruits as we departed the base," said Francine.

"Gene and I, along with several other couples were waiting in line at a bus stop outside the Welcome Center. Suddenly a group of about twenty young Marines ran up. As the bus stopped and the driver opened the door, these young Marines began pushing and shoving. They were determined to get on the bus ahead of all the other people that had been waiting."

They shouldn't have tried that. If there's one thing I can't stand, it's a bully.

According to Francine, Gene unbuckled the dress belt on his uniform, pulled it off, and wrapped it around his fist. Using the big buckle, he began beating, whopping, kicking, throwing and pulling the brash Marines away from the bus door.

In a few minutes it was over.

"All of the people who had been waiting in line got on the bus first," said Francine. "The smart-alecks got on last. Some didn't get on at all."

"There wasn't but about twenty," Gene recalls.

The young Marines had gotten first-hand experience of what a real Marine Raider was like. All had bruises and there were more than a few that had bloodstained uniforms.

The bus ride back to Mobile was delightful and uneventful. Gene and Francine were enjoying each other's company, but outside of that, Gene was not enthused.

It wasn't that I didn't love my family or had any bad feelings about Mobile or the environment. We had gone through so much training, and all of this training was still in me. I considered myself a first-class Marine, and it wasn't like anything I had learned back home.

The American Flag Atop Mt. Suribachi, Feb. 23, 1945

Third Marines Come Ashore on Iwo's Black Sandy Beach

Third Marines Cleaning Out Japanese Caves on Iwo Jima

CHAPTER IX

HOME TO AN INNER HELL

Reunions with family and friends continued for two weeks. But the most singular thing that puzzled me was the general apathy toward myself and other service men that had returned from the conflict. I had seen with my own mind so much death and waste of life, and I quickly sensed the futility of trying to reconcile the past two and one-half years of my life with the present.

"Life was made even more miserable by his physical condition," said Francine. In addition to the breakdown of his mental outlook, he had to endure problems with his feet, legs, body shrapnel and the continued effects of malaria and dengue fever."

There was an ache inside. It was an emptiness that was with me for days and nights. It was a hurt and inability to understand why, after giving so much of my life, other people did not realize what we had gone through. We who had been there listening in the night for the whoops and calls that we knew were coming, knew what it was all about. We had pain inside from hearing the cruel silence that followed a battle, and realizing you would never hear one of your buddies speak to you. Not knowing why the people acted the way they did was sometimes worse than being in battle. Not knowing these things seemed timeless; not knowing took forever to wear itself out in me.

"A private hell was developing inside him as he attempted to readjust to family life," said Francine.

Our baby girl, Shaaron, was born December 31, 1943. I learned of her birth in a letter while on New Caledonia. Having a girl hadn't really sunk in while I was fighting. The first one had been a boy, and I never got to see him. Getting to see and hold my daughter for the first time when she was two years old was pretty stressful for me.

After being home less than a month, the family went to a Mardi Gras parade. Mobile has some of the largest street parades in the country. Only New Orleans had longer and more elaborate floats.

It was a night parade, and we were standing right on the curb in front of one of my mother's restaurants across from Bienville Square. Francine was next to me and I think some other family members were in back.

I was holding Shaaron on my shoulders. She had her legs wrapped around my neck. Large flaming torches lighted each float in this night parade. As one of the floats approached us, Shaaron became frightened and peed on me. As soon as I felt the warm water streaming down my shoulders, I took her inside Momma's restaurant and spanked her.

"This upset me," Francine said. "I knew he wasn't used to children and I understood, but I knew I wasn't going to put up with that kind of behavior."

The next day, Sharon took a large picture down from a table of Gene in his Marine uniform. After showing it to him, she said, 'you're not my daddy. This is my daddy. One day my daddy's coming home.'

This upset me so much I had to leave the room. The incident had been almost unbearable. I was sorry for the spanking the night before, but I didn't know how to make Shaaron understand. Francine kept telling Shaaron that I was her daddy, and that I was the man in the uniform in the picture, but she didn't understand.

"She could not understand that her daddy and the man in the picture were one and the same," said Francine. "But it's because they were so much alike. To this day, they get along, but they still clash because of their tempers."

In the Marines, I respected authority, and was a team player, but back in Mobile, I resented the "chicken authority" displayed by some of the locals.

I didn't have much respect for those people that had never gone overseas. I had taken enough orders from some fine folks that were no longer with the firm, and I didn't need any more orders from those little so and so's. I have never gotten used to somebody taking advantage of a little bit of authority they have been given.

A few weeks after returning home, I was delivering some produce to one of mother's restaurants. I had parked in an unloading zone. Suddenly, a taxi driver came running up to him and said, 'you can't unload here.' I knew I was parked legally and ignored the taxi driver and continued unloading the truck.

Pretty soon this little joker leaves and when he returns, he's got a policeman. My mother came out and started apologizing for me. I said, Momma, don't try to beg off, I've got a right to do what I'm doing.

According to Francine, who witnessed the incident, Gene grabbed the taxi driver around the neck with just one hand. "He lifted him off his feet and was just holding him in mid-air. His feet and legs were dangling. Gene was shaking him like a feather. I was afraid his eyeballs were going to pop out of his head."

The entire incident should never have happened. The policeman marched me to the jail which was just across the street, but I got upset over policemen and people who overlord others that has never gone away. I respect the police that do a job right, but I will not put up with them overlording others to this day.

If the Mobile police officers and Mayor were educated well enough to be put in their positions of authority, then they should have been able to lead the people without acting in a chicken-manner. My outlook on the misuse and unauthorized power is the same today. I had a hard time with some of the authority figures back then.

Ellis Wilkins, recalls some incidents involving Gene right after he returned home.

"His mom had a little money and, when he came back, she bought him a brand new tandem wheeled Chevrolet truck, one of the finest vehicles in the town for him to haul produce," Ellis said. "I would hear the tales about him racing Harris Tillman in his old red Dodge. Harris could outrun Gene even though his Chevrolet was newer and state-of-the-art for hauling produce.

"I've seen him go out and bring that truck in loaded down and not take it to market. He'd go in and wait until the produce was hardly fit to sell. On one occasion, bunches of turnip greens were scattered all up and down Moffett Road. He really had troubles. He was messed up big time.

"One night, several years later, was the only time he ever talked about his war experiences. He told about how he went on a submarine to scout an island to determine the enemy troop strength. He said he was so close to the Japanese soldiers, he could hear them. And he said he was in mop-up operations against the Japanese in caves after the troops had landed. The Japanese were entrenched in caves, and they were smart enough that they knew how many shots an American weapon could fire before it ran out of ammunition. So he got the Seabees to extend the clips on his weapons. He would then stand in front of the cave; fire the given number of shots. Then when they would come out to retaliate, he would mow them down."

I found that men who had taken over jobs from those who had gone into the service didn't want to relinquish them. Some of us who offered to give our lives weren't able to get our jobs back. But most of the times, if we got our jobs back, the fellows who were our bosses were the ones who stayed behind. They collected the overtime and other goodies, while we were working for thirty dollars a month. There was nothing fair about that.

"Even though he was around many people including me, his daughter and family, Gene withdrew emotionally," said Francine. "He couldn't seem to accept the fact about what had happened. He had been such an alert, alive person with a purpose in life, but now that was fast slipping away. He needed a foothold in life that he wasn't finding.

"It was an adjustment for me. After so many years apart, I was hoping for some stability in my life, but Gene wasn't able to contribute much to our personal relationship.

"The two of us were having to adjust. I wasn't used to living with a husband, and by this time I was determined nobody was going to tell me what to do or how to live."

During the winter, Mobile, Alabama, did not have a lot of activities for young couples, but there were many movie houses.

"I had asked Gene to take me to see a movie at the Saenger Theatre," continued Francine. "We went in the car and both of us had on short sleeves. When we came out, the streets had iced over. An ice storm had passed through and we didn't even know about it. We got back in the car and drove to my sister's house in Baldwin County to see what the ice looked like on one of the hills. I had seen ice like that, but Gene hadn't. We almost froze to death, but it was fun seeing and feeling the coldness of the ice that was on everything.

"We continued to live with Gene's mother while we attempted to adjust to each other. Gene's Uncle, Sam Johnson, who owned an interest in his mother's restaurants, realized Gene's situation and offered a plan to help him."

By this time, my mother had four restaurants. There was a shortage of raw oysters. My uncle discussed a plan with me that seemed pretty good. He offered to buy a truck so I could buy and haul oysters from the southern part of Mobile County to their restaurants. Since I was having problems with my feet and couldn't stand on them all day, this seemed like something I could do. And besides, I would be out of everyone's way, so I said O.K.

Gene really hoped this would help him adjust because he was still having a rough time. Every time a firecracker went off, he would duck or jump underneath something. The Marine Corps survival skills he had been taught were no help in civilian life. In addition to his nerves, he also was undergoing extreme physical pain.

There were days he couldn't wear shoes. His feet would be swollen and sometimes the toes would pop open from the jungle rot. And at other times, a piece of shrapnel would work its way out of his body, but the coral infection was the worst.

Even though he was not able to walk for many days on end, suffered terrifying flashbacks and nightmares, he never received any compensation from the U. S. Government. The best treatment he got was from a local United States Public Health Service in Mobile.

They thought for a while that I was going to lose my right foot and part of my right leg. I was trying to get my life back in order, settle down and raise my family, but I couldn't do anything because I was still hurting. You can't begin to start something new when you're in physical pain like I was.

CHIEF WILEY CHATOPA

As Gene continued to try to get his life back in order, his uncle, Sam Johnson continued with the plan to buy and haul fresh oysters..

The plan Uncle Sam presented was for me and a helper to drive a circuitous route from Mobile to the small oyster shops bordering the Alabama Gulf Coast in the south part of the county.

We would stop at all the little fishing villages, Bayou La Batre, Coden, Heron Bay, Alabama Port and Dog River, buying fresh oysters. After buying up a truckload, we would return to Mobile and sell them to local restaurants, including those of my mother's. The roads were mostly unpaved and sometimes we had to spend the night and return to Mobile the next day. Helping me on the route was a big Indian from Oklahoma.

Wiley Chatopa was his given name, which meant something like, "Cunning Dog," but his American name was Willie Anderson, after his adopted family. We called him Chief. He weighed in at about three hundred twenty-five pounds and stood six feet, seven inches. He was a huge fellow with an arm reach of over seven feet.

Chief had just recently moved to Mobile. He had been sentenced to death in the Oklahoma electric chair for killing a man. It seems he got in a fight, and put another fellow's lights out with just one punch. He was on Death Row, but before the execution could take place, the Governor of Oklahoma reviewed the case, and believing it was accidental, pardoned him. He left Oklahoma right away. I guess Chief decided the best thing for him to do was get out of town before a lynching party caught him.

Our relationship worked well. Whenever I had to go into the hospital with my feet, Chief was able to drive and run the oyster route without me. Handling ninety-pound sacks of oysters was no problem for the big man. Maybe another reason we got along so well is the Chief enjoyed a pretty woman.

Chief was smart and he had good common sense. He could con the buffalo off a nickel. Sometimes we'd be going through the countryside picking up those oysters, and Chief would see a bunch of women's clothes hanging on a clothesline and he would tell me that we had to stop there one day. When I would ask him why, he would say,' look at all those drawers and bloomers hanging on the line. There must be six or seven women living there.' Sure enough, when we stopped, there would be several girls there.

During one of our runs, I met a young oysterman named J. B. Todd. His father had been killed when he was fourteen, and J. B. took care of himself and his mother catching oysters. I admired his reliability, and soon developed a close relationship with him.

I took a liking to this kid because he was always trying real hard to take care of his family. He had strong arms like Popeye's and was usually as barefoot as a yard dog. His feet were so tough he could walk on oyster shells without getting cut. It looked like the skin on his feet was a quarter inch thick. I could always depend on J. B. He had been working seven days a week for three or four months and I felt sorry for him. One day I told him I thought I had some clothes that would fit him, and I asked if he wanted to ride to Mobile?

I had intended to see that he got a pair of good shoes and pants and send him back home. Instead, J. B. asked if he could stay in a small shed out behind our big house. He remained there until he turned twenty-one several years later, and married. In the meantime, Chief had started courting J.B.'s mother and the two of them began living together.

During this time, we began to notice how the crabbers were complaining about a lack of crab bait. Any kind of meat could be used to bait the traps, so Chief hit upon the idea of cornering the crab bait market.

Meat was still pretty scarce back in the spring of 1946, so we went to the butcher shops and made them a deal. We would furnish them with a barrel of brine and if they would put the beef tripe, (cattle stomachs,) in these barrels, we would pick them up every week and pay them a penny a pound. They weren't getting anything for it at the time, so most shops jumped at the idea.

We went by at least once a week and dumped that stuff in the back of the pickup and took it to Coden and Bayou La Batre to the crab processors on our way out of Mobile. We were able to resell it for five cents a pound. We made good money, but boy was that a smelly mess. Finally, after a few weeks, somebody else starting offering the butchers more money, and we lost out. The Chief didn't mind because he said the women complained about the way he smelled.

After losing out on supplying crab bait, the two entrepreneurs decided to go into the scrap iron business.

We'd go around and find old abandoned sawmills that were rusted and buy them, usually for as little as three or four hundred dollars cash. We would then dismantle every thing and haul it to the junkyard. Chief couldn't do any cutting or burning with a torch, but he could sure tote scrap iron to the truck after I cut it up.

During this period, Gene and Francine continued to live in his family home, along with his mother, grandmother, and sometimes a guest or two. It was usually an intimate and happy group. On weekends, there might be as many as thirty relatives and friends who would visit.

J. B. Todd continued to live in the small building in back of the main house, but he ate many of his meals with the Tapia family. One day, he and Gene got into a wrestling match in the kitchen. It just so happened that Francine was cooking and their playing began to annoy her.

" I was trying to get dinner ready and they were jostling each other around and it got on my nerves," she said. " Gene would come over and slap me on the rear end and stuff like that. I asked them to get out so I could finish cooking, but they kept on. They never paid any attention to what I was doing. Finally, I told them to knock it off and get out.

"But neither of them was ready to call it quits. By this time, I was furious. I picked up a dining room chair and headed for them.

"When I did this, J. B. ran out the door, but Gene was cornered, and to keep me from laying that chair across his head, he dove under the dining room table."

Gene's grandmother, "Gangy", who had been upstairs quilting heard the commotion and came downstairs.

"When she got to the kitchen, I could tell she was mad," Gene said. "She dipped snuff, but she was always discreet about it. But this time she went over to the kitchen sink and spit in it, something she had never done before. Then she came over to the table and bent down and said, 'there ought to be a law against a man hitting a woman.'

Gene replied, "Grandma, what in the flying hell do you think I'm doing under this table? Does it look like I'm hitting a woman?"

MOONSHINE RUNNER

In addition to buying and selling oysters and hauling off old sawmills, Gene had found a good part-time job; one that suited his spirit for adventure.

In the rural South, illegal whiskey had been made for years. In Alabama the sale of alcoholic beverages was strictly controlled by the State. There was less than a dozen State-operated liquor stores in Mobile. These were the only stores that openly sold wine and hard whiskey. Only a handful of grocery stores were allowed to sell beer. No alcoholic beverages were allowed to be sold on Sunday. This made the manufacture and sale of homemade brew very lucrative.

Private clubs were the only source for most people who wanted a good drink. Commonly referred to as "honky tonks," "roadside taverns," or "juke joints," these taverns provided a ready-made market for bootleg and homemade whiskey because they were very loosely policed by the Alabama State Revenue Commission. A fifth of "State-Store Bourbon" cost ten dollars, whereas a gallon of good "moonshine" whiskey could be had for the same amount.

The time and place was perfect for a young person like Gene, because the roads were narrow and more crooked and there wasn't nearly as many policemen as there are today.

Gene had a friend who operated a "corn whiskey still" in a swamp about ten miles from his home. While he had grown up around it, he had never been involved in its manufacture or sale.

This friend and I had been making whiskey all night. We came out of the woods early in the morning. If you didn't come out on a different path from the one you went in on, you would soon get caught. The revenue men didn't get up too early, either. We were tired, and I think I had about eighteen or twenty gallons loaded in my Plymouth coupe.

Whenever Gene left the woods and hit Howell's Ferry Road, he pushed the accelerator to the floor in case there was a Federal Agent or other law enforcement agent watching for him.

As I came to the Gulf Mobile & Ohio Railroad tracks on Orchard Road I was running pretty fast, because I knew someone was after me. That was a pretty rough crossing with a high hump between the two sets of tracks. As I hit it, the car sailed up in the air. Those glass jugs filled with whiskey in the back started bouncing around and most of them broke.

Gene knew most of his load was gone because he began to smell it. As he looked back in the rearview mirror, he could see the trail of whiskey behind him.

That's when I really took off because I knew that now, I had to outrun them.

He made the remaining three miles to his home on Moffett Road without being caught.

I zipped in the back yard back behind the dairy barn and began hosing the car down. We washed it out good and got all the broken glass bottles. Then, we just sat there, like nothing had ever happened. I had lost the police because they never came by, but I lost the load of liquor also.

He was always coming up with something to make his car run faster. That's the way the whiskey running business was—you had to have a car faster than the police in order to get away every time. He learned how to turn the car around without using brakes, in case he ran into a roadblock. Most of the time, the police he would meet on the road, he was able to outrun them.

The Tapia family was well respected throughout the neighborhood. A few days after losing the load of liquor going over the railroad tracks, he and his family had gone out to eat.

We were in the White Spot Café on Springhill Avenue in Crichton, and Mr. Harry Sanders, the chief deputy of Mobile County, called me outside and said, 'Son, just be real careful.' Our second daughter, Rebecca had been born October 15, 1946, and from then on, I quit making whiskey and just hauled it.

Making whiskey was hard work, but it was interesting.

The interesting part kept Gene motivated. He was still searching, and this was the only outlet his adventuresome mind could relate with at the time.

After being warned by Deputy Sanders, Gene established a regular route with several of the local taverns. Occasionally, he received an order from a dealer in New Orleans, Louisiana, and would deliver an entire truckload.

Being strong and husky with a fast car didn't always insure success in the illegal whiskey trade. Especially in some of the neighborhoods he delivered in. One such area in Mobile was known as Wheelerville.

When his route took him into the clubs and barrooms in this area, Francine often accompanied him.

"You bet I was worried about him," she said. "We weren't worried about somebody stopping us and taking our money or the whiskey. It was the club owners that concerned me. A lot of times they didn't want to pay.

Only once did Francine have to go looking for her man.

"Gene always kept a .44 Colt in the car," said Francine. "One day when he didn't come right back out I thought something might have happened to him."

Francine grabbed the big Colt Revolver and marched inside the building. Much to her relief, Gene was standing next to the bar talking with some old buddies.

As soon as the people saw Francine holding that big .44, they scattered. Some went out the back door and others tried to hide under their tables. I never had any problems after that in the Blue Spot Lounge.

Pretty soon, the demand for oysters dropped, the number of old sawmills dwindled and the police were watching Gene on his whiskey runs. He decided it was time to look for a regular job, even though he was still struggling with life. The months had turned into a year, and he was still lost. By the latter part of 1947, his entreprenuering skills had played out, leaving him still more depressed. The only improvement was in his feet and legs.

People have looked at me and wondered why I did things I did. Hell, I knew running whiskey was illegal. In the back of my mind, I knew if I got caught I was going to jail. That thought always bothered me in addition to what it would have done to my family. What most folks can't feel is the pain and problems I had back then.

The coral and shrapnel in my legs kept me in such bad health I couldn't work most of the time. The doctors spent hours working on me, but none of them knew anything about treating jungle rot or coral cuts. Jungle rot affects you in different ways. A lot of people have rashes, but my problems were in my feet and legs. A Dr. Patterson from Washington County told me I was going to lose my right leg and foot, it was so bad. And I still have bouts of Dengue Fever and malaria that leave me listless.

Gene's physical condition caused problems for the entire family. Since his mother had four restaurants, she usually left early in the morning. The burden of keeping house, cooking and taking care of the two daughters, Shaaron and Becky (Rebecca) was squarely on Francine's shoulders.

"One morning, I had just put on a blue dress and was getting ready to take him to the Marine Hospital," she said. "His foot was swollen twice its normal size and he couldn't drive himself. Aunt Beatrice Headley had spent the night in the front room. She had opened the window to spit and didn't close it back. Underneath the window was a pile of oyster shells. Becky was leaning out the window as I was getting dressed. She was begging to go with us, but I said, No darling, you can't go with us. I have to take daddy to the hospital and we might have to stay a long time."

All of a sudden, Becky disappeared.

I was combing my hair in the mirror, and after a few minutes I wondered what happened to my baby. I got up, looked, and she had fallen out that window, hit her head on the oyster shells and split it wide open. She had gotten up, but blood was gushing out all over her blonde hair. It scared me to death.

Francine was just learning to drive, but she picked up her two year-old daughter, ran to the car and shouted back at Gene, "I've got to take her to the doctor." Francine drove to front of the White Spot Café and parked on the street.

I ran to the door and hollered for Ms. Ada. She ran out and we headed to the doctor. I made three circles around his office because I didn't know how to parallel park. Finally, a man that worked across the street at a service station saw the problem I was having and he let us get out and then parked the car for us.

After the cut on Becky's head was sewn up, Francine went back home, picked up Gene and took him to the hospital where his foot was lanced, then she drove back home.

Gene visited several doctors at the United States Public Health Service Hospital in Mobile, but quite by accident, a young intern just out of medical school took notice of his problems. According to Gene, Dr. Ben Pringle didn't have a lot of credentials, but he had the latest training, which included the latest treatment for jungle rot and coral cuts. Gene had to pay for his treatments with Dr. Pringle.

He told me it was going to be a tough battle. He said we had to work through seven layers of skin. Finally, after several months, he got that seventh layer of skin off, and the treatment progressed as he said.

I was struggling. If it hadn't been for my wife and Momma, I wouldn't have made it. I was in bad shape most of the time. I think the whiskey business was a terrible burden for my family, particularly because quite a few people knew about it later. I quit it because if I had been caught and sent to the penitentiary, it would have been so devastating for my family.

STOCK CAR RACING

Even though Gene's feet and legs were never cured from the two diseases, he did reach a point where he could walk without too much pain. Life became bearable and he was able to hold down a regular job, once again.

He went back to work on the night shift at the Gulf Shipyard in Mobile as a special pipe fitter apprentice. At about the same time, the sport of automobile racing was growing in the South. For over fifteen years, drivers had raced their cars in southern cow pastures on Sunday and at State Fairs.

The nation was going through a period of tremendous change. Just a couple of years out of the war, everything was getting back to normal. In fact, everything was going well. The economy was on an upswing, and the country was in a good mood. The heroes had shifted from the battlefield to the ball field and racetrack.

. Stock car racing was experiencing the greatest popularity it had ever seen. Dirt tracks sprang up in cow pastures, behind factories, and more and more drivers were racing in front of more and more fans.

While most of the glory in racing now rests in the major marketing areas, there were hundreds of small quarter-mile and three-eighths-mile dirt tracks in Florida, Georgia, Alabama, Mississippi, Louisiana and Tennessee in the 1940's. Most of these had been cow pastures at one time, and usually races were held on Sunday afternoons.

Prior to the formation of the National Association of Stock Car Automobile Racing (NASCAR), a Southern or Gulf Coast racing circuit stretched from Macon, Georgia, west to New Orleans, Louisiana, and from Panama City, Florida, north to West Memphis, Arkansas. Within this region, there were sixty or seventy short tracks that put on weekly racing shows.

Tracks weren't very elaborate. Most lacked lights. Usually someone who wanted to build a racetrack would lay out a track, get some earth moving equipment and start grading an area. Sometimes a few wooden bleachers would be built, but mainly people stood around in front of their cars or on the backs of pickup trucks as the cars circled the track in front of them.

There were no concession stands. Maybe some enterprising individual would bring some iced-down Coca-Colas or RC Colas in a number three washtub, and sell them from the back of a pickup. The only bathrooms would be self-made in the nearby woods or trees.

Even though a tanker truck might spray water on the track surface during intermission, there was always dust. Some tracks added a layer of oil, but by the time the feature race began, there would be holes in the track and dust clouds might reach several hundred feet. A lot of people would come with their Sunday best on and leave all caked with red dust.

Between 1946 and 1956, five tracks operated in the Mobile, Alabama, area: Hartwell Field, behind Fort Whiting; Wolf Ridge Road Speedway just west of the Mobile City Limits; Satsuma Raceway, north of Mobile; Braswell Stables Raceway, off U. S. Highway 90 in Tillman's Corner; and Lakeview Speedway in Eight Mile. Two tracks, Lakeview and Braswell Stables, hosted NASCAR-sanctioned events.

The Lakeview Speedway was a six-tenths mile dirt oval track that was built around a lake. Overlooking the racing facility was Cochran Stables. Constructed in 1946, the track put on a racing show every Sunday from March through November. The track featured two classes of cars, modifieds and strictly stock. Jimmy Golden, Johnny Tillman and Walter Cochran owned it.

It was the largest and best known of all Gulf Coast tracks. Located west of Mobile, off U. S. Highway 98, it was accessible and offered bleachers for fans to sit in. Instead of the usual red dirt, it had a sandy track. The area in front of the grandstands was covered with heavy oil, which protected the fans from some of the dust. The oil was obtained from ships that docked at the Alabama State Docks in Mobile. It was known as bunker sea oil.

The owners would pay to have someone go to each ship in port and pump out their bilges into a truck. At the time, the bilges were just pumped overboard into Mobile Bay and the Gulf of Mexico. The heavy bunker oil was then poured on the track. It was almost like a light coat of asphalt, except after a rain, and then it was very slippery.

After NASCAR became organized, Lakeview and Braswell speedways hosted several big NASCAR races, but in the middle and late 1940s they were still a proving ground for racers like Tapia.

Since the end of World War II, automakers had been frantically converting their assembly lines from tank and truck production to building family cars. Demand far outstripped supply; so most of the cars that ran at Lakeview were pre-1940 model Fords, Chevrolets, Dodges, and Plymouths. Some of the same cars that ran in those years were bootleggers' cars and they were much faster than most race cars.

In reminiscing about his life at home after the war, Gene said, "Most of my days were long and hard. My spirit was sick and sore. My wartime experiences had left things in a chaos."

Even though the physical condition of his feet was improving, he often felt as if life had been squeezed from him. He found himself doing a lot of heavy thinking, but the right solution never seemed to pop up. He resisted the obvious solutions like drinking and wild living, but faced daily struggles to keep his emotions buried. Often, he could not respond enthusiastically to life. He had known how to handle his body in combat and competition, but now his whole life had been thrown off

After two years, Gene became increasing concerned about this lack of "centeredness" towards life, and those around him. But in his most disillusioned moods, he never lost sight of his role as a father and husband. Still at odds with himself, he accepted an invitation from a friend that would change what he would do for the rest of his life.

Somebody invited us to go out to Lakeview Speedway to watch these car races one Sunday. There wasn't much to them. Most of the twenty or thirty cars were driven to the track. A few didn't even have a roll bar. I was kind of enjoying them and made the statement that I could probably do well in one of the cars.

A friend of mine looked over at me and said, 'No Gene, you're too big, and besides, you'd never make a good race car driver.'

He shouldn't have said that.

The next day Gene sought out Lawrence Nolan, a local garage owner. Nolan had only one good arm, but he had a reputation of being able to build fast race cars. Nolan's response to Gene's request to drive his car was "No, I don't need another driver."

Determined, Gene asked two of his friends, Darryl Foster and Joe Burton, friends of Lawrence Nolan, to intervene in his behalf.

I bugged Mr. Nolan for weeks. Every time I had a little spare time, I would go by his shop and talk racing. One Saturday, in the spring of 1948, I had some time to kill, so I dropped in again. He looked at me and said, 'Do you really want to race? Would you like to go to Chisholm Speedway in Montgomery to a race?'

He said Burt Branch, who was a reliable promoter, was putting on a big race that Sunday, and if I wanted to go he would give me a try. I knew there would be some big names, but I also knew what I had done with cars on dirt roads in Mobile County.

Gene was elated. He went home immediately and told Francine.

"I didn't like the idea of him racing," she said. " We still had all kinds of problems; we were still adjusting to each other, he was just then getting back on his feet, and he wanted to take up this crazy and dangerous game of racing. I thought to myself, how stupid can a woman be? I didn't know if that might be the final straw."

Most race car drivers wives' are like Francine, scared for their man to race. She says the fear was greatest when the race started.

"This was one of the biggest moments in our lives," continued Francine. I knew I had to make a decision. I had to either get into racing or get out of the marriage.

Francine went along with her husband's plans for the next day. At six o'clock the next morning everyone had gathered at Nolan's garage in Crichton, Alabama. The car that had been prepared was a red and white 1936 Ford coupe with the No. 36 painted on the door. It had a tow bar fastened on the front bumper. A Chevrolet van was backed up and the No. 36 was hooked to the rear bumper. The racing team was ready to roll.

We had to take the wheels off and put different ones on because the height didn't match the van. It took us 5 1/2 hours to go the 175 miles up U. S. Highway 31 to Montgomery. By the time we got there it was noon. That was just right, because you couldn't start any earlier because of the church services.

NASCAR BIGSHOTS

The name NASCAR has become a household word for millions of Americans. We all know the names of our favorite drivers, both past and present, and practically all-racing fans know that it is the France family that has brought American automobile racing to its present heights. But in the spring of 1948, Gene Tapia had never heard of NASCAR or where it was headed. He was feeling a challenge and had to see it through.

In December of 1947, Bill France Sr. had organized a meeting at the Streamline Hotel in downtown Daytona Beach, Florida to discuss the makeshift facilities and lack of cohesiveness that confronted both drivers and fans.

France had come to Florida from Maryland years earlier and had operated a local service station and promoted events on the city's famed beach course that he often raced on himself. From that meeting, the National Association of Stock Car Racing was born. Few knew when the meeting adjourned if the organization would be successful. In fact, there were skeptics who believed it would never work.

Not even France, who believed a sanctioning body was exactly what the sport needed, could have envisioned what NASCAR has become today. On February 15, 1948, the first NASCAR-sanctioned race was held on Daytona's beach course. Red Byron, a stock car legend from Atlanta, won the event in his Ford Modified.

Less than a month after Red Byron had won the first NASCAR-sanctioned event in Daytona Beach, Florida, Gene Tapia, a rookie driver from Mobile was putting on a beat up football helmet to go up against Byron and other drivers who would eventually become NASCAR Legends.

All these early NASCAR drivers were there, people like Byron, Buck Baker, Gober Sosebee, Dick Linder, Jack Smith, Curtis Turner, Sara and Frank Christian, Speedy Thompson, and Tim, Bob and Fonty (Fontella) Flock. As I began to study the Montgomery track, I saw it looked like a dirt road I had been practicing on back in Mobile.

Most of the drivers at Chisholm Speedway were from Georgia. Gene called them the "Atlanta Gang," because most of them raced at the big Lakewood Speedway and other tracks around Atlanta, Georgia. For most novice drivers attempting to compete against these seasoned racers, it would have been intimidating, to say the least.

I knew who these drivers were. I had read stories about them in the Mobile Press Register and magazines. These were the big shot drivers out of Atlanta. Everybody at Montgomery that day knew they were watching the cream of the crop. They were at the top of the ladder. I asked myself, what am I doing up here with this group of men?

That was also the first day Gene Tapia had ever sat in a real race car.

The driver who impressed the young rookie most was Buck Baker, a driver from North Carolina. Baker went on to win the NASCAR Grand National Championship in 1956 and '57 and forty-four poles and forty-six major events during his career. He was also the first driver to practice that Sunday in March and Gene eyed his moves on the track carefully. The car he was driving was a modified Ford with a flathead V-8 engine.

That fellow Baker lit that flathead Ford up and sailed down the front straightaway. When he got to the turn, he just tossed it toward the corner and began steering like the devil. And he kept a big rooster tail of dirt coming up all the time. From that time on, I admired Buck Baker.

When it was his turn to practice, Gene tried to run the same grooves as he had seen Baker running. The car slipped up several times in the corners, but the 36 car stayed on the track, and after a few laps, Gene began to get the feel of the car against the track.

When qualifying results were posted, Buck Baker had turned the fastest time and would start on the pole.

Rookie, Gene Tapia had the third fastest time.

DON'T MESS WITH MY MAN

The Chisholm Speedway was a one-half mile dirt track built around several dirt pits. The center of the track had deep pits and sink holes that contained weeds, briars and was home to hundreds of cottonmouth moccasins. The drivers raced along the edges of this quagmire.

After allowing himself to become accustomed to the track in two heat races, Gene was ready to pour it on when it came time for the feature event. Since racing tires had not been invented, his crew put on a new set of recapped tires they had purchased from Slade Tires in Mobile. They were the best type of racing tires available in 1948.

The team was all set to go racing.

Things had worked out the way we had planned. The green flag came out and I put my foot to the floor. I knew I didn't have the experience those hotdog drivers did and I had sense enough to realize that. I let a couple get by and was running in about the middle of the pack and feeling pretty good about myself after a few laps.

Then things happened real fast. The X9 car driven by Dick Patton got into the back of me and knocked me off the track and into the water. I didn't get hurt, and it was kind of funny. Sometimes you have a feeling that time has stopped and you have to wait and see what's going to happen. It's almost like your mind hasn't caught up with you until it's all over.

As I went sailing off into that water, the car stirred up a bunch of moccasins. Those snakes were swimming around all over the place, licking their tongues out at me. I didn't know which way to go, but I sure didn't like the predicament I was in.

Francine, who had been sitting in the grandstands on the outside of the track, saw what had happened. As soon as the No. 36 hit the water, she jumped up from her seat and ran across the muddy track. Cars were still flying around it, and several had to dodge her as she darted across the ankle-deep dirt and mud track amid the shouting of officials.

"I was heading for my baby," she said. "The officials started shouting at me to get back, but wild hogs couldn't have detoured me."

As she came across the pit area through the weeds, briars, snakes and water, she noticed a tall man standing on a flatbed truck. "Lady, take off your shoes and wade out to him," he shouted.

The man turned out to be James "Big Jim" Folsom, the future Governor of Alabama.

"Big Jim helped me get across all that water," said Francine. "The thing I remember about him was his feet and voice. You could have heard him hollering into the next county, and he had the biggest feet I've ever seen on a man."

CHAPTER X

AN ANGEL WITH LIGHT

Gene survived his baptism into the Chisholm snake pit. After the race, Johnny Martin, owner of the X9 car that had knocked him into the water came by as Gene was sitting on the sidelines. Looking toward his car owner, Lawrence Nolan, he said, "It looks like you got a driver, Nolan."

Even though Gene had not been able to finish the race, a fire had been lit inside him. He discovered the old killer instinct. It's an instinct that every good race car driver has. Without it, you're not going to make a good race car driver.

The drive back to Mobile was long and agonizing for Francine.

"Gene was everything I wanted in life," she said. "I was proud to be married to him, and I had given him all my faith, hope and love. There were times during the war when I didn't think I would ever see him again, but I prayed every night that God would allow him to come home.

"I felt betrayed. Seeing him fall in love with racing was like I was faced with another competitor. First, it had been Alaska, then Uncle Sam, and now I could see it was happening all over. He was falling in love with racing. I didn't know if it was possible for me to live with it now that we had a family.

"And it was at times like these I thought about our lost baby. It usually made me cry and when I brought it up to Gene, he would get depressed for a few days."

Gene was elated over his new hobby and pastime, and even though Francine was very unsettled over what was happening, her uneasiness did not affect the two girls.

"Right after Daddy started racing, we had gotten this little rabbit for Easter," said Shaaron. "Everybody used to slide down the banister on the steps coming down from upstairs, so I thought the rabbit should be able to do it. But he fell off on the way down and didn't get up. His little eyes were open and I said, Momma, he's not dead. But he was. After crying a lot of tears, we went outside and had a funeral for my rabbit.

"We had some Wisteria vines right close to the house, so I thought that would be a pretty place to bury him. After getting a pillowcase from Momma, Becky and I dug a grave and gave him a real proper funeral. Becky just stood around, but I said, "this rabbit to dust, and things like that."

"I think there was a change in Daddy when he started racing. It seems like the tempo of things picked up around us. We didn't always get to go with him to the track but I believe it made a change for the better in the way we lived and got along."

Unlike today's drivers, Gene and the ones who started out in the early days of the sport didn't have water bottles; fire suits or specially designed safety seats. If a car would run, the driver drove it. He figured out what to do to make it run faster. If he was sliding off the seat, he tied himself up. And sometimes, the steering wheel would fall off. If it did, the driver would have to put it back on as he raced.

The drivers today couldn't cope with situations like that. I don't think most of them would have the desire to compete like we did. Don't get me wrong, I enjoyed the money and prestige of winning a race, but hell, I would have paid someone just to let me race. That's how much I loved it.

Because I qualified well, it meant I usually started near the tail end of every race and had to go after all of them. When you can trick or fool a driver into going one way and you get by him on the other side, you've done something. The elation of coming from behind and winning is something else. It was a thrill that consumed me.

Gene had made a commitment to racing. It was an honest commitment. Unless another driver showed himself by using dirty driving tactics, Gene Tapia raced him clean. Practically all his victories were legitimate.

"Mr. Clean is the best way I know to describe Gene Tapia," said All-Pro Series owner and promoter Bob Harmon. "He never tried to mess up anybody's equipment or wreck them on the track. That is, unless you messed with him first. Then, because he had so much driving talent, he could take you out in a heartbeat.

"In all my years of racing, I've never known a better driver or one who has shown as much sportsmanship as he has. In stock car racing, it's win at any cost, but Gene always had the attitude that you could do it honestly."

The next weekend Gene was back in the No. 36 car, this time at Lakeview Speedway. He didn't win, but he gained valuable racing experience that can only come from sitting behind the wheel of a race car.

Some of the best drivers in the country raced at Lakeview. I think the shows were sponsored by the Pensacola, Florida Dust Busters. One of the organizer's of them was Fred Brundidge.

I can't remember them all, but, "Madman" Bob Thompson, Fred Vannoy, Norman Gonzales, Bill Hightower, Bill Osborne, Burt Freeman, "T'Bone" Shelby, Jake Hatcher, Luverne Macks, Carl Beverly, Lamar Crabtree, Leroy Morgan, and Fred Moore were some of the early drivers that came over from Florida.

Eddie Niedermeier was the flagman and spokesman for the Mobile drivers.

Cooley Barnett, C.T. Weldon, Woodie Wilson, Joe Slaughter, Charlie Merrill, Harold Munn, Glen Hobson, Doug Wimpee, Bill Howell, and Reuben Barnett were regular local drivers.

"I had been thinking about it all week," Francine said. "I didn't want to do anything rash. I had to think about the family. Sometimes when the old thoughts came up, I moved mechanically, numbed by memories of the past, especially about the loss of our first baby."

However, the loss of their child in a Memphis hospital in 1942 also affected Gene.

"I'm sure I was always searching for that lost son," Gene said. "Whenever I got around boys and young men, I was always wanting to help them or explain to them something about my life. There were so many times I felt ashamed for not being home. Had I been here, I feel like things would have been different."

Two weeks after returning from his first race in Montgomery, he was one of the fast qualifiers in the modified class at Lakeview. The field was inverted, which meant the fastest cars started from the rear. This allowed slower cars a better opportunity to win and provided more of a show to the spectators.

There was between fifteen and eighteen cars that started the race. About halfway through the race I had been watching the drivers ahead of me and I was seventh or eighth. Boy, that was fun passing those other fellows.

Being able to pass so many cars in such a small number of laps caused his adrenalin to flow.

I saw that I had a chance, and I really went after them.

Gene had the accelerator pedal all the way to the floor. The flathead Ford's engine screamed. He was throwing up a rooster-tail all the way around the track. As he passed another car, the dirt he kicked up would pile up on its windshield and inside the car.

All of a sudden, I was having the time of my life. It wasn't too long before I caught the leaders, and suddenly there wasn't anyone in front of me. I was leading the race. It had been so much fun getting up through the pack, that when I found myself out front, I was surprised.

After winning his first career race Gene Tapia didn't walk around Mobile declaring himself a great driver. He knew it would take lots of hard work, time in a driver's seat and scraped knuckles. In more ways than one, he knew good racers were made, not born. But strangely, he had found something much more important inside himself.

Even though, he was a sociable person, Gene says he often felt shy.

I accepted what I had been given and I savored it. I knew what I was capable of doing, and I didn't go around tooting my horn, showing off or bragging. I was finding something I had been looking for. Racing was the thing that got my feet back on the ground from all that baloney I had been through. All the hard times and stress and trying to figure out who I was began to disappear. Suddenly, there was something I wanted to do. I knew I had to race. For the first time, I could see the light and was feeling some peace inside my soul.

Francine didn't share the same feelings as her husband, but she made it easier and safer for him to race. After reading a magazine article on how to make drapes and tablecloths fire retardant, she bought some of the liquid. She mixed the liquid with starch and soaked his uniforms in it, and afterwards pressed them. Not only was he smartly dressed, but he was the first person in the area to have fire-retardant uniforms. Every race day morning she pressed his uniform and picked him up at work. Often Gene would drive to the track, but if it had been a rough day, Francine might drive.

Most of the time, she took the two girls. During the races, she and Becky and Shaaron would sit in the stands with friends. Often Gene's mother accompanied them.

On weeknights, Gene would go directly to the race car shop before he came home. While he never stayed out late or came home drunk, Francine was feeling like she and the family were being avoided. When the depressing feelings of despair became unbearable, she would talk with her best confidant, Gene's mother.

While Francine was emotionally unsure of what was going to happen in her life, Gene was now beginning to get his back in order. He had joined Local 119 of the Pipefitters Union in Mobile and worked out of it most of the time. But occasionally, he and Francine had problems.

Often, the problem was other women. Gene had developed a large fan following, many of who were women. After the races, Francine would be in the pits and could manage when young girls or women would try to come on to her husband.

Neither Gene nor Francine were heavy drinkers but they liked to go to party at clubs with other couples. One club they frequented was the Diamond Horseshoe Club next to Lakeview Speedway.

A LAP GIRL

Janice was built like a brick house. I mean she had everything in all the right places, long legs, a fine set of lungs, and the best thing about her was the cute behind she sported. She was a fine looking woman, but she was also a big flirt. Her husband owned one of the cars that I drove.

Francine was on the dance floor when Janice came over and sat in Gene's lap. Francine spotted the pair through the smoke and dim lights and came to where the couple was sitting.

Arguing with any woman in a bar or restaurant can drive a man crazy. But when you get one like Francine, you've really got a problem on your hands. At home I could have banged on the table and we would have shouted at each other to make a point. In the spot, however, where we were, everybody was watching and I knew they were going to be talking about whatever happened. I had to clench the table and the beer bottle in order to keep from banging my fists on the table. Holding back the desire to scream and tell Francine I didn't have anything to do with her coming over and flopping down in my lap made me red in the face.

Francine didn't accept Gene's version of what happened.

" I didn't care what people said or thought," said Francine. " I was not going to take a back seat to any woman. Gene was my man and that's the way it was going to stay."

Francine stood back, looked at Gene and Janice, who was now on the other side of the room, and said, "I'm leaving. I'm going home." She turned, and headed for the door, leaving Gene and his two buddies sitting there.

"I felt like a red-faced idiot," Gene said. "Having to sit there and deal with the stares of the other customers, many of whom I raced against, and wondering what was going to happen when I got home."

Francine threw the door open and walked out at a very fast pace, not looking back.

"That made me even madder," Gene said.

Even though he was mad, Gene started out the door after her. By this time, Francine was almost out of sight in the darkness. She had taken off her shoes, and as Gene approached her, she drew one shoe back as if she was going to throw it at him.

Man, I didn't know what to do except follow her. She had taken her high heel shoes off and wasn't looking back. She intended to walk the three or four miles home. Pretty soon, Leroy Jones, the fellow we had rode with came up in his '36 Ford and between the two of us we calmed her down enough so she would get in the car.

But that wasn't the end of it. It was pretty hectic around home for a couple days. She was pretty miffed, but I finally convinced her there wasn't anything between Janice and I.

SERIOUS RACING

In the fall of 1949, the owners of Fuller Pontiac in Laurel, Mississippi, asked a local radio announcer, "Fats" Harvison, to help them locate a good driver from Mobile to run a factory sponsored Pontiac at the Laurel State Fairgrounds.

The track was a one-half mile oval that raced on Saturday nights. It was located near the Laurel Airport. At the time it was one of the best tracks in the South because of its good racing surface and fan accommodations.

This was the first factory-backed sponsorship that I had heard of. The car was a big 1949 or '50 Pontiac sedan with a straight-8 flathead engine. That was the only time I was guaranteed one hundred percent of the purse. I just went up on kind of a lark, because I didn't think that type car would run.

But they had the right gear in that thing that allowed the engine to build up the right amount of horsepower, and I had a wonderful time in that big old heavy car. I could make the rooster-tail fly. When I would pitch it into the first corner and get on the gas, the engine would just whooooom and shoot down the back straightaway. I would do the same thing at the other end of the track and the fans loved it.

I remember Milton Tilley of Lucedale, and Charlie Merrill of Mobile were two drivers that were tough to beat at Laurel.

There are no records available, but Gene does not ever recall losing a feature race in the maroon and yellow Pontiac.

That was one of the most lucrative racing deals of my life. I won watches, meals, tires, rings, sets of tires, bedroom suites, and all kinds of prizes. I had so many watches that finally I began giving them away to the mechanics.

After a few weeks, Gene was earning as much money racing in Laurel as he was at his regular job. But it wasn't just money and trophies that the handsome ex-Marine was winning. He was also accumulating a large fan following.

"He always had so many fans around him after the races," Francine said. "I mean, they would be five and six deep all around him. And I had to watch the women around him. One evening three women who worked in Laurel got mad at their boss because he wouldn't let them off to see Gene Tapia race. They quit their jobs to come and watch Gene race."

"The people in Laurel fell in love with me, and I fell in love with them," Gene said.

KANGAROO COURT

But not all racers are winners. Gene discovered that not everyone liked him or his racing. To get to the Laurel track from Mobile, Gene and his family traveled up U. S. Highway 98 to Richton, Mississippi, and took a back road into Laurel.

The area from Lucedale, Mississippi, which is just inside the stateline to Hattiesburg, was a very rural area. There were a few small family farms, but it was mostly flat swampy land with a lot of pine trees. People who lived in the area made their living logging or cutting pulpwood in the pine forests. There were several small towns along the route. The business district consisted of a gasoline or filling station, small store and post office. In between the towns there were only scattered farmhouses.

In general, it was and still is an economically, underdeveloped region. Two of the small towns between the Mississippi stateline and Hattiesburg are Richton and Beaumont.

Late one Saturday evening, Gene was heading to Jackson, Mississippi for a regular night of racing. As he approached the small town of Beaumont, Mississippi, he noticed a George County sheriff's car ahead of him. The driver was weaving all across the road. He was apparently drunk.

I wasn't going all that fast, so when I got the opportunity, I zipped by him. As soon as we had passed him, he started to run me down. I stopped and waited for him. He didn't have on any uniform, but he had a badge.

Gene and his family were forced to follow the deputy to the house of a Justice of the Peace in Beaumont.

As we pulled into the driveway we had to wait for a lady and a bunch of pigs to cross. We go up on the front porch and there are twelve rocking chairs all lined up. There was some latticework on the porch to keep the pigs and chickens out of the office, and sitting alongside the building were six or eight snuff-dipping men, whittling with their pocket knives. They had to chase all the pigs and dogs off the front porch before court could begin.

The old staggering deputy brought me up before this Justice of the Peace, and he fined me twenty-seven dollars and fifty cents. In Beaumont, Mississippi, is where I learned the meaning of Kangaroo Court.

Well, I got over it. We went on to Jackson and I won the feature, so it wasn't too bad.

A normal feature race at the Jackson and Laurel tracks was 25-laps. This is because people would become bored if one driver was leading the entire race. And 1940 vintage cars couldn't stand up like a modern race car. The night's events would consist of a five or six lap trophy dash, two six to eight heat races, and the feature event.

About once a month, the Laurel track and most other tracks would run an Australian Pursuit. The top six or eight qualifiers would line up single file. The slowest car would start in front and the fast qualifier would be on the tail end. The field would run two laps after the race was started. Every lap after that, the car at the end would be given the black flag, meaning he was out of the race. Racing continued until all cars except the leader had been black-flagged.

Not all cars were legal. Even back then all tracks had a set of rules and inspectors to enforce their rules after every race.

Jeep McDonald was a good friend of mine, but sometimes he didn't run exactly according to the rules. One night he came in with his Ford and everybody knew his engine was too big. The first lap I took the lead with ole Jeep right on my back bumper.

About two laps later, Jeep lost a left front wheel. When he lost that wheel, he fell back a little. The hub wasn't digging in the dirt, so he stood on the gas. He ran that entire race and passed me for the lead.

He was running wide open when he took the checkered flag, but when the race was over, he never stopped at his pit. He just kept right on going out the pit gate and went home. He knew he was illegal, but he just wanted to outrun me. And he did it on three wheels.

Gene raced for Fuller Pontiac for nearly one year. At the end of 1950, the Laurel Fairgrounds Speedway was known throughout the southeast. The young, personable driver had helped put Laurel, Mississippi on the map.

Not all local racing was confined to race tracks. Gene recalls one incident that caused him to get locked inside the Laurel Airport. It involved Smith Orr, owner of the Jaguar dealership in Laurel, and Laurel track promoter Pee Wee Reeves.

Pee Wee had a modified Model T with a big block Chevrolet motor. The two got into an argument over whether Pee Wee's Model T or Smith Orr's Jaguar was the fastest. To settle it, we go out to the airport and start fooling around and racing on the runway. We zipped all over the runway for about an hour. That Jaguar would run 140 mph and the Model T wasn't a slouch either.

When Gene and the other men decided to leave, the gate was locked.

We couldn't get out. I didn't drink, but some of the others were three sheets in the wind. The caretaker had locked us up and called the sheriff. The sheriff didn't want to come out, but he finally did. After awhile, he talked this caretaker into turning us loose.

Gene, driving the Jaguar, beat the track promoter in the Model T, but he promised himself he would never again allow himself to get in such a predicament.

What brought the Laurel racing deal to a close was the fact they couldn't get enough Pontiacs to meet the demand. I sold a lot of Pontiacs for Mr. Fuller. The deal was very rewarding for me. I gained a lot of friends, made money and furthered my racing career. I can't say enough good things about the people of

Laurel, Mississippi. They are some of the finest people in the world.

The one bad moment at Laurel was the death of Fred Rawlings. He was a wonderful young driver. He was killed because a green driver came out of the pits while he was on the track qualifying. Fred elected to wreck rather than hit the driver. He ran off the track and hit some trees rather than ram into the driver who came out in front of him.

It was at times like this when Francine would begin to cry over the loss of their baby boy in 1942. Coming home from Laurel one night, she asked Gene to try again and find their son.

We had hired one detective, and he wasn't able to turn up anything. But I hurt just like Francine.

The next week, Gene found another private investigator, who was a former policeman and paid him in advance to provide them with information on their missing son.

He reported to us several times, but it was all dead ends. After about three months, the investigator just left us hanging. We never heard from him again.

Gene continued to race on Saturday nights at Laurel after losing his Pontiac ride. William J. Hogeland of Atlanta owned a six cylinder Plymouth that Gene won with on a regular basis.

As a mechanic, this man was far ahead of his time. He knew just the right gear ratio to get the most out of a car. We put a little Plymouth together, numbered it 67 Jr., and took it to Laurel. It sounded like a bumblebee, wheeeeeeeeee, going down the straightaways. We turned 7,000 RPM's all the time. We won some races, but it wasn't long before some of the other teams caught on to our gear ratio and they started running different setups.

In one of the races in the 67 Jr., a wheel came off just as Gene finished the race. He was able to keep it under control, but the wrecker had to lift the front end off the ground and tow the entire car with Gene in it back to Victory Lane.

In the fall of 1950, Gene received a notice to report to the Draft Board in Montgomery for a physical and possible induction back into the Marines.

After they began to give me a physical it didn't take long for them to realize it would cost them too much to get me back into a good physical, fighting condition, so they sent me back home.

When Gene returned home after failing his physical, the couple was still searching for something to do together.

I'm sure I put a big strain on her, but we kind of liked each other. And we wanted to grow up together. We were always able to talk. She let me handle my emotional problems, but I stumbled a lot and she picked me up. And not only her, but my mother was the kindest person in the world and she understood me.

Operating four restaurants in downtown Mobile, Gene's mother was exposed to many returning servicemen who told her what had happened on Guadalcanal, Guam and Iwo Jima.

On her tombstone it says, 'A best friend to many.' Many people called her their best friend because she would listen to their troubles and if they asked for advice, she would give it, and it was never bad.

Everybody was good in her book until they showed her different. But she'd give them one and sometimes two chances. On that third chance, if she told you they were an SOB, you could write it on the wall. That fellow was what she said he was.

NEW YORK, NEW YORK

Gene had remained friends with a fellow Marine named Charles Christian from Mineola, New York, after his discharge. In 1950, he and his wife came to Mobile on a visit. While in Mobile, he talked with Gene about going to work for him in New York City. He had two contracts, one with Dun & Bradstreet, the other with the legal firm of Goldman, Horowitz and Chernow.

Christian's contract with Dun & Bradstreet was to investigate firms and companies that were attempting to establish credit with member merchants. It would be a big change for Gene. Instead of wearing jeans and khaki shirts, he would be dressed in a business suit.

Gene was told his job would be investigating stores and giving written evaluations of their financial accountability, and whether they should be considered a good credit risk.

The move sounded good to Gene, but Francine wasn't overjoyed with leaving the only security she had ever known.

Noting her concern, Gene said, "By golly, Francine, this would be a pretty big move."

Francine smiled. "We've been through a couple big moves in the past haven't we. This one shouldn't be any different from the others. It won't get us down."

In October 1950, the Tapia family left their southern friends behind and moved to a large home with nine acres, known as the Dowsey Estate in Mineola, New York. The large two-story house had an iron fence completely surrounding the estate, and seemed the perfect home for the Tapia family.

Gathering information suited the ex-Marine. After a few months, he was assigned the job of delivering legal summons to merchants, and this was a task that was unacceptable to him. Less than a year after arriving in New York, Gene called it quits and headed south.

After returning to Mobile, he took a job at a local garage, wrecker service and body shop. Harold "Bud" Erb was not only a racer, but he had the reputation of driving fast on the highways, often outrunning the Alabama Highway Patrol. He always had souped up cars and the only two speeds he knew were fast and faster. A local farmer, who lived on the Irvington- Bayou La Batre Road, once remarked that it took two people to announce when "Bud" Erb came by; one person to say, "Here he comes," and the other to say, "There he goes."

I didn't have to do a lot of work, most of what I did was answer the telephone. One day, three people were killed in a wreck involving a 1950 Mercury. The car was damaged pretty well, but Bud bought it and made a race car out of it. He had another Mercury, a 1951, that he wanted to rebuild, but didn't have enough money.

Gene and William Hogeland thought the car would make them a good race car and they talked Chester Sapp into buying and sponsoring the car. Hoagland went to work on the engine and race setup. The gear ratio they settled on was 5.05:1.

That car would fly after Hogeland got through with it. We won many races with that car.

By making modifications on the 1950 Mercury, Gene was able to compete in three different classes: NASCAR Grand National, now Winston Cup, Sportsman, and Modified divisions.

The tracks they competed on were NASCAR-sanctioned and scattered from Macon, Georgia to Metairie, Louisiana.

Back in those days we didn't have money for a tow truck. We drove that car to most of the races. We put a muffler on it and drove it on the road, sometimes all the way to Macon, and then back home. Sometimes we didn't add a muffler because people liked to see and hear stuff like that. Sometimes it had a windshield on one side and some times it didn't. But it always had that big number 66 on the door.

The No. 66 traveling team consisted of Gene and William Hogeland. Early one Sunday morning, the car was loaded down with spare tires and toolbox. The team headed out before daylight for Macon, Georgia, 275 miles away. Their route was over crooked two lane country roads.

We ran a NASCAR Grand National race in Macon in 1951. Speedy Thompson was the winner, and as soon as it was over we headed back home. On the way back to Mobile, it turned cold. We didn't have money for motel rooms. I had a blanket that I was covered up in on the back seat, but Hoagland was driving and he was about to freeze. His fingers had started turning blue.

We stopped at some roadside joint to try to get something to drink. This was Sunday and all the beer was covered up. Stores couldn't sell beer or whiskey on Sunday. Hogeland was looking around in the cold drink box, and down underneath, covered up, he spotted some beer. He reached in, grabbed that beer, and started tossing bottles of it to me. That got him warmed up enough to drive the car on to Mobile.

Sometimes at the big NASCAR events, Gene would win five or six hundred dollars. Since most of the large races were held on Sunday, it meant he wasn't always back home in time to get to work on time Monday morning.

Very seldom did I have problems on my job. Most of my working buddies were my foreman or superintendent, but they were also my race fans. They liked me and I liked them and we always got along. They understood. But I always did my share. When I got to the job, I put out enough to take up the slack for not being on time.

People like to talk about racing, and, about nine o'clock, we always took a coffee break. They usually asked me to stay away from the coffee pot because the other workers would want to spend too much time talking about racing and be late getting back to work. I knew what the situation was and had very few problems with my bosses.

Whenever Gene was to race on a Thursday or Friday night, he would take a clean set of racing clothes with him to work in the morning. As soon as his shift was over, he would shower and change into his clean clothes. Francine would meet him at the gate and usually drive to the track in their large Chrysler Imperial. This allowed Gene to let his seat back and get some sleep on the way.

If it hadn't been for Francine, I wouldn't have been able to do the things I did.

KING OF THE COW PASTURE

There were several tracks along Highway 90 between Mobile and New Orleans, but Gene's favorite was a half-mile, dirt oval in Metairie, Louisiana.

Louisiana people, especially the Cajuns, are clannish. The King Bee of all the racers at the Metairie track was Jimmy Furr. Another fellow that was a good racer was Jay Gonzales. I always had fun with these people. We got to know these people and developed a lot of respect for each other.

But gaining the Louisiana racers respect didn't just happen. Gene first had to show them what he was made of.

Really, the place wasn't much more than a cow pasture. Sometimes in the evening before we raced, a bunch of us would have to run the cows off the track. The first time we went over, the flagman let everybody except me get in a lot of practice laps. When it came my turn to practice, he black-flagged me after only one and one-half laps. He wanted me to get off the track. I couldn't believe it.

But Gene wasn't through warming up or feeling out the track. He hadn't driven 150 miles to be told he couldn't practice the same as the other drivers.

I wasn't through practicing. He had given everybody else all kind of practice time. Huh, I knew I was going to get in some more time, so I kept on practicing. Pretty soon he ran out on the track, waving the flag and acting like he was chewing on nails. He shouldn't have done that. I pointed the nose of that Mercury right at him and put the gas pedal to the floor. Vroooooooooom, there I went, heading straight for him. He got the message pretty quick because he joined the bird gang. He never messed with me again.

There was this Cajun lady named Bougalee. She was married to a race driver named Jimmy Burt, who was in the whiskey hauling business. Bougalee was just a doll. She was just as cute as a brand new button. She would get to talking fast in French, and I couldn't understand her. We didn't see her over the winter months, and when racing started the next year she had a little baby with her.

"Bougalee, where did you get that young 'un?"

"I got him wit de Green Stamps," she said.

Joe Booker, Clint McHugh, Arthur McMillan, and Pappy Crain were some other fellows I loved to hang around with after the races. Clint was killed a few years later in West Memphis, Arkansas.

One night a special Match Race was set up between Jimmy Furr and Gene Tapia. Furr drove a small roadster while Gene continued to race his heavy 1950 Mercury.

They put us side by side. He was on the inside and I was on the outside.

Whoever won that Match Race was going to win a great big trophy and be recognized as the champion.

Jimmy had already decided he was going to spin me out. We went into the first turn and Jimmy laid the bumper to me in the left rear. He nearly spun himself out. He came back and tried it a couple more times. I wasn't worried, I was just going to outrun him. I didn't want to embarrass him. The next time he tried it I decided to help him. I kicked the tail-end of that big heavy Mercury a little bit and zoom, zoom, zoom, his little roadster spun about three times.

From then on Jimmy Furr and Gene Tapia were buddies. After winning the race, Gene was given the title, "King of The Cow Pasture."

While Gene enjoyed racing success and loved the drama of competition his family was enjoying a quiet, happy time.
The children had their own life. They had pets and when Gene wasn't home, they enjoyed being around Mr. Diering, the caretaker.

"He was a wonderful old German," said Shaaron. "His wife had died many years earlier, but he would always play with us and he was always giving us candy or some little something. On holidays he gave us presents. He was like a grandfather to us. Daddy's father was deceased, and mother's father wasn't around, so we accepted him as one of the family.

"He had what we called a German-speaking parrot. That bird could curse you out, and you would never know what he was saying."

In addition to gathering eggs and helping do other chores, the girls helped feed the cows.

"But sometimes we had surprises," said Shaaron. "I remember once I was reaching in a nest to get an egg and a snake slithered across my hand. And we had a rooster that chased me. Every time I was out close to the chicken house, he would come running and attack me with his spurs, and it hurt. Daddy told me not to take it. Finally, I got up enough courage and got a stick. The next time he came after me, I beat him within an inch of his life. He never bothered me after that."

In 1952, Gene became reunited with his original car owner, Lawrence Nolan. At this time, Nolan was running the No. 40. Gene and Leroy Jones, another Mobile driver, were racing car 41 throughout Alabama, Mississippi, and Florida as a two-car team.

These early tracks were located in Kosciusko, Hattiesburg, Jackson, Laurel and Meridian, Mississippi. By this time, racing had become so popular that more and more tracks were lighted. By now there were too many for all to race on Sunday, so a racing schedule was made where one driver could run at a different track each night. The racing week began on Wednesday and ran through Sunday night.

On Labor Day, 1950, NASCAR ran its first long race at Darlington, South Carolina. Over 25,000 fans showed up to watch the cars run on the one and one-quarter mile track. Stock car racing was suddenly magic in the Southern states.

Even though he never competed on the Daytona International Speedway, Gene raced in many of the NASCAR Grand National races (now called Winston Cup), but to race once a week was not to his liking. He competed against Lee Petty, Cotton Owens, Fireball Roberts, Jim Paschal, Buck Baker, the Flocks, and all the early NASCAR drivers.

First, I realized I had a family to support. Second, you had to have a big sponsor to run at Darlington, Atlanta and Charlotte, and we didn't have one. But, most of all, I loved racing. Staying in Mobile with my family, I could race four or five times a week. That, to me, was a whole lot better than racing just one time. I loved racing and I had fun.

I could have gone with NASCAR using the equipment I had and I'm sure I would have done good. But I had a family and Hogeland had a family. There wasn't that much difference between what NASCAR had to offer and what I had around here at the time. It was better for me as a driver and Hogeland, as a mechanic to run the local circuits.

We did NASCAR a favor by promoting good racing with stock cars at the little tracks. This allowed the drivers and tracks to develop and become a part of NASCAR later on. We were responsible for the survival of NASCAR in Georgia, Alabama, Mississippi and Louisiana because they didn't have all that much to offer back then.

Gene and his team took the Mercury off the Grand National circuit and selected the tracks that paid the largest purses to win. Sometimes they might race five nights a week. Other weeks, they might choose one special race that had a large purse.

In late 1952, NASCAR attempted to increase its Sportsman Series. It sent out flyers and enlisted many local drivers.

Life was pleasant for me, and even though I was busy with my family and racing, I looked forward to each coming day. The flashbacks from the war still occurred, but everything seemed to be going right. The girls were able to get almost everything out of me they wanted, but I loved it. The family was finally living as a family should.

EARLY RACING PHOTOGRAPHS

First photo:
Top: Buck Baker, the fast qualifier at the 1948 NASCAR 100 in Montgomery, Alabama, Gene's first race.
Lower: Car owner, Lawrence Nolan and Gene.

Second photo
Top: Gene is in the outside car as the field rounds the fourth turn at Lakeview Speedway in Mobile.
Bottom: Another car, driven by Leroy Morris comes up on Gene's No. 36 and he rolls over four times. His helmet flies off his head and out the window. Fans thought his head had been knocked off. He was able to climb out, with only bruises.

Third photo
A group of Lakeview racers in 1952 or 1953.

Fourth photo:
Top: Gene and car No. 47 sponsored by Vigorlube, the forerunner of STP.
Lower: A 1934 modified Packard with four carburetors.

Fifth photo: After winning a race at Laurel Faigrounds in the 67JR, a wheel came off before he crossed he finish line. He won the race on three wheels.

Sixth photo
Top: The 1950 Mercury he won the 1953 NASCAR Florida State Championship and Mississippi State Championship with.
Bottom: Ellis Pallisini on top of one of his early V-8 racers at Laurel Fairgrounds.

Seventh photo:
Top: The P-80, a 1933, 6-cylinder, straight drive Plymouth, patterned after Cotton Owens' original NASCAR racer.
Bottom: The No. 327 School Bus in which Gene won the 1963 Southeastern Modified Championship at Montgomery, Alabama.

Racers at Lakeview Speedway, on Following Page:1952 or 1953

Back row: Bill Osborne, Leroy Morris, Albert Rice, Fred Moore, Joe Slaughter, Lenny Boyette, Ruben Barnett, T-Bone Shelby, Jake Hatcher, Gene Tapia, Glenn Hobson.

Front row: Bert Freeman, Charley Merrill, Carl Beverly, Laverne Macks, Bill Howell, Doug Wimpee, H.E. Hawkins, C.T. Weldon, Woodie Wilson, Lamar Crabtree, Flagman, Eddie Niedermier.

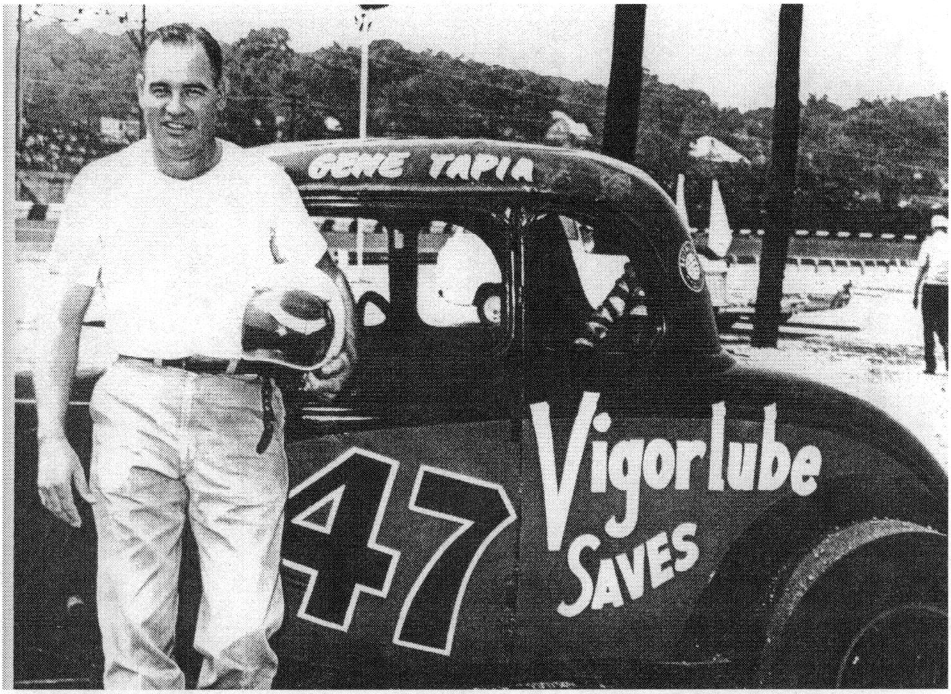
GENE TAPIA
47
Vigorlube
SAVES

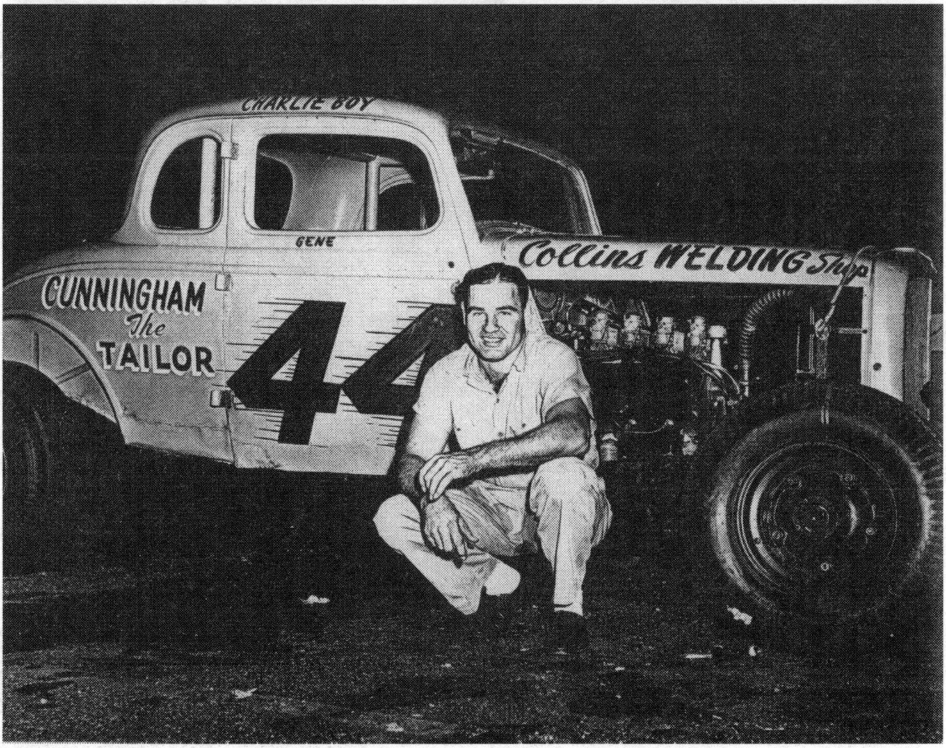
CHARLIE BOY
GENE
Collins WELDING Shop
CUNNINGHAM
The
TAILOR
44

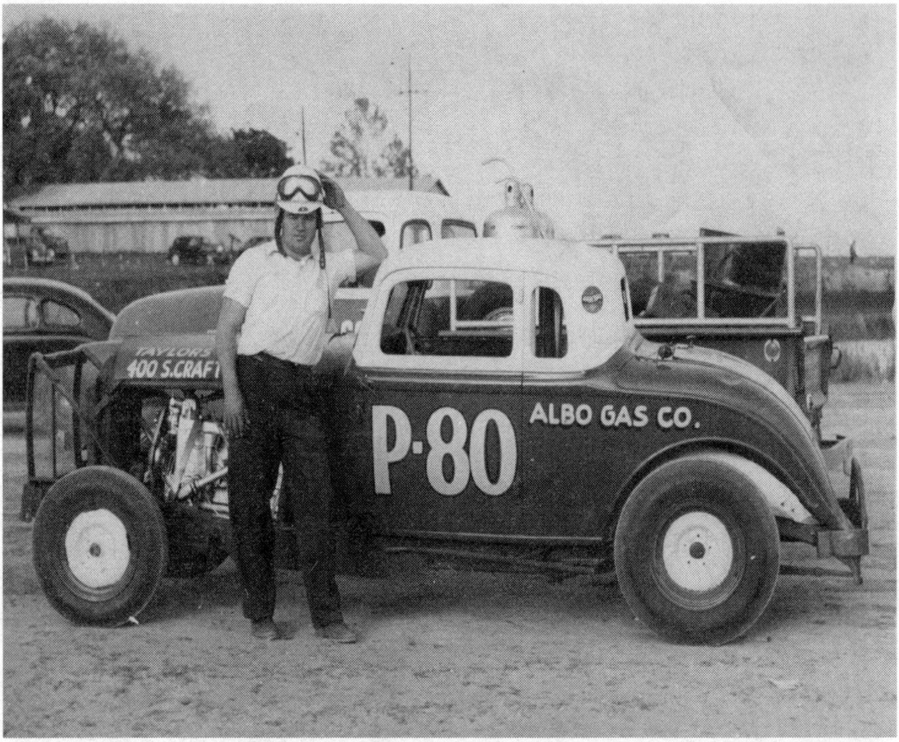
TAYLORS
400 S. CRAFT
P-80
ALBO GAS CO.

327

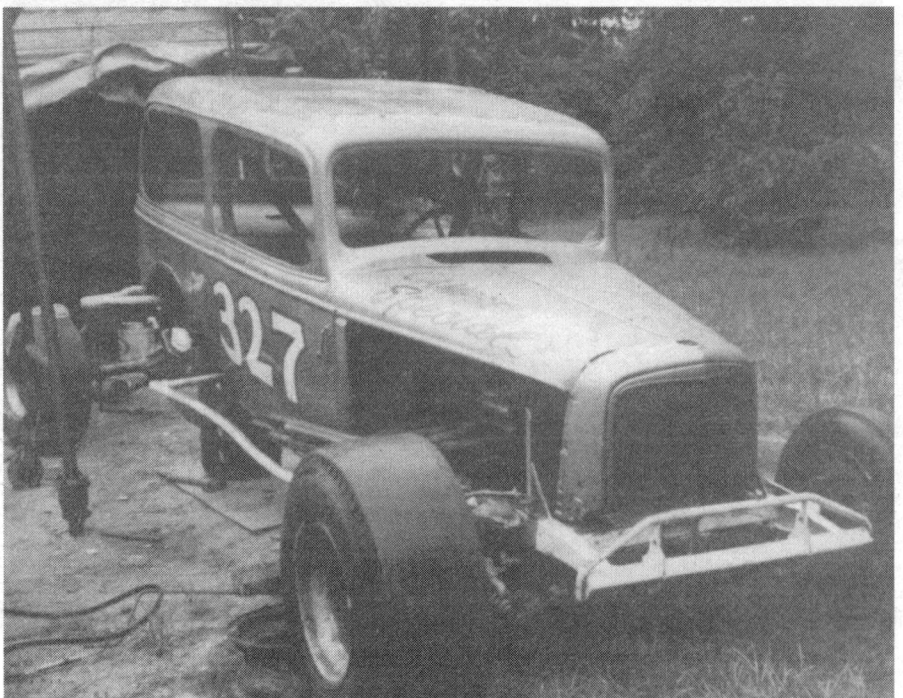

Flagman, Eddie Niedermier, Gene Tapia and Gene Jackson

Standing: Pete Wesphaul; Seated: Gene Tapia, Marvin Johsnon, Guy Taylor, Hubert Gilley

Buddy Bielarski, John Ardis Sr, Bill Osborne

Jake Hatcher of Pensacola, Florida

Perry Farnell's No. 80 Hudson Super 6, rests on its roof on the front straightaway at Lakeview.

The crew of modified No. 109, driven by Bill Howell

Bill Cleveland, Lakeview announcer and stuntman

Bud Erb's Ford sitting in the lake

Start of race at Lakeview. The car being worked on was No. 45 driven by Doug Wimpee Sr.

Cooley Barnett's No. 62 comes to rest against the fence

Gene Jackson, Ed Strahley, Walt Wortham

Bert Freeman's Rainbow 22

Drivers racing around Lakeview Speedway on Sunday afternoon.

Charlie Merrill's No. 66 after he flipped it. The car was rebuilt in time for next Sunday's races.

Ellis Pallisini and his father, Guido Pallisini

Bobby Garrison, Lee Fields, Charley Barnett, Chris Barnett. Lee Fields was the owner/promoter of Mobile International Speedway, Mobile, Alabama, from 1972-1999.

CHAPTER XI

A DEATH AND REBIRTH

By 1952, Gene had succeeded in getting his feet firmly on the ground. He was happy working as a boilermaker out of the local union in Mobile. Gene, Francine and their two girls continued to live in the Tapia home place, along with his mother and grandmother. On any given day or night there might be as many as four or five others visiting. And on weekends, the family might swell to twenty five. They were a big family with lots of socializing and eating together.

A serious problem was just over Gene's horizon. He was about to experience a problem at home, one that threatened to pull him back down into the abyss. It was a situation he had to face head on. And if he, personally was to survive, it would require all his emotional abilities.

His mother worked every day managing her restaurants and Francine handled things in the home. John Diering, the old

German, still took care of the cows, chickens and farm duties. The two girls were doing well in school, everyone was healthy and life was looking good for the Tapia family.

My mother didn't think too much of racing when I first started, but later, she fell in love with it and went with us every opportunity she got. I think one of the reasons she liked it so much was because of the wrestlers that used to come in her restaurants.

These wrestlers got to coming in her restaurants, and finally she asked me to take her to a match at Ft. Whiting in Mobile. She recognized a couple of the wrestlers because they had been coming in to eat with her. What bothered her was when she would see a bad one fighting it out with a good one, and then both of them would come in the next day and eat together. Even though she loved it, I don't think she ever fully understood the wrestling game.

It was a sideshow to watch my mother and Francine carry on as they watched a wrestling match. "Oh, he's killing him, he's killing him" they would shout. One wrestler named Henry Harrell, from Jackson, Mississippi ate pretty regular and we got to know him real well. One night they got Henry in a big hold and was about to choke him. Momma and Francine got to shouting, "Turn Henry loose, let him go. You're killing him, Awww, please."

Old Henry looked over at my Momma, winked his eye and threw the fellow off him and took the match.

Gene got to know most of the wrestlers because they came into the restaurants. The Southern wrestling circuit in the 1950's consisted of Pensacola, Florida; Mobile, Alabama; and Gulfport, Laurel and Jackson, Mississippi. As Gene's racing career moved forward, most of the wrestlers came to watch him race whenever they were in town.

Some fans mistook Gene for a wrestler, because he was built like one and in good physical condition. Many fans mistook Gene for Henry Harrell.

A cracker jack motorcycle rider named Glenn Hobson was leading the race one Sunday at Lakeside Speedway. Glenn could do things with a motorcycle that very few other men could do. Momma was sitting in the stands watching the race when Glenn fell. He got up, cranked it back up and won the race. From then on Momma thought Glenn Hobson was the best.

Later on he became a race car driver and drove for Marvin Johnson. He and Marvin had one of those relationships that each knew what the other was thinking.

After that, Momma started going with me. She went to Laurel and Jackson, Mississippi, and all the tracks whenever she could. She was still in the restaurant business but by that time she could designate authority to someone when she wanted to take off. Uncle Sam Johnson had one-half interest in them, so she didn't do it all by herself. In the stands, she was as excited as Francine.

By September 1952, Ada had sold the restaurants in downtown Mobile and concentrated her time to one single restaurant in Brewton, Alabama, a small town sixty miles east of Mobile near the Florida and Alabama Stateline.

She had gotten a stomach ache and after several days went to doctor Frank Woods. The doctor ran a lot of tests, but back then they didn't have the medicines or the cures we have today. The doctor told her it was cancer and she should get her house in order.

The Tapia family home had always been visited daily by dozens of people, especially on weekends. Miss Ada was so well liked and had so many friends that there was hardly a quiet time.

"Even before Miss Ada got sick we had from seventeen to twenty five people over for dinner," said Francine. "Once the folks found out she was at home, we had people over all the time. There were kinfolks and friends. Her reputation as a cook had preceded her. Those friends loved to sit under her table. And most of them would contribute something."

According to Gene, there was always fresh butterbeans, peas, corn, okra, cucumbers, potatoes, turnips, cabbage, snap beans, and tomatoes that the family grew.

"We could seat twelve people at one table," Francine said. "There were two other tables, plus a small one for the children.

"Right after a breakfast of grits, biscuits, bacon, sausage, ham and eggs, we started dinner. If we went to church, we would get everything ready in advance. Usually, we ate after twelve thirty in the afternoon. This was to allow everyone who went to church time to get here.

"It might seem like a lot, but Miss Ada could get in that kitchen and prepare a meal like you've never seen within an hour. She could make the best desserts: lemon pie, apple pie, banana pudding, bread pudding, rice pudding, and all kinds of cakes. You name the dessert and she could make it.

"The kids didn't eat outside. We had a special inside table for them. We always had between six and ten children, oftentimes, many more. But there wasn't any shouting or screaming. When they sat down to eat, they didn't act ugly, they knew what to do. Once they finished, they could go outside and play."

"We didn't have too many thugs at Sunday gatherings, said Gene. "They might be from all walks of life, but the talk was good. Usually all the adults were sensitive to others and this made for good fellowship, and kept the family bonds intact. People treated each other more reverently back then, than I think they do today. That doesn't mean we didn't get in a bad word every now and then. Old brother Carl Atkins was a preacher, and boy I loved to hear him tell jokes. I guess if you were invited to sit at my Momma's table you had learned a certain amount of respect for life and the people in it."

As the weeks turned into months, Miss Ada's health began to slip. She began to spend more time in bed. As her strength diminished, Francine grew in spirit and strength.

Gene worked long hours, because of his mother's mounting debts and business problems with the Internal Revenue Service. He was home only at night and one day during the weekend.

I worked as many hours of the day and night as I could to help pay our bills and my mother's bills. She had let some tax problems slide and her brother Sam was supposed to have taken care of some of them, but didn't. By this time the tax bills had added up and the government was going to make a deal and forgive part of the debt. They had paid a tremendous amount of money and just couldn't make any more payments.

Francine waited on Mommy hand and foot. She was her constant companion. We couldn't get anybody to relieve her. Even though we had plenty of kinfolks that lived around us, none of them would lend a hand.

The Tapia family had electricity and running water, but no electric washing machine. The home was crowded during this time but not cramped. In addition to the seven persons living inside the house, Chuck Christian and his family from New York lived in a house trailer in the front yard. By this time Francine was the person in charge.

"There was some kind of crisis nearly everyday," she said. "I recall one incident that really scared us all. It wasn't funny at the time, especially to Gene.

"It was his custom after he came in after work to go in the bathroom and read the newspaper. That day I had left a can of Glade aerosol spray next to the natural gas heater."

According to Gene, what happened next was like a flashback from his days in the Marine Corps.

I was sitting on the throne and I began to hear a little hissing sound. I didn't pay it too much attention. I looked around but couldn't see anything, so I just kept on reading the paper. Pretty soon, I heard it again. About that time the entire bathroom just went ka-boom, and blew up.

The gas space heater had ignited the fumes from the leaking aerosol can and Gene was caught with his pants down.

I came out of there with my britches down around my ankles. I mean I was getting with it. My whole bottom was singed. All I could think about was the Japs had bombed our house, and I had to get everybody out.

Gene was working at Cortauld's, a large industrial plant twenty miles north of Mobile. As he left for work, he had a deep feeling inside him that would not go away.

When I left that Sunday morning to go to work I knew she was in bad shape, and I needed to be at home. I started the job at seven, and about eight-thirty I went to the foreman and told him I had to go home because I felt like my mother was dying.

He left the jobsite and headed home. According to Francine, he burned up the engine in his car driving so fast to get home.

Just as she drew her last breath, I was standing there next to her.

A LOST BALL IN HIGH WEEDS

Three days after the funeral, John Diering, the German caretaker came to Gene one morning.

We were sitting at the breakfast table and Mr. Diering asked, 'What be happen to me?' in broken English. Mr. Diering was like an old second-hand granddaddy to all of us. I told him, Mr. Diering, my mother told you, you could stay here as long as you wanted to, and the deal still goes. As long as we've got this place and a place to stay, you can stay here with us.

We sure weren't going to kick him out because of the loyalty he had shown to our family. He had a son that lived in Pascagoula, Mississippi, but he wasn't able to take care of him. Mr. Diering was like an old secondhand granddaddy to us. Every Easter he bought our kids a big chocolate Easter Egg.

With Miss Ada's death, the big moment everyone had been dreading was now gone, but the entire home was very depressing. The matriarch of the Tapia family had performed her service and duties well, but now that she was gone, could the family hold together or would it become dysfunctional? Did Gene and Francine have the emotional strength required to get on with their lives or would they succumb to a depression and even separate?

"It was an atmosphere of dread," Gene said. "Because the most loved one of the family had suddenly disappeared. My mother was the best thought-of person in that part of the country. We had a lot of family and friends like Leroy Jones that tried to get us out of the state we were in, but it took a long time. After a few weeks, my brother came back and tried to help me pay off some of the lagging bills. I went back to work almost immediately and that helped me get over it."

While Gene was preoccupied with Miss Ada's financial problems, Francine was dealing with a deep emotional trauma.

"The physical burden was gone," she said. "What I had inside me can't be described after Miss Ada passed on. I don't know how long the hurt stayed with me. I had such a heavy heart. You see, everything I knew at that time had been learned from her. She was also the best friend I had ever had."

"When she died, everything was in a quandary," Gene said. "I was the Executor of her will, but I was still young and having to work a lot of hours trying to pay off all the bills."

Gene's efforts were not good enough to keep the Internal Revenue Service from seizing fourteen acres of family property and a house that was registered in his mother's name.

They took the land and a house that was supposed to belong to me, but we were able to retain about twelve acres of land and our old home.

Throughout his mother's illness, Gene continued to race whenever time and circumstances would allow it. Once her death was behind him, he had to get his mind clear again. The illness and problems associated with her personal and business problems had gone on for over a year.

Stock car racing and two women are what had saved me when I came back from the war. That might seem like a strong statement, but it is a true one. My mother and wife never gave up on me. They helped me work through things until I was able to get a better grasp on the world. I dearly loved my Mommy, and I did all that I was able to do to make her life comfortable. There were a lot of money problems that she left and I was determined to pay them off and keep her name clear. I still had Francine and my two girls, and for their welfare, I had to move forward.

Gene made good on his promise. He was beneficiary of a three thousand dollar insurance policy.

Doctor Woods did not charge my Mommy for any of his calls or services, but I paid him a thousand dollars out of the insurance money. He had been so kind and good to her. It took me seven years, but I managed to pay off all of her debts.

BACK ON THE NASCAR CIRCUIT

Part of the money Gene paid off his mother's debts with came from racing. By the mid 1953, things had really gotten rolling and stock car racing was headed for the big time because car manufacturers were discovering the sport. It was just natural for Detroit to capitalize on 'fan loyalty.' But Gene Tapia wasn't concerned about factory sponsorship or big money purses, he loved the sport for what it was—the thrill of it and the competition factor.

If you had to pick a time to race in Grand National cars, that was the time. The purses in NASCAR's Sportsman Division in Florida were larger than what they were paying around Mobile and southern Mississippi. We raced on all kinds of speedways, mainly in northwest Florida and as far south as Tampa and St.

Petersburg. A lot of times we would make two or three races in one weekend. If we weren't racing in Florida, we would be in southern Georgia and Alabama.

He went every week during the 1953 season and accumulated enough points while racing in Florida to win the 1953 NASCAR Florida State Sportsman Championship.

Most of my Florida racing was between Pensacola and Panama City. I never got to Daytona Beach. There were several times I was scheduled to drive, but something happened and I couldn't make it to Daytona.

In 1953, he also sped around the tracks in Mississippi like blue blazes, winning enough races and accumulating enough points to be named Mississippi State Stock Car Champion.

Gene loved racing, but he had discovered how to balance his racing career with the needs of his family. One night after working overtime, he came home to be told Shaaron had something to tell him.

She told me the outside water pipe faucet was leaking. It was cold outside, so I told her I would fix it the next day. Then she told me it was leaking pretty badly. I asked, how bad? After another few minutes I learned they had been practicing driving in the front yard and backed over it.

When I got out there, water was shooting up as high as the house. That faucet had been there for forty years, and they just had to pick that one spot, on the coldest night of the year to back over it.

The temperature was below freezing, and by the time I got it repaired it was almost midnight.

Gene decided to go to work late the next morning, but Francine's car would not start. The only alternative was for Gene to take his daughters to school in his black and yellow Mercury race car.

"Daddy went out to the garage and began revving the engine," said Rebecca. "Oh no, we can't go to school in a race car. But Momma said, 'Honey, it doesn't matter as long as you get there.' Shaaron and I pile into the race car and we go to school.

"As we come pulling up to the front of Forest Hill School in the race car, we see all the boys are running towards us. The boys were thrilled, and Daddy being the showoff he was, revved the engine up. Shaaron was embarrassed, but I think we received more attention that day from the boys than we've ever had in our entire lives.

"The kids came running out of the classroom, and Daddy talked with them, because he always talked with kids, no matter what their age. He's always said, 'Don't be ugly to a child, because they won't ever forget it.'"

There were always pets around the place. Dogs, cats, opossums, birds, raccoons and even turtles had free run of the property. The back half of the property was still wooded and swampy and was home to several types of small wild animals.

"We had this turtle, named Sam," said Shaaron. "He used to come up every day and eat out of the dog food bowl. Several months later, we noticed there was several small, baby turtles followed him. We had to change Sam's name to Samantha."

Since Shaaron was the oldest, she was supposed to be in charge of her younger sister, and other children that frequently came over to play.

"Daddy always told me not to go to the back of our property that was swampy," said Shaaron. "We had a type tall grass that grew near the water that was filled with a foam rubber substance and we loved to play with it. One day, Henrietta Gunn, a girl that lived next door, wanted to go back and get some of this grass. I was afraid to go, but she kept calling me chicken until Becky and I finally decided to go with her."

The three girls headed for the swamp with Henrietta in the lead, followed by Shaaron, and then Becky.

"There was a path, but the grass was over our head," continued Shaaron. "Pretty soon, Henrietta began to say, 'I'm stepping on glass, ooh, and it hurts.' I looked and didn't see any glass, but I decided it was time to turn around and go back to the house. On the way back, Henrietta fell down. We didn't know what was wrong, so we ran to her house and told her big sister, who ran down to where she lay.

"Henrietta was taken to the hospital and treated for several snakebites.

"As soon as Daddy came home, Momma began to tell him what we had done and how we had taken Henrietta back into the swamp and she been bitten by a snake and was in the hospital.

Boy, was Daddy hot. He took me out back and tore my butt up with a switch."

Gene continued to race every opportunity he had, sometimes five nights a week.

Back in the late 1940's and 1950's NASCAR wasn't all that big. It was drivers like the ones in Mobile that kept it going. I found out that if I went to one big NASCAR race it would take me all week to prepare for it. Most of the time drivers took home one to four hundred dollars. That wasn't as much as I could make staying home after doing all that traveling and paying all those expenses.

And most of all, I wouldn't be away from my family. I could have gone NASCAR with the equipment I had and done real good, but I needed to be around to mind the store. But there wasn't all that much difference between what NASCAR had to offer me at the time and what I had around here.

One reason Gene chose to stay close to home was because of the guilt over losing their son. Whenever Francine would bring it up, he would get depressed, often for days. To break free of the guilt feelings, he would work. If he wasn't working around the house, he was at the race shop.

Things were hectic at home. I don't see how I did it. But like I said, I couldn't have done all these things if it hadn't been for Francine. We had two girls, but we were getting along fine. But I was always busy. If she wanted to see me, she had to come down to the shop on the corner of Old Shell Road and Florida Street where I was working on the race car. That was the biggest problem.

When I got off work in the afternoon, I would go to the shop and we would talk about racing. Most of the work was done by other folks. I made suggestions, but I did very little work. I learned real early that if you allow it, your family and friends would have your head stuck under the hood of a car doing freebies from 'can to can't.' So I told them I wasn't going to do that. I was the driver. That was the only way I could handle it.

While Gene did not always win every race, he won his fair share, and learned to take the good with the bad.

Back in those days some drivers liked to fight just as much as they liked to race. There were times when the best driver never won. Some of the best drivers weren't too good at fighting, and they knew if they won the race they would have to prove it after a race. Instead, they would settle for a spot back in the field.

I tried to race every driver out there clean. When I went out on that track, I had a plan to win the race. Now, I didn't always win the race, but that was my goal. If a fellow didn't want to race me clean, that was all-right, too, because I knew how to take care of him.

By 1953, a new track, Five Flags Speedway, had opened in Pensacola, Florida, seventy-five miles east of Mobile. The track raced every Friday night. Francine would pick Gene up from work and drive him to the track.

"I would just make it in time to warm the car up, qualify it, run it and then come back home. Saturday we would race in another town. And then on Sunday, we would go to another track. But later, we got to racing five nights a week.

Wednesday we went to West Memphis, Arkansas. Thursday night it was Laurel, Mississippi, and Friday, it was Pensacola, Florida. Saturday we were at Mobile, and then on Sunday, it would be Opp or Montgomery, Alabama. Sometimes, we'd travel through five different states just to race each week.

The girls and Francine went, too. They would have to sit in the grandstands once we got to the track, but they had lots of friends to socialize with before the races.

Once the racing began, the Tapia fans cheered for their driver.

"There was a professor from the University of South Mississippi that was driving one night," said Shaaron. "He was involved in a bad, bad wreck and his car caught on fire next to the grandstand wall, right in front of us. I couldn't see the car number, and I thought it was Daddy's car that was on fire, and I went berserk. Finally, my Mother spotted Daddy's car and began shaking me until I understood it wasn't him.

"We really never got in any fusses that I remember with fans. I would always walk away if someone was saying ugly things because Daddy had always stressed not to get in arguments over racing.

"Daddy was our hero, but we liked Red Farmer, Ellis Pallisini, Marty Robbins, Donnie Allison, Freddie Fryar, and Larry Schaeffer, who I really liked."

Both Francine and Gene met many new friends at the track. His job with the Pipefitters Union meant he sometimes had to live out of town during the week. One particular job he worked was near Butler, Alabama. While working as a purchasing agent, he met Bernice and Jim Chandler, a Birmingham couple that had seen him race.

I was buying a million dollars worth of materials for the job from the Chandler's company and one day this lady saw my name on a purchase order. Bernice Chandler called and asked if I was the same Gene Tapia that drove a race car at the Birmingham track. I had to admit it was me. From then on, the Chandler family and I established a friendship that has lasted forty-seven years. They made it possible for me to race in north Alabama and Tennessee, because they allowed me to stay in their home.

I would come in with my dirty clothes all caked with mud or dirt and they never said a word. They fed me and once in a while I would be allowed to contribute, but they wouldn't accept much. Every race track I raced at, they were there.

As long as Gene worked and raced in north Alabama, he stayed with the Chandlers. Whenever possible, the Chandlers watched Gene race. They and their son, Ricky, became three of his biggest fans.

One night I was racing in Clinton, Mississippi, and the Chandlers were in the stands. The flagman favored some local drivers, and on the start of the race, as I would begin to move up from my rear starting position, he would throw the yellow flag. It is very dangerous to put out a yellow on the start, because everybody is all bunched up, the adrenalin is pumping, and there is a risk for a major wreck. It's dangerous.

The flagman threw the yellow flag three times. Francine, who was sitting next to the Chandlers, recalls what Jim Chandler did.

"Jim knew what the flagman was trying to do," she says. "He wanted to get Gene knocked out of the race, so a local driver could win. When the flagman threw it the third time, Jim got up and walked to the flag stand. I heard him tell the flagman, 'If you cause my friend Gene Tapia to get hurt or killed in this race, your ass is mine, because I'm going to kill you.'

"Buddy, the next time the cars came around the track, that flagman did what was right; he threw the green flag. I'm glad he did, because Jim would have hurt that man."

Aside from their passion for racing, the Tapias' were a typical family by the late 1950s. During the summer of 1959, Gene raced sometimes as many as four nights a week.

I was always coming and going. I didn't have much time for socializing. I didn't drink, so most of my time was spent racing, thinking about racing, or working. Back then racing was part of making a living. I made almost as much money racing as at my regular job, sometimes, even more. I raced and I raced hard. That's the only way I could do it.

Quite often fans would ask me why I wouldn't take a drink with them. I would tell them in jest about a conversation I had as a boy with my granddaddy. He said, 'I know you might like whiskey and women, but you can't have both. Just remember, you can drink whiskey when you're old and can't handle the women.'

One night in early 1958, when Gene came home, Rebecca had a surprise waiting.

"He came in one night and was acting like Mr. Macho Man," said Rebecca. "I thought to myself, OK, I'm going to fix his goose."

As Gene went to hug Rebecca, she grabbed one arm, leaned under him and flipped him right over on his back.

Gene was laying on the floor when Francine came in. She asked, "What's the matter with you?"

"She caught me with a good move," said Gene. "It didn't hurt, and as I lay there, I remembered what I had done to my dad when I was about her age and he tried to teach me to box. I guess I deserved it."

A few days later the entire family was going to Birmingham, Alabama, where Gene was to compete in a big race. The route they were taking was over a two-lane highway. Their car was a big Chrysler Imperial. Rebecca was driving, Gene and Shaaron were in the passenger seat, and Francine was in the back.

"Daddy had told me to build up some speed because there was a line of cars we were going to have to pass," said Rebecca. "I did exactly what he told me. About the time I pulled out to pass, a car was coming head-on. This idiot that was behind us moved up and wouldn't let me get back in line."

Rebecca turned hard right, got in front of the car in back, and took off on the right hand shoulder of the road, throwing gravel on all the other cars as she picked up speed.

"I passed all the cars on the right hand side between the telephone poles. I went around the entire line of cars and got in front of everyone."

Gene was very quiet during the event, but Francine was screaming and almost had a heart attack.

"My God," said Francine. "Pull this car over and let me drive."

Francine drove the rest of the distance to Birmingham.

THE KING OF ROCK AND ROLL

While Gene reveled in showing off on the track, he was reserved off track. Occasionally, he would drink, but he never allowed himself to become intoxicated. All bars in Mobile County that served whiskey and other hard alcoholic beverages had to be incorporated as private clubs. Legally, to enter these clubs one had to be a member, but the membership rule was very rarely enforced. According to Francine, one night, Gene and his regular racing gang decided to go to the Rose Club on Telegraph Road in Plateau, Alabama. The night's events strained their marriage.

We had to go to a hot-rod meeting at the Rose Club one Sunday night. We were adding new rules and making some changes to the old ones at Lakeview Speedway. After the meeting ended, several fellows insisted that I go with them to hear a new singer named Elvis Presley down at Radio Ranch on the Cedar Point Road.

Parker McMillan, who was one of my mechanics, said, 'Come on, we're not going to stay long. Ride with us, and we'll bring you back whenever you get ready.' I didn't really want to go because Monday was a workday and I had to get up early.

We made it and Elvis was very good. It was the first time I had ever heard him. During a break he came over and sat at our tables. He wasn't but about nineteen years old, just a good boy.

As the midnight hour approached Gene realized he had to find a way back to his car at the Rose Club. All his racing buddies were enjoying the beer, booze and Elvis.

Nobody wanted to break loose. They wanted to listen to Elvis sing some more, and nobody wanted to take me back to my car. This lady named Eva Neely, who was a nice, and decent lady was getting ready to go home. The fellows I was with asked her if she would take me to my car. She said, 'Sure,' so we left the Radio

Ranch and headed back to the Rose Club. On the way we discussed my family, my history and things like that.

It was nearly 2 a.m. when the pair arrived at the Rose Club and his car. Parked about one hundred feet away was another car.

"Pardon me, Gene, but isn't that your wife walking across the parking lot," Eva said.

Francine and another one of the husband's wives, Jeannette Taylor, were waiting.

"When I got up to the door on Gene's side, he turned as white as a sheet," said Francine. He looked over at Eva and said, 'Uh, uh, what did you say your name was?'" You talk about mad, I was mad. Boy, he got in his car and made it to the house before Jeannette and I did."

By this time Gene had accumulated a large fan following. He tried never to short them when they wanted to talk. But It reached a point he had to start filtering the calls because he couldn't talk with all of them.

There was much socializing and visiting between the families that Gene raced with every week.

"We were very close to Donnie Allison, Red Farmer and Marty Robbins," said Rebecca. "We knew Bobby but he didn't come around very much. Daddy helped him get started in racing. Donnie and Red would come down very often and go hunting with daddy. Donnie's favorite saying was, 'You want me to show you a trick?' He always seemed to bring some pants that wouldn't fit, and I would have to hem them up.

"One time, he and his wife, Pat, came with their twin babies to spend the weekend. We didn't have a place for the babies, so Momma made them beds in dresser drawers, and that is where they slept, right next to their momma and daddy's bed."

CHAPTER XII

ANOTHER TWIST OF FATE

Even though it was a busy household, with a pleasant and happy atmosphere, there seemed to be a small void in Francine's and Gene's personal lives over the loss of their baby boy in 1942. Even though Gene did not talk about it much, he often felt himself acting as a father to other boys. Several times they had hired local private detectives and individuals in hopes of finding him. Each time the answer that came back was without hope. The Christmas of 1959 was especially bad.

One day Gene decided that since the legal channels of finding the baby were not working, he would try a different approach.

I hit upon the idea that if the underworld fellows could find whoever they went after, why couldn't they help us find our boy?

Gene knew just the right person to begin with. There was a part-time race car driver who had connections with some of the leading underworld figures in the south and east coast. As a last resort, Gene and Francine enlisted the help of this mafia figure.

There comes a time in most folks lives they forget about pride and doing things the proper way if they have exhausted all other ways. I knew a man who was real close to me. He was an associate in a way. He was one of the few people that knew about the boy.

After giving him the meager information they had about Georgia Tann and her operation at the Memphis Children's Home, and what other private detectives had told them, the man left.

After several months they received a called, but all he could tell them was he and several friends were working on it every opportunity they had. But as summer turned into winter, both of Gene and Francine had quit talking. Their hope and optimism was just about used up.

A few days before Thanksgiving, I received a call on the job from this man. He said he had some information and wanted to meet me somewhere that afternoon. He wouldn't tell me on the phone, but it was about my son. He believed he had located him.

I don't remember exactly where we met, but when he told me about my son it was almost unbearable. I had the feeling that a heavy weight had been placed on my shoulders, and a tight rope was around my chest.

His associates had found a man named Larry Eugene Cheney, who was born September 24, 1942, the same day as our son. He told me a lot of other things about this boy, and from all indications this was our lost son.

When I asked where he was, he replied, 'The Oklahoma State Prison in McAllister, Oklahoma. He is serving two consecutive life sentences for killing two women.'

I asked him if he was sure this was our son, and again he replied, 'yes.'

My whole body melted after hearing that. I didn't know what to say. I wasn't able to think. People don't know how they will react until something like that about your family hits you.

"Gene came home that evening and wouldn't talk with anyone," Francine said. "I don't believe he went to work for several days. I had no idea what was wrong with him, but I knew something was troubling him. The girls noticed it too, and asked me what was wrong with daddy. He usually worked hard in the evenings and on weekends, but he suddenly stopped doing anything and just stayed to himself. We hadn't had any kind of fuss or argument, so I didn't know what was bothering him, but I knew it was something major. Little things didn't affect him long."

For several months Gene sunk into a deep depression and lost interest in life. According to Francine, she tried to arrange a doctor's appointment for him, but he refused.

There wasn't any medicine available that would cure what ailed me. It was knowing and experiencing the shame that I had brought on the family. It wasn't bad enough that I had left to pursue adventure, but now my own son was a murderer and in jail. I couldn't bear to tell my family and because I didn't want to bring any more shame on them, I kept it all inside myself.

Gene kept the secret buried within him for over twenty years before telling Francine.

SAGA OF THE SCHOOL BUS

In 1954 Gene had teamed up with a childhood friend, Ellis Wilkins. Their racing association lasted over twenty years. It was during this period that Gene would have his greatest racing success.

"We were pretty well involved from start to finish," Ellis Wilkins said. "Gene started driving about the time I started building cars and we were pretty much together from then on, one way or the other. We never did have a whole lot of money to build cars with. But through his skills, he took what I gave him and won an awful lot of races.

"We raced with some of the best. One of the unique things he did was take an old 1934 sedan and turn it into a race car. The thing looked like an old school bus. Now, this was after the supermodifieds, or 'skeeters' were in. These were the highly modified and fast cars with wings and the whole nine yards. We called this 1934 sedan the "School Bus." It was the only car that I ever saw get a standing ovation when it came onto the track. Fans loved it. When we would come over the top of the track as we entered the speedways, people would stand up and cheer, because we took that car, raced against the big names in supermodifieds, and won.

"The high point of the car's history came in 1963 in Montgomery, Alabama. They decided they were going to have a "Skeeter Night" in Montgomery and they invited supermodified cars from throughout the southeast for the Southeastern Championship. They allowed us in with the school bus, but when we went through the pit gate, the guy that checked us in said, 'What are you bringing that thing here for?' I said, notice how flat it is on top? We can sit on it and watch the races.

"We parked next to the Gober Sosebee car out of Georgia, and their engine is setting over behind the left front wheel and I'm hearing those cars running around the track and I began to meditate on the question the pit gate man asked. He said, 'why are you here,' and I began to wonder, too. Gene took our old car out to qualify and it didn't sound near as terrific as those other cars, but he qualified third. We raced throughout the night and ran the feature for the Southeastern Modified Championship for supermodifieds."

In most stock car racing, the field of cars was inverted, which meant Gene had to start near the tail end of the line of cars.

"They had some awful fast cars with some of the country's best drivers," Gene said. "I couldn't stay with those big boys out of Charlotte and Atlanta on the straightaways. They just had too much power. But when we went into the corners I was able to gain on them. It didn't take me long to work my way towards the front. But right on my bumper was Jake Hatcher of Pensacola, in his No. 35 Cadillac.

Jake and I stayed hooked up most of the night. Finally, I got the lead, but Jake was right on my bumper. We both were evenly matched, but since we had raced against each other so much, I knew his moves and what he was going to do. He tried, but I was able to block him. He and I finished one-two, and when we crossed the finish line the closest car behind us was about a fourth of a lap behind."

Ellis Wilkins was elated. "One of the first people out of the stands to congratulate Gene was Gober Sosebee, one of the most respected NASCAR drivers in the southeast," said Ellis. "Gober was so happy that, that old underdog car had cleaned house that night that he almost danced a jig on the front straightaway. We had run against the best and won."

Gene had won the 1963 Southeast Modified Championship title.

"One of my friends, Nero Steptoe, came over after the race, congratulated me and said, 'It was just one old man outrunning another,'" Gene said.

Even though Gene and Ellis had been racing for several years, their operation was less than big-time.

"I was mechanicing under one of the oak trees in Gene's yard and in one of the dairy sheds until we finally got a good sponsor," Ellis said. "We didn't have any money. I think we did very well under the circumstances. Finally, we landed Campbell Piping and Construction and then we started to do very well. The way we really got into the business is one weekend, a lobe on the engine camshaft ground off. A boy that had formerly been on Bobby Allison's crew remembered there was a cam they had taken out of an engine, because it didn't run too well. He said at least we could use it to run that weekend. It was still in Hueytown, Alabama, so they put it on a bus and sent it down to Mobile. They stipulated that it be installed exactly the way the manufacturer said.

"Well, when it got here and I saw how Chet Herbert said install it, I told Gene, we might as well stay home, there was no need trying to run. He said, put it in the way you think it should go and I'll suffer the consequences. So, I did. Neither Bobby nor Donnie Allison had been outrun that season. We went to Five Flags in Pensacola that weekend and whipped them all day.

"Monday morning, I called Chet Herbert, who was Bobby's sponsor, and said, 'I kicked your boy's butt this weekend and I want you to sponsor us because I was running your product.' He asked what we ran and I told him. He said, 'Oh no, that camshaft won't run that well and we've taken it off the market." I said, well, that's what we ran and we kicked your boy's butt. He asked how we did it? So he wouldn't think he was talking with an Alabama dirt farmer, I told him. That was a big, big mistake. They took the cam back, we didn't have anything to replace it with and Bobby started kicking our fanny.

"I went to Red Farmer and said, Red, there's something wrong with this. He said, 'Call this phone number in San Diego.' It just happened it was Snyder Engineering, the company that had built the California State Champion's car. They sent us a camshaft and three or four weeks later Gene set a new world's record. Three or four weeks later, every manufacturer was setting down on Campbell's doorstep wanting us to run their product.

"I could always make an engine turn faster than the parts could stand. When I got the chrome vanadium rods I figured I could turn that baby on. But it broke the rod bolts. And Gene is part of all that. He was able to drive the car that fast to do all those things. I think we made a good team. We were very successful until egos got in the way, then the team just kind of split up. Gene went one way and I went another.

"We utilized all our resources. I worked in the engineering department at Brookley Air Force Base and had access to engineering type knowledge and data, plus the engineers that worked in the department. I would call on them for certain projects on the car. When we got into airfoils for handling purposes on the car, I knew the most efficient airfoil was a propeller blade. I asked an engineer in the engine department to get me the half section of a propeller blade. That became the shape of the airfoil or wing we ran on top of the car. Just as there is prop wash off a propeller, when Gene would run on a damp night with high humidity it looked like that car was dragging a sheet. Just as you know your own kid when it cries in the mall, I knew my own product after you've put it out. And a car from Mobile was sold to someone in Texas that had an airfoil on top of it made from my form blocks. The next year at Indianapolis, a Texas car from Mr. A.J. Foyt had my airfoil shape on the back of it. We've been pretty deep in the racing business.

"Gene could have been a national racing figure, but he wanted to race more than once on Saturday or Sunday like NASCAR does. He often drove the racecar to tracks all over the southeast, raced the car, and then drove it back to Mobile. Gene loved to race, and just being able to race one time a week didn't suit him."

One night, Hooker Hood, a well-known supermodified driver from Memphis, Tennessee, was walking through the pits prior to a race at Mobile International Speedway in Irvington, Alabama. Clarence C. Hood Jr. acquired the name Hooker at the age of six. He was petting a young calf when the calf's momma came along, hit him in the stomach and knocked him through a fence. As he laid on the ground the cow continued to butt and hook him.

His racing career started on motorcycles in the mid-1940s. From the bikes, Hooker moved to midget cars, then stockers, and finally into supermodifieds.

Old Hooker was walking through the pits and I saw he had a pencil and piece of paper. Pretty soon, he came by me and asked how I spelled my name. I asked him why he wanted to know how to spell my name. He said he was making a list of every driver whose butt he could whip. I said, why Hooker, you can't whip my butt, so there's no sense in writing it down. He just said, 'OK, I'll just scratch yours off.'

I never had any problems out of Hooker on the track after that.

JOE CASPOLICH

Joe Caspolich from Long Beach, Mississippi, is one of the charter members of the elite NASCAR Winston Cup Unocal Drivers Club at Darlington Speedway. Like Tapia, Caspolich served his country during World War II and then turned to racing after the war ended.

"I turned my fifteenth birthday in the Army," Caspolich said. "When I came home on my first leave I didn't have enough money to get a new car and all I could afford was a 1939 Plymouth with a bad motor. Back then parts were hard to come by because of the war. I used a file and sandpaper to grind down the crankshaft. My father, who was a good mechanic, thought I was crazy, and said I would never get beyond Gulfport, which was only twenty-five miles away. But I made it to Fort Bragg, North Carolina, and back home, and the old car was still running."

Caspolich tells of his first organized automobile race. "On one of my furloughs home I was traveling to Lafayette, Louisiana, to visit some relatives. Just west of New Orleans, I saw these cars racing out in a fenced cow pasture. I went over and there was an old GMC car that was faster than the others. I made the statement, 'If they had a good driver in that car, it could be a winner.' The owner was standing next to me and overheard the conversation, and asked if I could drive. Of course, I said yes.

"He put me in the car and I did win the race, but when the checkered flag was dropped, I didn't know what it meant, so I kept on racing. Then they gave me a red flag, and finally, the black flag. By this time all the other cars had pulled into the pits, so I figured the race must be over, and I stopped, too. The officials really talked to me afterwards using some strong language.

"I think Gene was one of the greatest drivers I ever raced on the same track with. Of course, we always called him "Pappy" Tapia. Quite a few of the old drivers, along with Gene, used to come over to the old dog track in Gulfport, Mississippi. When we weren't racing in Gulfport, Joe Fazio, Joe Booker, myself, and more of the Mississippi drivers would get together and go over to Lakeview in Mobile. The first time I saw Gene, he was in a little six-cylinder GMC 'skeeter.'

"I never will forget in the first race at Lakeview Speedway how Gene, who was on my right, whipped across the hood of my car and looked at Woodie Wilson's car. When they got in the corner they didn't see me because I was in that little Skeeter. When they came together, I went flying out in the trees. From the track the trees looked like small pine saplings, but come to find out, they were just the tops of tall pine trees. My old car went off the track, hit one of those tall pines and when I came down, the old car just broke half in two.

"I guess that is one of my first memories of Gene Tapia, but I've kept the picture of his car, the EZ-1. I never will forget that car. He had it up in Laurel, Mississippi, one time. We were running on the half mile Fairground track, and to me, I think Gene is a super guy. He's country and I guess about the only thing he loved to do as much as racing is hunting. He tried to get me to go hunting with him when I first came to Mobile. But we never got together.

"He and Ellis Pallisini were real good friends. He got in touch with me when Woodie Wilson Sr. passed away a few years ago, but I missed the entire funeral.

"Back then I think everyone raced harder and had more fun than they do today. Gene was one of the fellows that liked to have his fun, but he raced you hard and clean on the track. I guess you could have called us Gypsies, because we went from track to track and neither of us really had a big sponsor. But in another way, if one of us needed help or anything, the other one was always right there to help."

In 1950, after winning a race, Caspolich performed a gesture to a young boy that would save his life in later years.

"This young teenager came up to me after I had won a race in Louisiana in the late 1940s," Caspolich said. "He kept hanging around and so finally I handed him the trophy I had won."

In 1957, during the NASCAR Southern 500 at Darlington, South Carolina, Caspolich was involved in a serious wreck on the track.

"I was leading the race when another car came down on me," Caspolich said. "It took the track personnel over one and one-half hours to pull me out of my Ford. Every bone on my left side was broken. I was pronounced DOA (dead on arrival) at the Florence, South Carolina, General Hospital. After covering me with a sheet, they wheeled me into a room with two other bodies. My wife was standing outside when this young intern from New Orleans came up.

"He introduced himself to my wife and told her he was the young boy whom I had given a racing trophy to years earlier, and wanted to pay his respects. As he uncovered me, my arm dropped from the stretcher. He discovered I wasn't dead and wheeled me back to the emergency room. The doctor said afterwards, 'Don't thank me, thank God, because you were dead.'"

By the late 1950s and early 1960s, Tapia's name was known throughout the Southeastern United States. Whenever he was on hand to race, he was always the one to beat.

"I never got to start up front," said Gene "It was usually because I qualified so well, and since the field was inverted, it meant the faster cars were sent to the tail end of the field."

Sometimes he would have to pass twenty or more cars to win but fans loved him. He had acquired the name "Pappy," not only because he was older than most of the drivers, but he looked out for younger drivers and would usually offer up free advice.

Promoter Skip Wetjen opened Mobile International Speedway in 1964. It was a first-class half-mile asphalt oval, that was billed as "The Quarter Million dollar Speedway. Wetjen was the Director and President. The other officials were: Superintendent: Phil Wendt; Announcer: Blackie Gripp; Chief Steward: Charlie Merrill; Flagman: Eddie Niedermier.

The early supermodified drivers, their hometowns, and car numbers: Bobby Allison, Hueytown, AL #1; Fred Moore, Pensacola, FL #R-1; Doc Kelly, Birmingham, AL #2; Cecil Wyatt, Mobile, AL #77; Hoot Gibson, Pensacola, FL #6; "Yankee" Bill

Riggs, Pensacola, FL #7; Ellis Palisini, LeLand ,MS #V8; Jimmy Senter, Mobile, AL #10; Friday Hassler, Chattanooga, TN #15; Jim Busby, Lipscomb, AL #F16; Armond Holley, Columbus, MS #22; Bill Mooty, Moss Point, MS #29; Woodie Wilson, Mobile, AL #30; Dale Hammac, Mobile, AL #38; Freddie Fryar, Rossville, GA #48; Paul Vanderley, Biloxi, MS (owner) #60; Pete Gulsby, Theodore, AL #65; Jake Hatcher, Pensacola, FL #70, Phil Wendt, Irvington, AL #73 & 38; Al Monday, Pensacola, FL #75; Hugh Richards, Mobile, AL #76; Lucky Mayes, Gulfport, MS #88; Donnie Allison, Miami, FL #88; Bob Herrin, Biloxi, MS #91; Red Farmer, Hueytown, AL #F97; Wayne Niedeckin, Abilene, TX #99; Hooker Hood, Memphis, TN #99; Ival Cooper, Jackson, MS #248; Joe Fascio, New Orleans, LA #280; Jack Ellis, Birmingham, AL #706.

Sonny Black, Nig Persell, Jimmy Riddle, Clyde Johnson, Jack Ellis, Bill White, and Lenny Boyette were other super modified drivers that competed on the half-mile asphalt oval.

In addition to supermodifieds, the track ran two other classes of cars; late model modifieds and pacers.

Some of the 1965 late model modified drivers: Donnie Allison, Jackie Evans, Jerry Lawley, Bob Burcham, Art Hastings, Bo Fields, Friday Hassler, Jerry Myers, Charlie Griffith, Freddie Fryar, Bill Sternenburg, Joe Lee Johnson, Jack Hardin, "Cowboy" Plummer, Red Farmer, Bobby Allison, Ed Grady, and Joe Burcher.

Early pacer drivers, hometowns and car numbers: Vince Emmons, Mobile, AL #Diamond 1, Rat Lane, Prichard, AL #2; J. C. Perry, Prichard, AL #03; Harold Lowe, Birmingham, AL #03Jr.; Ronnie Rivers & Charles Drake, Grand Bay, AL #5; J. C. Mason & Buddy Rogers, Prichard, AL #06 (Big 6); Jimmie Lee, Mobile, AL #6; Howie Hubb, Holdsfield, NY #8; Donald Adams, Pascagoula, MS #11; Ronald Woodruff, Mobile, AL 315; Layman Harden, Prichard, AL #X15, and Rufus Johnson, #71.

Racing was good at MIS, but the only problem was some nights Wetjen couldn't pay the winner's purse.

More than one time Skip would come to me and ask me to help him because his crowd wasn't all that great. I usually had a little extra money on me and I didn't mind because we needed a good place to run and Skip ran a pretty good show. But he always paid me back.

The financial problems associated with his mother's death were over and the entire Tapia family had made a transition from the problems of their early life. Gene was receiving regional and sometimes national recognition. It pleased his daughters, Sharon and Becky, when he would take them to school in his race car. Gene usually sat outside the school and signed autographs.

SUPERSTAR MARTY ROBBINS

Through Gene's racing, the family made many new friends from all walks of life. One in particular was Marty Robbins, a Grand Ole Opry superstar. The entire family became well acquainted with him, but he always refused their request to sing while at their home.

Robbins made no secret about his fondness for driving race cars. When he was asked why he would risk his singing career by climbing behind the wheel of a high-powered racing machine, Robbins would flash a bright smile and say, "It is as much a passion as my singing and writing." Even after suffering a heart attack, he continued racing.

By the time Marty Robbins came to Gene for advice, he had already spent many nights driving midgets. One night Robbins was singing at the National Guard Armory in Prichard, Alabama. Doug Powell, a Prichard policeman, had been assigned to be Robbins' bodyguard. Powell was also a crewmember on Gene's No. 327 supermodified racing team.

"It was a Saturday night and Doug wanted to go racing," said Gene. "He mentioned to Marty about racing at Mobile International and he said Marty's ears just lit up."

Powell loaded Robbins on the rear of his Prichard Police Department's big Harley Davidson and headed to the Tapia home. Just as Doug and Marty wheeled into the Tapia's driveway, Gene and Francine were getting ready to leave.

It was the weirdest pair on a motorcycle I had ever seen. Doug was dressed in his black leather jacket, but he had a cat on the back that was dressed in white pistol-leg pants and pointed-toe shoes that were turned upwards. His collar was all turned up and he had wavy Spanish-looking black hair.

After being introduced, Gene still wasn't impressed because he had never heard of Marty Robbins. After reaching the track, Robbins watched every move Gene made during practice and qualifying in the No. 327.

I finally began to reach top speed and the rooster tail of vapor began to come off the top of the air foil and old Marty hadn't never seen anything like that. He was just amazed. That got his attention, and every time he could come, he came back. That really hooked him on racing. I didn't really teach Marty how to drive. He watched me, and he learned from watching me. Bobby Allison took a liking to him after that and built him a race car."

The Marty Robbins concert in Prichard was late getting started that Saturday night.

In all, Robbins competed in thirty-five Winston Cup races between 1966 and 1982 with his fifth-place finish at Michigan in 1974 being his career best. In addition to Tapia, Robbins admired Richard Petty and Donnie Allison.

Robbins said the highlight of his career came at the old Fairgrounds Speedway in Nashville, Tennessee.

"It was in the late 1960s, I think Coo Coo (Marlin, Sterling Marlin's father) had only lost two races," Robbins said in a magazine interview. "One of the wins went to Red Farmer, and I don't know who beat him in the other race.

"I said that if I ever got in front of him, I wouldn't let him get by me. Well, one night I got ahead of him. There was only one way I would ever beat him. He was a better driver, and he had more power than I did.

"So I came out of the turns in the middle of the groove. There was no way he could get by me. He certainly couldn't pass me in the turns. I wouldn't look back at him. I knew if I did, I probably would let him pass.

"Well, they gave me the checkered flag (after winning the race). I took it and kept going, out the back gate. I hung that flag in my office where everyone could see it."

Marty Robbins died of a heart attack on December 8, 1982 at the age of 57.

THE NASCAR STRIKE

Gene had pretty much given up the big Sunday NASCAR events in favor of the smaller tracks that allowed him to race four and sometimes five nights a week. He was a staunch advocate of American Labor Unions, but in 1960, he refused to back Curtis Turner's plan for a driver boycott against NASCAR. Turner was one of NASCAR's earliest and most controversial drivers, winning seventeen races during a career that spanned from 1949 through 1968. Turner was suspended from competition by NASCAR president Bill France Sr. during the 1960 season. Turner was the first president of the Charlotte Motor Speedway (now Lowe's Motor Speedway), and needed a loan from the Teamsters Union to repay creditors. When France got wind of his scheme, he banned Turner until near the end of the 1965 season.

NASCAR put their thumb on Curtis Turner and wouldn't let him run. NASCAR was and still is a dictatorship. That doesn't mean they are always bad, it's just the way NASCAR is. When Big Bill France said you weren't going to run, you might as well park it. You couldn't run at any NASCAR track in the country. I was involved in what Turner wanted to do, but I didn't go along with his methods. I never felt like a strike was necessary. The drivers had a lot of grievances, but a strike would have penalized the fans, and that's why I didn't go along with it. NASCAR would say one thing, and then do another. They would promise you the world, but usually they never delivered. While they had these problems I just quit running with them. I could have a lot more fun and take home more money by running local shows and circuits, so that's why I didn't stick with them.

While Gene usually got along well with drivers on and off the track, he never developed a liking for Elmo Langley, a former driver who went on to become a Winston Cup pace car driver.

Elmo had been a whale of a driver but NASCAR had hired him to help organize many of the smaller tracks. In fact, they were even organizing the supermodified drivers. They would run the Grand National (now Winston Cup) cars and supermodified and Sportsman cars all on the same track.

One night I was at Pensacola and got in my car to warm up like I had for years and Elmo shut me down. He wouldn't let me on the track. He wouldn't talk about it, so we just said, "We'll go to the house." He was overbearing and told us he was running the show. I said, "Cap, I don't even know you. Who are you, and what do you mean this is your show? We've been running here for many years, and I've never seen you in my life." He began to tell me he was Mister NASCAR.

Gene immediately developed a dislike for Langley because of his overbearing attitude, but he stayed and raced. He ran third in the late model feature and was the winner of the special 200-lap supermodified feature.

Mister NASCAR didn't show himself after that race, and it's a good thing he didn't.

Langley suffered a massive heart attack in November 1996 while chauffeuring Buddy Baker around the 1.54-mile Suzuka Circuit Speedway near Nagoya, Japan, prior to the NASCAR Thunder Special 125. Langley was dead before the ambulance arrived. He died doing what he loved.

TOP-TEN NASCAR DRIVERS

Buddy Shuman could do more with a race car, especially in the modified division, than any driver. I admired the way he could go through traffic. He was a traffic expert. The first time he saw Francine, he fell in love with her and wanted to kidnap her. He went to work with Ford Motor Company testing seat belts and other automobile safety devices. He was in a hotel room in Atlanta when it caught fire and burned him to death.

Buck Baker was my idol. I loved to watch that fellow drive. He could really put on a show. If you could follow Baker around a track, you had really done something. Buck Baker was one of the best.

Fonty, Bob and Tim Flock were three of the early drivers that were very good. All three of those men were excellent racers. They also had a sister, named Ethel that raced.

I was driving the P-80 car in a race one Sunday against the Flocks. After I won the race, Fonty came up to me and after introducing himself, said, 'I bet a dollar-bill on you.' He took the bill out of his pocket, ripped it in half and gave me half of it. 'I bet that dollar on you, now when we race again, I'll bet another dollar, and each of us will have one dollar.' I carried that torn up dollar bill in my pocket for years. Fonty and I became fast friends.

Gober Sosebee could drive just about anything. He ran all type cars, and I never met a finer driver or gentleman.

Speedy Thompson got his first win at Macon, Georgia, in 1953. His name really fit him. He was a wild Indian who wasn't afraid to run a car wide open. He also helped Bill France Sr. into developing NASCAR into what it is today.

Jack Smith was a Georgia driver that originally drove a Ford. But he came to Birmingham and drove a Studebaker that would fly. He would burn the tires up and they would cut the power down, but still, he kept burning up tires. He never won a Grand National championship, but was always near the front. He would drive you clean, but don't ever get in a crap game with him, because I've watched him clean house with some real pros. He could somehow roll sevens and elevens consistently. Don't shoot craps with Jack Smith.

Billy Carden was one of a family of drivers that I had an awful lot of respect for. The entire family raced over in Georgia and North Carolina. He had a brother, Lewis, who was a slingshot driver. I never had any problems with any of them, but I heard there was more than one driver that had to fight several Cardens.

Lee Petty wasn't a good modified driver, but he was a whale of a good late model driver who won three NASCAR Grand National championships. He was a late model expert.

Fireball Roberts never won a championship but he was also one of the best and most popular racers before his death in 1964. He got the name, 'Fireball,' because he was an outstanding baseball pitcher before he started racing.

Those fellas had nerves of steel. Their nerves were better than the equipment they drove. And there were so many more good drivers that I have so much respect for, but those are some of the fellows that really stand out in my mind.

GULF COAST RACERS

But I admired the local drivers that ran the weekly shows with us. Many of them could have held their own with NASCAR's biggest drivers. The reason they didn't move up was family commitments and lack of a big sponsor.

Whenever Woodie Wilson of Mobile would show up at one of the NASCAR shows, the first thing they would say is, 'hell, here comes that Alabama Gang.' He was always the one to beat.

Wilson only ran five Grand National races in 1961, but that was enough to win him Rookie of The Year honors.

Drivers must love to race, otherwise they wouldn't be in the sport. However, Wayne Niedeckin was in a class all by himself. He not only loved the racing game, but it was also his "bread and butter."

Other drivers usually had either a sideline or regular job to keep groceries in the house and all the bills paid, but if Niedecken crashed, or didn't finish a race, the cupboard went bare.

The driver of the No. 99 yellow supermodified was a consistent winner. Being his own driver/mechanic/sponsor, he didn't take a lot of unnecessary chances on the track. Some people liked air conditioned offices, but Niedeckin liked a good track and fast race car.

Speed Scoop News was the weekly magazine published by Speedway Inc. It published race results of Mobile, Laurel Memphis, Montgomery, Opp, and Pensacola tracks. The following is a recap of a race run July 7, 1966 at Laurel Fairgrounds.

LAUREL,Miss.—Gene Tapia found Laurel Fairgrounds Speedway to his liking last Thursday night and picked up most of the marbles.

However the exciting racing program was marred by a spectacular crash by Red Farmer in the No. F-97, which sent the red head to a Laurel hospital with multiple injuries.

Farmer, who hit the guardrail coming out of the fourth turn in the second heat, suffered cuts and bruises along with possible back injuries. He was taken from the car unconscious.

Red was making a bid for the front position when he crashed, and Hooker Hood went on to win the race, after a lengthy delay, having led all the way. Yankee Bill Riggs also skidded into a rail, but the mishap occurred after the checkered flag.

Donnie Allison won the first heat in his new No. 41, followed by Ival Cooper in No. 22, Tapia in No. 27, and Bill Roynon in No. R-1.

Rufus Johnson was on hand for the Pacer competition and he treated the Laurel track like he owned it, winning both the fast heat and feature.

Johnson's only serious threat came from Rat Lane, who has been driving real well of late at Laurel.

Lane finished second in both the fast heat and feature.

Roynon, another driver who like Laurel, won the Match race, followed by Armond Holley in No. 30 and Tapia.

Carlson Hill took over on the second lap of the second pacer heat and went on to victory over Kenneth Shirley in No. 97 and Jimmy Pitts No. 1.

Tapia, tired of running near the front, but not on top, moved out to a sizeable lead in the Black Flag race and got the win. Ival Cooper took down second, when Bobby Allison lost a rear end on the last lap.

While Johnson was winning the Pacer feature, some of the other cars were fighting it out for the runners-up spots to provide excitement. Johnson and Lane lapped the rest of the field.

Roynon was leading the supermodified feature when his engine started smoking, prompting pit stewards to give him the black flag for his own safety and that of other drivers.

With Roynon in the pits, Tapia was the new leader, and went on to take the win plus the big money

KING OF THE SUPERMODIFIEDS

No early driver made his mark in southeastern stock car and supermodified racing quite like Gene Tapia. By 1966, he had been racing and winning at short tracks from Tampa, Florida to Memphis, Tennessee, and all over the South. His fan following was tremendous. It reached a point that he asked family members to screen his telephone calls, because so many admirers were calling him at home.

But two of his biggest achievements were still on the horizon. The popularity of supermodified racing was nearing its peak in the late 1960s. Ten years earlier, NASCAR had widened its scope by sanctioning races in South Dakota, Nebraska, Iowa, and other midwestern states. For those people who doubted that NASCAR would take over the American stock car racing scene, they were about to believe otherwise. But until 1970, the faster and lighter supermodifieds were the choice of fans and racing promoters.

The circuit that Gene Tapia drove included Mobile International Speedway, a one-half mile high-banked asphalt oval. Later Winston Cup stars like Bobby and Donnie Allison, Red Farmer,

Ken Schrader, Rusty Wallace, Darrell Waltrip, Woodie Wilson, and many others competed there.

The 1967 World 300 for supermodified cars was considered the top supermodified event in the country. As prize money, it offered a $22,000 purse, which was much higher than most NASCAR events paid. According to Vincent Johnson, Sports Editor of the Mobile Register, all the top race car drivers in the country were on hand for the prestigious event. In all, sixty seven drivers attempted to qualify their cars for the forty starting positions-including Donnie Allison in Rod Perry's No. 119 of Miami, Florida.

The race, which was billed as the richest in the world for supermodified cars, got off to a bloody start that Saturday morning when Mort Anderson, thirty-two year-old father of five children, was killed when his car left the track during the morning warm-ups and practice for the afternoon time trials.

"Something happened and he sailed out over turn three," said Tapia. "He went clear out into what we called the death trap."

Unlike some race tracks, Mobile International Speedway did not have a protective outer fence. Anderson's car went airborne, then landed in a small canyon, about thirty feet below the racing surface.

The lightweight driver's seat in Anderson's car stripped its bolts and Anderson was hurled against the steering wheel when the car landed on its nose in the hard red clay. The car did not overturn, but it was badly damaged. Anderson died in an ambulance en route to a Mobile hospital.

Armond Holley of Memphis, Tennessee, won the pole in his No. 12 Ford, followed by Gene Tapia, Mobile; Ellis Pallisini, Leland, Mississippi; Bill Roynon, Tampa, Florida; Wayne Niedekin, Abilene, Texas; Rat Lane of Mobile; and Herman Wise, Atlanta, Georgia.

After the first 150 laps, the 1967 race was stopped, and drivers were given twenty minutes to change tires and make adjustments to their car. Back on the track, each driver went back to the same position he had before the race was stopped.

The race was basically two 150-lap dashes with speeds exceeding 125 miles per hour around the half-mile track. "Armond Holley had a 427 Ford that had been bored, and as soon as the green flag was given, he took off," said Gene. "I had decided to just lay back and be conservative. Within thirty or forty laps, he was a half straightaway ahead of me."

During lap 49, the car of California driver Donnie Hamilton caught on fire after being struck from behind by another car. There was an hour and forty-five minute delay while track officials fought desperately to extinguish the blaze.

The car had originally caught fire in a small ditch on the inside of the track, but was fed by the methanol fuel. Hamilton's crew ordered the car hauled out of the ditch by a wrecker, and trailing burning fuel, it rolled into the pit of the R-1 car driven by Bill Roynon of Tampa, Florida. Several other cans of methanol ignited, along with the magnesium wheels on Hamilton's car.

When racing resumed, Tapia stayed near Holley, who was still the leader.

When we neared the one hundred lap mark, I noticed I was closing in on him. Each lap I got a little closer.

Just before the 150-lap break, Tapia had pulled right up to Holley's rear bumper.

I watched him for a couple more laps and pretty soon, I saw his car flutter a little, and I sailed by him.

The crowd stood and cheered as Tapia made his pass.

Tapia went into the pits at the halfway point as the leader. His closest rival was Kentucky driver Wayne McGuire.

McGuire was one of the few drivers that had a Pontiac. He was turning that Pontiac more than he should have trying to keep up with the 327.

During the pit stop, McGuire's team decided to make some changes to their car.

Wayne couldn't catch me, so they decided to change gears in his Pontiac. He told me afterwards, he knew he would either blow the engine or win. That's all he could do, because he couldn't outrun me the way his car was setup.

During lap 210, the engine in McGuire's Pontiac came apart. He had wound it too tight, and was still unable to catch Gene in the 327.

I didn't know when Wayne went out. Back then we didn't have radios and things often got confused, because you couldn't see everything. I missed seeing Wayne. I kept looking for him and looking for him, but I never spotted his car. Finally, I figured he must be right on my bumper and about to catch me, so I really started romping on it. I mean I poured the coal to it.

By the time the checkered flag was given at two o'clock on Sunday morning, signifying the end of the race, Gene Tapia finished nine laps ahead of the second place car.

Tapia was almost unbeatable for the remainder of 1967. He successfully defended his World 300 supermodified crown the following year, beating out Wayne Ruittimann of Tampa, Florida, by three laps.

TOP: 1997: Charley Merrill, Harold "Bud" Erb, Doug Wimpee Sr., "Little" Joe Holly, Pete Gulsby, Gene Tapia

LOWER: Gene Tapia and Car Owner, J. T. Doughty After Winning The 1967 World 300 (The World's Richest Supermodified Race)

PHOTOGRAPHS OF FOLLOWING PAGES

First photo: Supermodified driver Lucky Mays.

Second photo: Gene Tapia after one of his late model wins and Jim Chandler of Birmingham, AL.

Third photo: Ellis Pallisini of Leland, MS carries the checkered flag around Mobile International Speedway, Mobile, AL.

Fourth photo: J.C. Mason Jr., Charley Grant and J. C. Mason Sr., after a feature late model win at Five Flags Speedway, Pensacola, FL, May 14, 1971.

Fifth photo: Flagman, Eddie May and Phil Wendt, supermodified and late model driver. Wendt helped build Mobile International Speedway and was the first driver to practice on the asphalt surface. Wendt is shown receiving the Late Model Hard Charger Award in 2001.

Sixth photo: Gene Tapia and the 327 Modified, in which he won the 1967 and 1968 World 300, and hundreds of other races.

Supermodified Driver, Lucky Mays

Alabama Auto Racing Pioneers Hall of Fame-1999

Doug Wimpee Jr., Tom Claxton, Bud Erb, Gene Tapia, and the author, Gerald Hodges-1997

CHAPTER XIII

THE CHECKERED FLAG

Having competed and won against the nations best drivers was gratifying to the forty-three-year-old driver, but as he enjoyed his successes in 1967 and 1968, he could also see the influence NASCAR was having on local racing. At the end of the 1968 season, Mobile International Speedway and several other tracks that made up the Gulf Coast Racing circuit, announced that the supermodifieds would be run on a limited basis in the coming years. They were replaced by the NASCAR late model series in 1969.

Browning and Furlow Plumbing of Houston, Texas, bought the No. 327 from J. T. Doughtry of Mobile in late 1968. Gene continued to drive it on a limited schedule at tracks in Texas, Louisiana, Mississippi, Alabama, Florida, and Tennessee, but he also drove a late model owned by J. C. Mason of Mobile.

A lot of tracks would put on a double show of both supermodifieds and late models, and I would drive both cars in a single night. We continued to do real good. We won our share of the races, and the family had fun too.

There were many nights Gene would win both feature events. But now that his girls were grown, they began to have concerns about him. Gene says he never had a serious racing accident, but his family began to mention to him that he needed to hang up his driving helmet.

I never got tired of racing. I still love it to this day. I think it's one of the finest sports there ever was. It's a team effort, and each member of that team is a cog in that link. If a cog doesn't mesh right and they don't have the same outlook, then the team won't operate properly.

That was what was happening with Gene's racing family. His team was no longer meshing.

I never did see the finish line coming, I was sort of forced into it. I had a lot of help getting out of racing. My family wanted me to get out, and I preferred to keep peace in the family.

In 1980, after 42-years behind the wheel, the King of the Supermodifieds received the checkered flag for the last time.

I guess I'd still be crawling in and out of a race car if I could. That's how much I loved it.

THUNDER AND LIGHTNING

After his driving career ended, Gene continued to hang around with old racing buddies and visit relatives but his number one pastime was hunting. During the winter months he visited with his good friend and former competitor Ellis Pallisini. At home, he hunted deer, turkey, and bear on over 4,000 acres of land belonging to the Bucks Outdoorsman Hunting club in north Mobile County. During the summer months, he and Francine traveled and visited friends and relatives.

On August 9, 1986, the couple left to visit relatives in North Carolina. Shaaron had her own home, but Rebecca continued to live with her parents in the old home on Moffett Road that was built in 1924 by her grandparents. On the evening of August 11, one of Shaaron's and Rebecca's childhood friends, Laura Jo Holly, was coming to visit and they were going out for her birthday.

"Laura and I were raised together," said Rebecca. "We've been friends since we were four years old. When we first became friends, we were so little we couldn't cross the street, but we would see each other in the grocery store and chase each other around the store.

"She was not only my friend, but Shaaron's friend, too. We all grew up together in the same neighborhood. Laura was getting ready to move to San Francisco, so we wanted to get together and have a good time before she left."

Rebecca didn't get off work until five-thirty, so Shaaron had picked up Laura.

"It was a real rainy evening," said Rebecca. "I was rushing around, because I remember I had to check on my car at the service station, then I went home and changed into some different clothes, real fast."

The threesome went to Twickingham Station, a popular Mobile restaurant. After reminiscing over old times, Sharon wanted to go to Crockmier's for a couple drinks before going home.

"I didn't know what it was but I had some type of gut feeling that told me to go home," continued Shaaron.

Finally, Rebecca yielded to the desires of her sister and Laura, and the trio went to Crockmier's and headed home about nine o'clock.

As Rebecca turned on to Moffett Road, she saw a lot of red lights and emergency vehicles.

"Oh my god, there's been a horrible wreck," said Rebecca. "Finally, as we got closer, I saw they were gathered at our house."

Shaaron says Rebecca turned directly into the path of a tractor-trailer and went up the wrong side of the highway toward their home. Two fire trucks were parked end-to-end to keep cars and pedestrians out of the Tapia yard. Rebecca gunned the engine and headed for the small opening between the two trucks.

"I scraped both sides of the car, and went flying down the driveway as far as I could," said Rebecca. "There were five fire trucks in the yard and a bunch of firemen standing around. I heard them say, 'OK, here they come.'"

As soon as the girls jumped out of the car, they were stopped by police and firemen who surrounded them and refused to let them go near the burned out shell of what was once their home.

Rebecca and Sharon began screaming.

"Oh, my babies, oh, my babies," cried Rebecca.

One of the firemen looked at the girls and said, "We're so sorry. We didn't see any babies."

"Sir, it wasn't babies," said Sharon. "It's animals. It was our pets. I realized he thought it was people."

Two of the family pets, Patches the cat, and one dog, Muffin, were inside and dead. The other dog, Smoky, who had been tied to the porch, survived.

"I was so upset," said Shaaron. "We had no way to reach Mom and Dad, nothing. The phone number had been on the kitchen table when we left. A fireman had been injured when he fell through the roof and had been taken to the hospital."

Finally, the firemen escorted them into the gutted structure.

"We saw one miraculous thing," said Rebecca. "As we came back through the living room, we saw an end table that had the family Bible laying on it. Everything else around it had been completely burned, but only the edges of it were singed. It stayed intact, and Momma still has it.

"And I saw an apparition of my grandmother. Nobody saw her but me, and I saw her three times. She was there walking through that house in a daze. She was just walking. I said, who's that person over there? They said 'What person?' Then I realized who it was. She was a tall, slender black-headed lady. She was just drifting through each room in the house, like she was checking out to see if her family was all right."

The piece of paper with the telephone number was still on the table, but only four numbers were legible. The girls were able to piece together the correct number and went to a service station and called their parents.

"Mother, there's been a fire," said Shaaron. "The table is still standing in the kitchen. I wanted to spare them as much as I could, but finally, it all came out."

Eventually, the Mobile Fire Department would discover the cause of the fire, but for three days, Rebecca was under suspicion for arson because she was the last person to leave the house.

"We got our clothing together immediately and headed home," said Gene.

The traveling time to North Carolina required twelve hours. It only took Gene eight hours coming back.

"From the time I saw it, I too, was in complete shock," said Gene.

Friends and neighbors had gathered around the Tapia home the next day to help clean away the debris and comfort the family.

"There must have been fifty people in our front yard when we pulled up," said Francine. "They had sat up tables and things outside, because the firemen were still checking it and wouldn't let anyone inside.

"Gene had been in that house since he was eight years old and together, and we had almost fifty years of our lives in it."

To make matters worse, the fire inspectors continued to treat the cause of the fire as arson.

"They kept pointing the finger at me," said Rebecca. "One inspector went out and got a gas can that Daddy used for the lawn mower. It had been setting by a tree, but he said it was on the front porch. That indicated I started the fire.

"Later, we discovered Mr. Harbin the insurance agent was behind those accusations. He was real nice when he first came, but when he found out our home was paid for; he started being a total jerk.

"He began to tell us we had to show receipts for every thing, even our underwear. It wasn't total replacement. He asked for receipts on a table my granddaddy had built in 1925. This meant more heartaches began immediately."

Gene Tapia now faced a new challenge. For the first time in his life, he and his family were homeless. All of what they had saved for was gone.

"We had no furniture, no beds or anything to sleep on," said Rebecca. "Shaaron got us an apartment near her. J & J Furniture delivered three beds that next night, and that's all we had. I had no clothes and Daddy and Momma had what was in their suitcase. I had to wash my clothes at night and wear the same ones for about three days."

Rebecca's coworkers at Alabama Shipyard and Drydock donated $225 for her to buy clothes.

"My Daddy was in total shock, and my sister had gone to pieces," said Shaaron. I realized I had to be strong, because Momma couldn't carry the whole emotional burden of the three of us."

The second night Rebecca was spending the night in Shaaron's apartment.

"Rebecca was still unable to cope, and I realized I needed some help," said Sharon. "So I called a prayer help line. I told the man that answered that my sister was going to pieces and what should I do, take her to the hospital and get her a shot? He said, 'Well, maam, I've been up all night myself and I haven't had any sleep and I really don't know what to tell you."

Sharon realized she had to take charge. She hung up the phone and eventually was able to get Rebecca calmed down.

"The one bright spot was our dog, Smokey, who survived," said Rebecca. "We slept at the apartment and Momma and Daddy went over to the place every day."

The insurance agent was not one of the Tapia family's favorite persons.

"He was giving them a hard time," said Shaaron. "I went over there and took him aside and said, look, this is my Momma and Daddy, and sister, and they have just been through a crisis. You are going to give them some money so they can buy the things they need. Finally he came up with $5,000 and they were able to buy other things they needed."

Gene credits a friend, Susie Gurganus; with helping them file the proper insurance papers. She came over and inventoried the entire household, then contacted the merchants where the furniture had been bought. After several months, she obtained receipts for most of their furnishings.

Fire investigators, led by Orville Shreve of the Mobile City Inspection Office, determined that lightning had struck the air conditioner in Rebecca's upstairs bedroom, and then ignited some of Gene's rifle and shotgun ammunition that was stored in a box. When the ammunition exploded, the entire end of the upstairs bedroom blew out.

"It is the most horrendous feeling I'd ever had," said Rebecca. "The loss of our home and to have nothing left but the clothes on my back is something I wouldn't want anyone to go through."

According to Shaaron, it was six months before the family regained their emotions and could function in society, but Gene slipped into a depression.

"A year later, you could talk to my Dad and he would answer you, but he was just there," said Shaaron. "He would eat only out of habit. He was oblivious to what was going on. He couldn't comprehend what was going on in the world around him. He was still in shock."

Shaaron arranged for a counselor to come talk with her father. After several visits, she told the family Gene would come out of the depression.

I did come out of it little by little, but it was a gradual process that took a long time. But I never got over it. That was my home. It was a big loss. I couldn't help it.

The burned-out shell of Gene's boyhood home still stands just west of Interstate 65 on Moffett Road. Next to it are several majestic, 500-year-old oak trees that stand like silent sentries guarding an old fortress. Gene refuses to tear it down.

Sometimes when I go over there, I still shed a tear.

For almost two years the family lived in an apartment. Finally, through the help of neighbors, they located and closed on another house and property about five miles north of the original Tapia home place.

With the children grown, and Gene semi-retired, the couple settled into what could be described as a normal retirement. There was nothing complicated about their lives; Gene hunted in the winter and fished in the summer, while Francine visited, kept house and continued to prepare meals for their many guests.

He and Francine would stroll in their backyard in the soft summer evenings as the sun set behind a row of trees and then return and sit together on a porch swing. Their usual time of retirement was somewhere between nine and ten o'clock. This couple was now boding to become as Gene put it, "Wiser, Refined, and Settled."

But now with a little more time on his hands, he would be able to search for the son he had never seen.

I just felt compelled to do it. And there was Francine and her faith. Somehow, she believed that one day we would get to meet and hold him.

J. P. Donohue, Norman Tew, Gene Tapia and Tony Dahlgren after a 1966 deer hunt.

Charley Merrill and wife, Ruth

Ellis Wilkins and wife, Virginia

A close friend of the Tapia family, L.G. Wilson

Doug Dunnam, Bill Ayres, Ellis Wilkins, Guy Taylor and Gene-1990

Francine and Gene Tapia, Susan Morrow, and Doug Parker take a break during a deer hunt, 2001.

Gene Tapia in his early driving suit.

CHAPTER XIV

ONE MORE MOUNTAIN

"Therefore I say unto you, whatsoever things you desire, when you pray, believe that you receive them, and you shall have them."
> St. Mark 11:24

    Both Francine and Gene Tapia admitted that the loss of their son on September 24, 1942 was the single most traumatic event in their marriage. Gene had given up hope years before, even though he continued to feel tinges of guilt. Francine, on the other hand, continued to pray, and never lost hope.
    Valentine's Day, 1990, had been uneventful for the Tapia family. Their children and some of the grandchildren had come over with presents, they'd had a big dinner, and now after everyone had gone home, quietness had returned to the Tapia home.
    It was Gene's usual custom after eating to go out in the den and sit down in his big velvety recliner and turn on the television.

Usually after thirty or forty minutes he was snoozing. This night was no exception.

Francine was through with the dishes and had set down in her own reclining chair a few feet from her husband. She was flipping through the television channels when suddenly an Unsolved Mysteries movie on the Lifetime Channel caught her attention.

"Gene, wake up, wake up."

Gene didn't respond fast enough so she jumped up and went over and began shaking him.

"What, what is it? What's wrong?"

"Oh my goodness, oh my goodness, it's a story about Georgia Tann. See, Mary Tyler Moore is playing the part. Wake up, wake up Gene, you've got to see this," Francine continued to shout. "This is about our child that was stolen in Memphis."

Gene Tapia woke up in a hurry. Right in front of the couple, a movie entitled "Stolen Babies" was on. As the two watched in disbelief, Francine sat on the floor next to her husband's chair and began to cry.

The documentary they were watching brought back the memory of unanswered prayers and what had happened nearly forty-seven years earlier. Francine and Gene had first consulted lawyers after their baby was stolen. They attempted to find birth records, only to be told they were sealed permanently. Frustrated, they hired several private detectives, but they never uncovered any facts about their son's birth. No leads were ever obtained as to his whereabouts. Then, in 1969, an underworld friend had told Gene that their son was serving two life sentences in the Oklahoma State Prison in McAllister, Oklahoma, for killing two women who had tried to swindle him out of a large farm.

Francine got up and sat on the arm of Gene's chair and put her arm around his neck. This program was causing them to relive the past. Francine couldn't stop crying and suddenly that old feeling of failure that Gene had experienced years ago returned. He could feel it in the pit of his stomach.

"Years ago, I had reconciled himself to the fact that I would never see my lost son," Gene said.

Mary Tyler Moore was doing a remarkable job of portraying Georgia Tann. And there was even the Memphis Judge Camille

Kelly, whom Francine had sought help from. Now, she could understand why the judge refused her requests. She and Georgia Tann were in the baby-adoption scheme together.

As the movie progressed, things became much clearer for the old couple. But they weren't expecting the next announcement.

When a commercial came on, Francine jumped up and went to her bedroom at the other end of the house to get some more Kleenex tissues. Gene continued to stare at the screen.

"Francine, bring a pen and something to write on. They've given a telephone number."

Not waiting for Francine, he reached over on the coffee table, grabbed a pen and started writing the number on the margin of the newspaper he had finished reading. By the time Francine came running back into the den with a pen and paper, Gene was standing up and very excited.

"We've got to call Francine. Here! This is the number, you call."

"Call who? For what?"

"There's a group of people that might be able to help us find our baby. They want people who lost their babies to call them. I don't know if they can help us or not, but call them."

Shaking, Francine dialed the number Gene had copied from television. It was the number of Tennessee's Right To Know, a non-profit organization devoted to helping adoptees find their roots. Because of its location in Memphis, the founder, Denny Child, frequently dealt with victims of Georgia Tann.

I guess I must have been the first person to call the number they gave. They took my name and number and asked a few questions and said someone would call us later.

Francine Tapia says she never closed her eyes one night in her entire life without asking God to let her see her child. Were her prayers about to be answered, or would this be another dead-end lead like so many they had pursued in the past?

Three days later, about seven o'clock in the evening, the telephone rang in the Tapia home.

"Hello, Mrs. Tapia, this is Jalena Bowling in Memphis, Tennessee."

"Lord, I couldn't believe it," Francine said. "After all these years, here was somebody offering to help find our son. I wanted to believe, but after so long, it's hard. It's not that I didn't have the faith, it just sounded too good to be true.

"She didn't tell us she would be able to find him but she told us she was going to try. There wasn't anything phony about her talk or attitude. She told us that she and two other women had set up a non-profit organization and in their spare time they searched out the parents of children stolen by Georgia Tann."

What surprised Gene and Francine about the first telephone call was Mrs. Bowling wasn't interested in any large sums of money.

"After we gave her all the particulars about the baby, I asked her how much money she wanted me to send," said Gene. "And she would never tell me, so I asked if one thousand dollars would be enough to get started. She said, 'No, that is too much.' I said, what about five hundred, and she said no, again. Finally, she said, 'Why don't you send me fifty dollars, and if I need any more, I'll let you know.'"

Jalena Bowling was not helping find stolen babies for profit. Even though she worked during the day and was a housewife at night, she had a special interest in helping reunite children with their birth mothers, because she too had been adopted.

"She called us several times and told us she couldn't find where our child had been registered in Memphis or Shelby County," said Gene. "She told us she might have to take a little trip and see what she could find in some of the surrounding counties."

Operating out of a small Memphis office, neither of the three volunteer women could devote themselves full time to gathering information. Even though they lacked time, personnel and money, all three had learned Georgia Tann's methods. When things got too complicated for her and Judge Camille Kelly, she would arrange to have the paperwork done in other Tennessee counties.

"One night Jalena called us and told us she had located his records in the Dyer County Courthouse in Dyersburg," said Gene. "Francine was on the other phone and all the time Jalena was talking, Francine was sobbing."

"I think I know which direction your child was taken. It looks like he went to New York, but I can't pin it down, yet," said Jalena.

Two days later Jalena Bowling called again.

"I think I've located the people who got your child," she said. "And they've still got an active number in Brooklyn, New York. But I've tried calling and don't get an answer."

Gene asked for the number and offered to check it out himself, but Mrs. Bowling refused.

"She said I would blow it, and if she were to continue, it would be done her way. I said, that's O.K. by me. You've already done more than anyone ever has."

A few days later, Mrs. Bowling called again and said she had attempted to trace him throughout the entire United States, but had come up empty-handed. She then asked for another hundred dollars so she could initiate a nationwide drivers license check.

Gene sent the money and a week later, on March 19, 1990 at eleven o'clock at night, he received another call.

"This time she told us she was pretty sure this was the one we were searching for. She asked what color eyes we had. Francine said, 'brown,' and I said, mine are blue."

"He goes by the name Robert Adelson, and I'm pretty sure this is the one,' she said. She also gave me his name, address, social security number, and telephone number."

In addition, Mrs. Bowling gave Gene specific instructions on how to make the first call. The next morning was the opening day of the spring turkey season in Alabama. For the first time in over thirty years, Gene Tapia missed opening day.

THE CALL

At exactly seven-thirty the next morning, Gene headed toward the telephone in the living room while Francine waited by the extension phone in the kitchen.

The morning of March 20 was brisk and cold in St. Louis, Missouri. In Maryland Heights, a suburb of St. Louis, Robert Adelson had finished dressing for work and was headed toward the door when he heard the phone. He stopped, placed his briefcase near the door and picked up the receiver.

The forty-seven-year-old salesman was totally unprepared for the news he was about to receive.

"Good morning," said Robert.

"Is this Robert Adelson?"

"Yes, it is."

"Were you born September 24, 1942, in St. Joseph's Hospital iin Memphis, Tennessee?"

There was silence as Robert Adelson pondered the question. "Yes, I was."

Gene had been instructed by Jalena Bowling not to be insistent or overbearing, and instead, ask him to write down their telephone number in case he thought it was a prank and hung up.

"This man said, 'before we go any further, do me a favor and write down this telephone number.' And he gave me his telephone number. And then he told me, 'your mother and I have been looking for you for forty seven years,'" said Robert Adelson.

Robert almost dropped the phone.

"Wow, that was some heavy stuff. That was a mind blower.

"He was worried I would hang up on him and my wife was saying, 'What do they want?' I was saying to myself, just relax and see what this is all about.

"And then he said, 'your mother is on the other phone. She and I were married before you were born, and we've been married all these years. You were not thrown away, you were taken from us. Can we get together and go over what happened to you?'"

By this time the ice had begun to melt between the two men. Gene asked Robert about meeting with him the following weekend.

"Robert told me it would be awful difficult for him to leave St. Louis, because he had just switched jobs," said Gene. "I said, we'll come up there.

"And you've got two sisters, can I bring them?"

There was another long silence before Robert replied, "O.K., bring them on, too."

Jeanne and Lester Adelson, his adoptive parents, had never kept the fact from Robert that he was adopted. The first book he ever owned was "The Adopted Baby."

"After the phone call, my wife questioned the validity and real purpose of the call," said Robert. All I could say was just relax, we'll find out soon.

"I was excited all during the week. I've always loved adventure, but this was an entirely different kind of adventure. I was anxious and wondering what I was going to find."

During the excitement of the telephone call, Robert was unaware that Gene lived in Mobile, Alabama. He assumed they either lived in or around St. Louis or a short distance away.

On Friday morning, when the Tapia Family left Mobile, the temperature was hovering around 40 degrees. The farther north they traveled the more the weather deteriorated. As they approached the Tennessee and Missouri borders, a full-fledged blizzard was blowing. The drifting snow that was blown across Interstate 55 made it practically impossible to drive. The accumulated snowfall reached one foot in places. Gene slowed, but he never stopped the big Lincoln until he reached the Hampton Inn in Maryland Heights, Missouri.

"The next morning I got up and put on my Sunday-best suit and went over to the hotel to meet them," said Robert. "I knocked on their door, and this beautiful lady opened it, introduced herself, and said, 'By the way, this is your family.'"

Francine's forty-seven years of prayers had been answered. It had been a long time. There was a lot to talk about. After introductions, hugs and tears, the two families talked for thirteen consecutive hours.

"As I understand it, I had an asthma attack on the plane," said Robert. "And this was very frightening for her. But she was able to get through it and made it back to New York without any further incidents."

Lester Adelson was a young executive who was on the move upward with Macy's. The family lived in Kew Gardens, New York, for the first several years of Robert's life. His outings consisted of being pushed in a baby carriage by both parents and other relatives.

Lester received a promotion and the family moved to 83rd Street and Central Park West in Manhattan in order to be closer to his work. Jeanne, who had previously been a model, did not work.

"I think all of my parents and grandparents gloated over me as a child," said Robert. "Every other Saturday, my mother's father would take me to the Museum of Natural History, and I loved it. Through those early experiences, I gained a strong appreciation for history. Many of those exhibits are still there, but the Indian and Dinosaur exhibits stand out in my mind.

"I can't remember a lot about this grandfather, except he came from Vienna, Austria, and lost and regained several fortunes in the ostrich feather business. He made money when the feathers were in favor, and lost it when they went out of fashion. I'm sure he had an accent, but I just remember him as Grandpa."

Just prior to Robert's entering kindergarten, Lester received another promotion and the family moved to a large white ivy-covered house in Mount Vernon, New York.

By this time, the Adelson's had adopted another baby, this time a girl.

Robert, meanwhile, was the typical boy who loved to play outside and have fun.

"There were some woods near our house that I liked to go into and play with older boys. We would gather chestnuts, drill a hole in the center and have chestnut fights. One time when we were gathering chestnuts, I ran across the road and was hit by a car. I was unconscious for two or three hours, and this caused Lester and Jeanne a lot of worry."

He had problems in the first grade. Even though it was thought he was dyslexic, there were additional learning problems. While running, he broke his left arm in three places. It did not heal properly and had to be rebroken three more times. Since he had a tendency to be left-handed, this caused additional writing and learning problems as well as a fear of doctors.

"The next three years was very traumatic for me," said Robert. "I fell behind in my work. Between the dyslexia and having my arm broken so many times, I was at a definite disadvantage with my peers."

Since Robert's family was Jewish, they did not normally attend church on Sunday. Instead, they would take drives in upstate New York. Aside from a kind of controlled workaholism, all too common in up-and-coming executives, which was Lester's milieu, the family constellation seems to have been free from major disharmonies. Robert remembers both parents as mutually supportive and highly mobile with a strong sense of familial self respect. This was particularly notable in the family's extensive intercultural and sightseeing schedule. But whether they were spending a quiet weekend at home or motoring around the surrounding New York countryside, they were very willing simply to have a good time together.

By the time Robert had turned eight, Lester was promoted to president of Bamberger's, a Macy's subsidiary, and the family moved to Morristown, New Jersey, a very rural area. Robert enjoyed the outdoors and was a physically active youngster.

"There was an old carriage house near our home that we played around," said Robert. "It was an old brick building with stalls for horses. And there was a ladder you could climb up to open the trap door into the loft. It was kept locked all the time because the owner kept some lumber and other things in it.

"One day we noticed the lock had been removed from one of the big sliding doors, so we decided to go inside and look around. It was dark and we were exploring and started to go upstairs, and suddenly we saw a fellow at the top of the stairs with a big knife. That scared us half to death and we all ran home and told our parents.

"Our parents called the police and this man we saw was a mental patient that had broken out of Greystone, a nearby mental institution, and holed up there. The police surrounded the building, but they never caught him. Apparently, he escaped over the roof and jumped off."

Growing up, Robert did not have a strong religious feeling, but participated in most Jewish ceremonies. For the most part, his childhood seems to have been warm, normal, and comfortable in the Adelson household.

Along with the innocent whirl and play of a healthy youngster, every now and then he used his very active mind to fulfill some goals. Once he used a certain amount of deception to land his first job.

"I had a friend that worked weekends and summers on the Dodge Estate," said Robert. "And I really wanted to work there. The lady that owned it was probably the second or third-richest person in the State of New Jersey. I talked with my parents and asked my father to drive me over to see if I could get a job."

After arriving at the Dodge Mansion or "Big house," Robert knocked on the door and was greeted by Mrs. Dodge's second husband, who instructed him to talk with the grounds foreman.

"My father remained and talked with the man while I walked a long way down to a greenhouse," said Robert. "I said, Mr. Dodge suggested I come down and talk to you about a position.

"The foreman asked if I knew Mr. Dodge, and I said, no. I

don't know him personally, but if you'll look up the hill at the big house, that's my dad talking with him now.

"He hired me on the spot, but about two weeks later he came back and said, 'You lied to me.' And I said what do you mean? He said, 'You told me you knew Mr. Dodge.' And I said, no, I said I didn't but that was my dad talking with him. And that was the truth."

Robert kept his job for nearly a year. He shoveled horse manure, dug potatoes, kept the gardens, and spent as much time in the woods as possible.

"Each year my family allowed me to go to a camp in Maine," said Robert. "One night we had been camping in the woods and after we came home, we heard this awful sound made by some wild animal. The next night I took a hatchet, some firecrackers, and a slingshot. Sure enough, about two o'clock in the morning we heard this creature again. I unzipped my jungle hammock, got out, grabbed a couple cherry bombs and fired them off into the direction the sound came from. I scared this horrendous monster away, but we found out later it was just a beagle dog that belonged to a nearby farmer and it was out chasing rabbits."

During one of his camping trips to Maine, he participated in a DRD, or Dead River Dash. This was a fifty or sixty mile trek in deep timberlands. Most of the time it rained. Once they reached a river that was normally fordable, it was raging and had flooded its banks because of heavy rains. A canoe was unfastened, but after two trips, the counselor was physically drained, so the job of ferrying ten more people across the river went to Robert.

He continued to be bothered by dyslexia and have reading problems while the family lived in Morristown. Lester had taken another job as head of Darling Shops, a woman's dress chain. Each day he commuted to work in Manhattan. Even though Robert was able to read, the family decided they would enroll him in some special programs at New York University in Greenwich Village.

Each day Robert and Lester would leave Morristown on their daily commute. When the pair reached Hoboken, New Jersey, Robert would get off the train and switch to the subway that would take him to the Greenwich Village area. Lester would catch a ferry and go to his upper Manhattan office.

"One day my father had given me money to get a haircut,"

said Robert. "Since I had something to do that afternoon, I decided to get my hair cut that morning, and I would tell my teachers the train had been delayed if I was late for classes."

The barber shop he was accustomed to using was part of the Sheraton Hotel on the edge of Greenwich Village.

Shortly after ten o'clock on the morning of Oct. 25, 1957, Robert was less than a block from the hotel when he saw a car pulled to the curb and stop. Two men got out and went into the barber shop.

"I thought with these guys going in ahead of me, it was going to be a longer wait than I expected," said Robert. "I stopped and debated whether to go in or wait until later, but after a second or two, I headed on towards the barber shop."

As the fifteen-year-old boy neared the entrance to the shop, shots rang out.

"I don't remember how many pops I heard, but instinctively, I knew they were gunshots," he said.

What Robert did not know was he had seen the two hired gunmen as they emerged from the barber shop after gunning down one of America's most notorious underworld figures, Albert Anastasia.

According to archives of the Laborers International Union of North America (LIUNA), Anastasia was one of the most ruthless killers in American organized crime. He personally murdered at least fifty or more persons but was responsible, as head of Murder, Inc., the syndicate 's execution squad located in Brooklyn, New York, for the killing of hundreds, perhaps thousands of victims for four decades

Shortly before WWI, in 1917, Anastasia and his nine brothers emigrated from Italy to the United States. A strapping boy, Anastasia was given a job on the docks and was a longshoreman by age sixteen, working alongside his brother, Anthony. Anastasia eventually came under the wing of Brooklyn gang boss, Joe Adonis, and it was through Adonis and his fabulous bootleg wealth that Anastasia was able to set up his own fledgling gang of bootleggers and killers at the dawn of Prohibition. By this time, Anastasia had been credited with killing at least five men in gangland wars over bootleg territory in Brooklyn. He made a mistake, however, when he boldly murdered a fellow longshoreman, Joe Torino, in 1920, in a dispute over the right to unload ships with precious cargoes. He was convicted and sentenced to death. Anastasia lingered on death row in Sing Sing Prison for eighteen months but he won a new trial when the witnesses reversed their statements and then suddenly vanished, and the thug-killer was released. Of course, Anastasia's gang members saw to it that the witnesses disappeared.

In 1940, when Brooklyn District Attorney Burton B. Turkus suddenly found several members of Murder, Inc., willing to turn state's evidence, Anastasia, too, went into hiding

As a Mafia don, however, Anastasia displayed an erratic, explosive nature and found it impossible to check his mercurial, murderous temperament. When watching a TV news show one day in 1952, Anastasia saw Arnold Schuster, an amateur sleuth who had identified the much-wanted bank robber Willie "The Actor" Sutton on a New York subway and informed police which had led to Sutton's arrest. While Schuster was being interviewed, Anastasia leaped from his chair and shouted to his goons, "I can't stand squealers! Hit that guy!" Schuster was murdered, according to the orders of the Mad Hatter, on March 8, 1952. When news of this mob murder reached the ears of Vito Genovese, the calculating Mafia don began to spread the word that Anastasia was unstable, a thug murderer who did not deserve the high rank he had achieved in the syndicate.

But it was Frank Costello, the so-called Prime Minister of Organized Crime that gave the order to kill Anastasia.

That vengeance was reaped shortly after 10:15 a.m. on Oct. 25, 1957, when Anastasia walked into the barbershop of New York's Park Sheraton Hotel. He waved at the shop owner Arthur Grasso as he sat down in the deep leather of chair four. Joe Bocchino, who had been cropping Anastasia's short, curly hair for years, covered him with the candy striped barber's cloth and began to clip at the gang boss's hair while a manicurist sat next to the chair and worked on the Mad Hatter's fingernails. Jimmy, the shoeshine boy, began to slap brown polish on the gangster's wing-tipped shoes. The two men that Robert Adelson saw get out of the car and enter the shop pulled .38-caliber revolvers and waved the shop people away from chair four. As they scattered in fright, both men began to blast at the seated figure.

Anastasia had been dozing in the chair, his eyes closed.

They popped open just before the first shot was fired. The gang boss raised his left hand as if to shield his head from the bullet which tore through the palm. Two more bullets smashed his left wrist and entered his hip. Anastasia let out a roar and struggled to get out of the chair, reaching, some reports later said, for a gun that he no longer wore. Bullets crashed into the barber's shelf in front of the chair, shattering bottles of hair tonic.

Another bullet struck Anastasia in the back as he stood upright for a moment, the barber's cloth still clinging to him. He sank to the floor, and one of the gunmen calmly walked up to the prone figure and fired a bullet into the back of his head, a coup de grace identical to the shot Anastasia had fired into the head of Joe "The Boss" Masseria in 1931. Their gruesome task completed, the two gunmen raced for the door and vanished. They were never apprehended, but as they exited the door, they spotted a boy walking toward them on the sidewalk.

"As those guys came out of the barber shop, they saw me and drove towards me in their car," said Robert, "I ran down alleys and one-way streets where they couldn't come. I was scared to death."

Robert ran and ran, until he finally was able to duck into the subway tunnel. He stayed in the "tubes" for several hours before going on to school. It wasn't until much later that he learned the men he saw were Mafia "hit men" and their target had been Albert Anastasia.

"But I knew how the mafia operated and I never told anyone about what I saw that day," he said.

By the time he entered high school, the family had moved to Scarsdale, New York. Even though he passed most of his classes, he says he was not a good student and had to struggle with most of his studies. This did not leave him enough time to play team sports.

"I regret not being able to play football," he said. "But with having to maintain an acceptable grade level, it was almost impossible for me to participate. Had I been able to play, it might have made a difference in my life. I was an excellent swimmer, but the school had no swim team, so I wasn't able to show those skills."

By his own confession, he was a bit of a hellion. He tormented his adopted sister on a regular basis. He once frightened her by locking her in a room for two hours. Because of the reading problems he had during his early years, he grew up believing he was a rather stupid person.

His biggest urge was to enter the retail business. This was probably conditioned in him because of his father's involvement and success in the retail industry.

At the age of sixteen, he went to work part-time for Macy's in White Plains, New York, as a stockman. Within a few months, he had worked his way up to the salesman. It seemed like he had found his calling.

During his senior year in high school, his grades were not good enough for college, so he joined the Navy after graduation. After attending boot camp at Great Lakes, Illinois, he was assigned to a Destroyer Escort, which was on patrol in the North Atlantic at the time. After serving a few months, he was reassigned to another ship, the USS Calcaterra, DER 390.

This was early 1962, and the Cuban Missile Crisis was about to reach its boiling point. The Calcaterra was reassigned to patrol duty in the Windward Passage, an area between Cuba and Haiti.

"We kept seeing more and more of these Russian missile ships," he said. "You could see all the missiles out on deck, because all they did was drape tarpaulins over them. We never attempted to turn any of them around, but we would ask them where they were going, and what cargo they were carrying, and things like that. And they would always tell us they had a cargo of fish they were taking to Cuba."

The Calcaterra was ordered back to its home base of Newport, Rhode Island. As the ship entered the harbor, President John F. Kennedy was giving his ultimatum speech to the Russians on the missiles they were bringing to Cuba.

The day after Robert enlisted in the Navy, Lester and Jeanne moved to Akron, Ohio, where he was assistant to the President of the May Companies, a major retailing conglomerate. As soon as he received his Navy discharge, Robert moved to Akron and began studies at Kent State University.

Robert and his family live in a St. Louis, Missouri suburb, and visits Gene and Francine on a regular basis.

FAMILY PHOTOGRAPHS

Gene's brother, Homer Jr.

Francine's sister, Dorothy Hays Brannon

Robert Adelson and wife, Phyllis

Robert's daughter, Tracey Michelle and grandson, Andrew

Gene's grandson, Scott Adelson

Gene's grandson, Robbie Adelson and son, Robert

THE FOURTH WOMAN

JALENA BOWLING OF "TENNESSEE'S RIGHT TO KNOW"

Gene said, "There have been four women that have had a profound effect on my life. The first was my mother. Second, it was my sister, that kept me out of so much trouble. The third was and still is the "Love of My Life," Francine. But the fourth was Jalena Bowling, who helped find our son. She furnished the light that helped end forty-seven years of groping through darkness."

THE GENE TAPIA FAMILY

Daughter, Shaaron Tapia Covey, granddaughter, "DeeDee" Covey Livings, Gene, Francine, daughter, Rebecca, and son, Robert.

CONCLUSION

MY THOUGHTS--FRANCINE TAPIA

If I had my life to live over, I don't think I would change it too much. I'd probably do the same things, just do more of them.

We've had a good time, a good life, and the Lord has blessed us with finding our son. I don't know of too many things in life that could be more rewarding.

I had a lot of unfortunate circumstances when I was young, and this may have developed my faith in God. All my life I went to church. When I was little, if we missed Sunday School, then we wouldn't get to do what we wanted to do the rest of the week. It was something that developed in me at an early age, and I just loved church.

When young people come to me that are getting married, I tell them a lot of times they're going to get into little arguments and fusses. But they shouldn't take it seriously or in a fatalistic way and begin looking for an easy way out or divorce. They need to cool it for awhile.

I have told Monte and Michael Stallworth, and other boys, they are going to find a lot of bitter things in life, but don't call it quits. If I hadn't waited things out, Gene and I would have been divorced years ago.

My grandchildren are pretty smart with good educations. They are heeding our advice and telling their children they are the most important things in life, because God gave them to them, and they are supposed to treat them with love and kindness.

My advice, not only to young people, but everyone is, don't let obstacles throw you. Sometimes when you go to bed things might look bleak, but wait until morning, things will change.

Wait it out. If you don't have the faith, then God will give you faith.

Francine Tapia, September 17, 2002

REFLECTIONS-GENE TAPIA

Early on Francine caught my eye, and she's never left it. She's had millionaires and famous race car drivers chase her. But I wasn't too far behind, and I wouldn't let them get too close. She's a beautiful woman and our marriage has always been so interesting. It's been a pleasant, beautiful adventure all the way through with her.

When I was young and in Dutch Harbor, Alaska, I was fortunate enough to have an older buddy, Homer Colson. He looked after me. All through life I have had some kind of help, usually from older folks. I believe I paid attention to the older folks more than most do.

I congregated with a lot of the older folks, and I gained a lot of knowledge from them. Even though times might have been rough, I was fortunate enough to have these people guide me along.

One of the best things that happened to me was in Portland, Oregon on the way to Alaska when I was hungry and starving. Mrs. Foster at the Western Union Station taught me one of the biggest lessons of life. She gave me ten dollars and said, 'always help your fellow man, don't expect repayment, just pass it on.'

War has in its way, advanced cicilization, and also torn down civilization. But it has also spurred on new thoughts and new inventions.

As far as war is concerned, if the politicians who started the wars were in a foxhole, it wouldn't take it too long to get settled. I never believed I would get off Iwo Jima alive. I had a job to do for my country, but a lot of luck was involved, and the Captain used up a lot of His angels keeping me alive. Every man on Iwo Jima was a hero, but the real heroes are still over there. They gave their all for their country.

Racing, along with my mother, sister, and wife brought me back to reality. I loved racing, and I wish I was still able to do it.

I would tell young folks to treat his fellow man properly, and conduct himself so that he would always be respected and respect himself. Love is what makes this world tick. If you can love God, country, and your fellow man, you've done a lot.

Gene Tapia, September 19, 2002